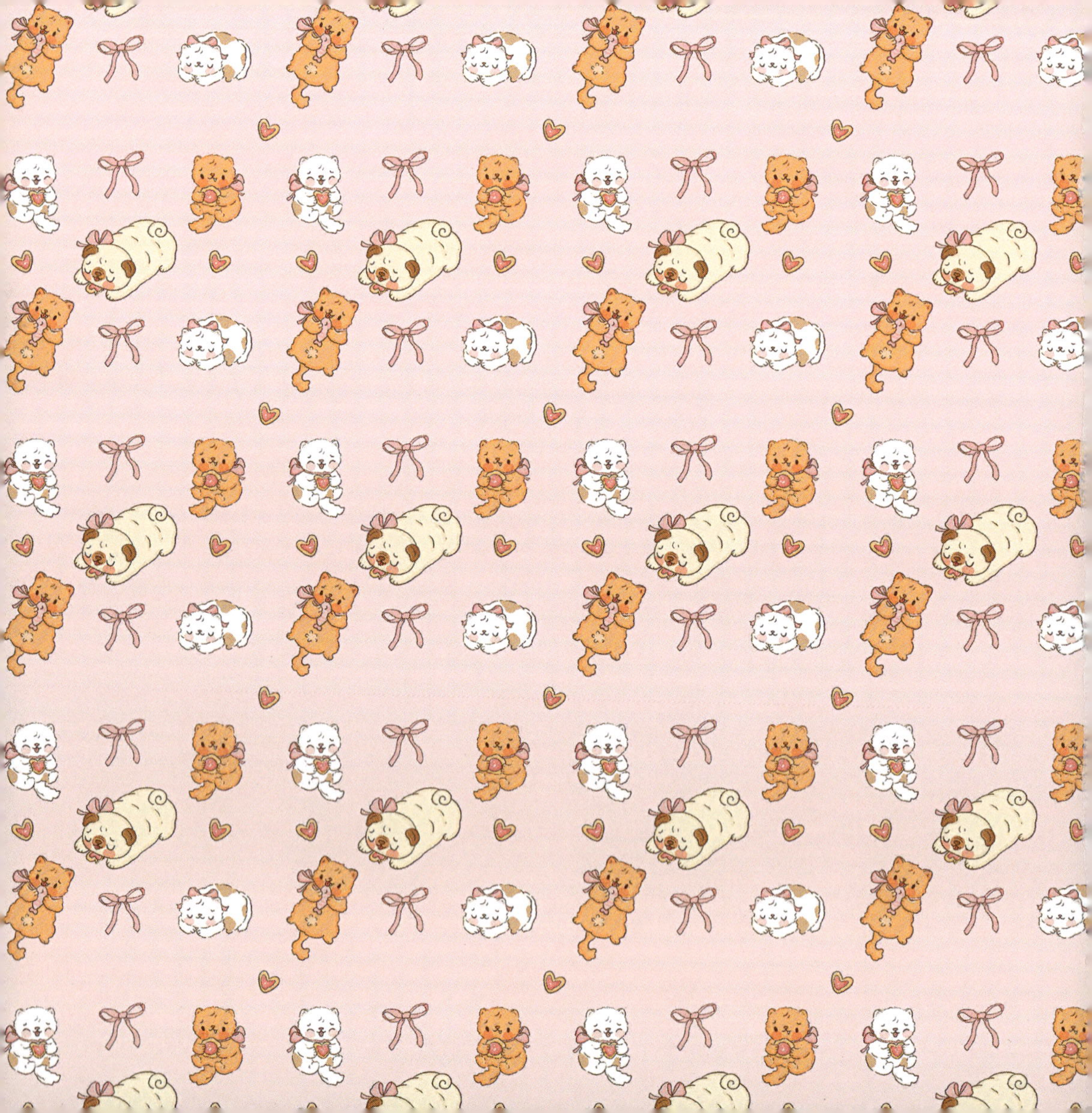

EBURY PRESS

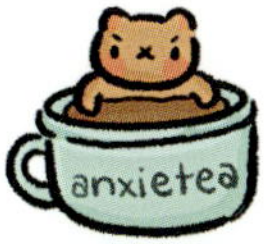
anxietea

the little book of big girl things

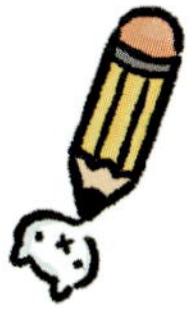

Akshara Ashok is an illustrator and the creator of *Happy Fluff Comics* (she could've thought of a better name). She draws some really serious stuff in a funny way. She discusses everything from silly everyday problems to body image, sex education, mental health and much more.

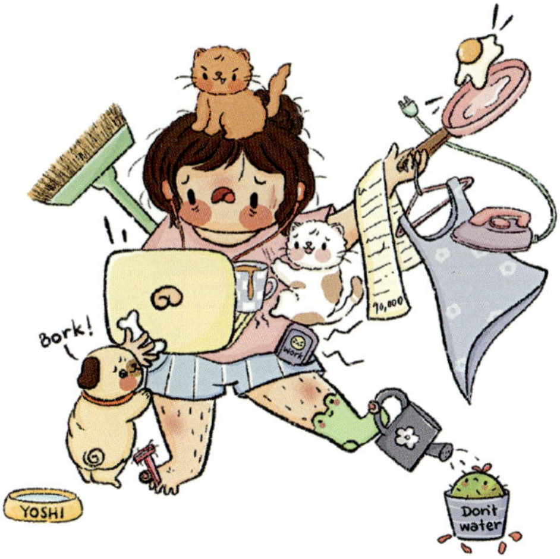
Bork!
YOSHI
Don't water

Akshara started making comics in 2017 when a mean professor yelled at her in architecture school and has made it her career ever since. Her goal is to help break taboos and stereotypes in society. She likes chonky animals, nuggets and lying in bed. She lives in Chennai with her sweet pug, two very grumpy cats and her crippling anxiety.

THE LITTLE BOOK OF BIG GIRL THINGS

AKSHARA ASHOK

EBURY
PRESS

An imprint of Penguin Random House

EBURY PRESS

Ebury Press is an imprint of the Penguin Random House group of companies whose addresses can be found at global.penguinrandomhouse.com

Published by Penguin Random House India Pvt. Ltd
4th Floor, Capital Tower 1, MG Road,
Gurugram 122 002, Haryana, India

Penguin Random House India

First published in Ebury Press by Penguin Random House India 2025

10 9 8 7 6 5 4 3 2 1

ISBN 9780143474265

Typeset in Century Gothic
Printed at Thomson Press India Ltd, New Delhi

www.penguin.co.in

Dedicated to everyone who has supported me & my work

thank you for giving me the love I never gave myself... 💗

flowers, lollies & tuna-flavoured kisses

contents

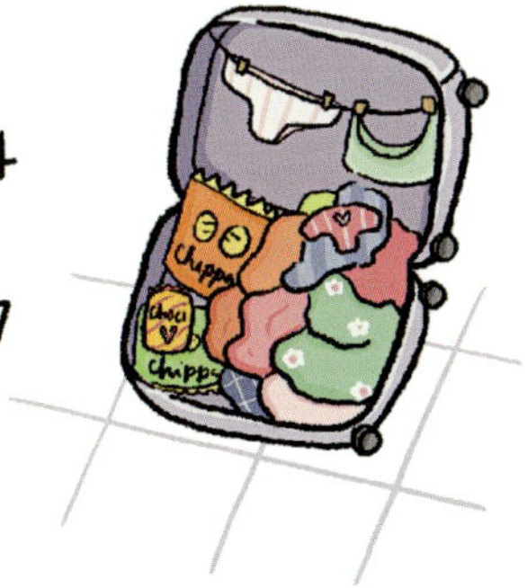

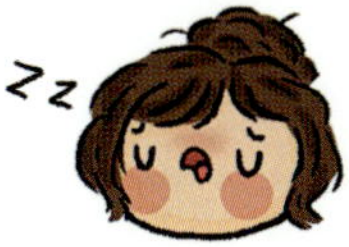

introduction

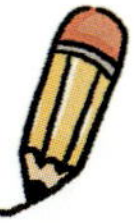

Hi! I'm Akshara & I'm

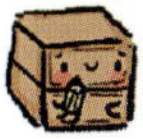

a professional (i think) draw-er...

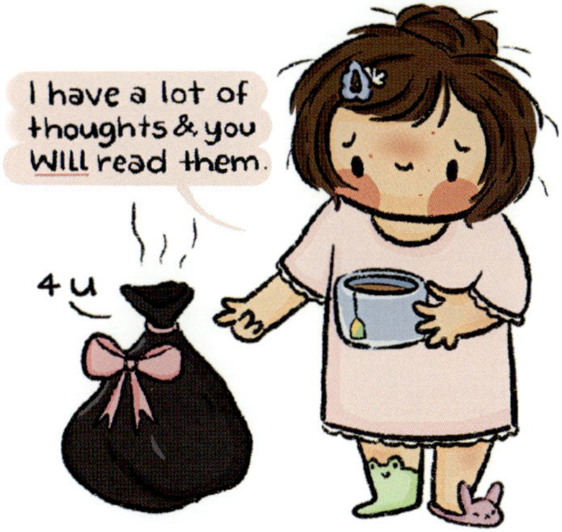
I have a lot of thoughts & you WILL read them.
4 u

this book is a mix of silly & serious feelings (mostly silly)

this book won't change your life (obvi-) but will make you feel less alone in this roller-coaster ride we call adulthood :|

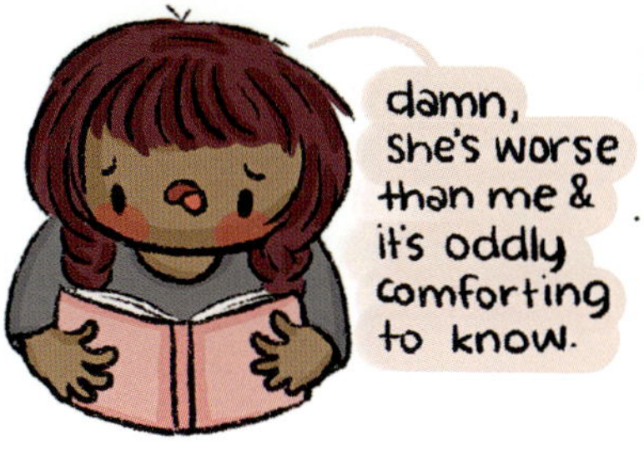
damn, she's worse than me & it's oddly comforting to know.

Alternate uses for this book:

Makes you feel better about yourself almost instantly.

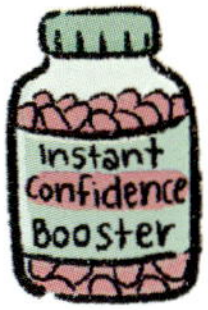
Instant
Confidence
Booster

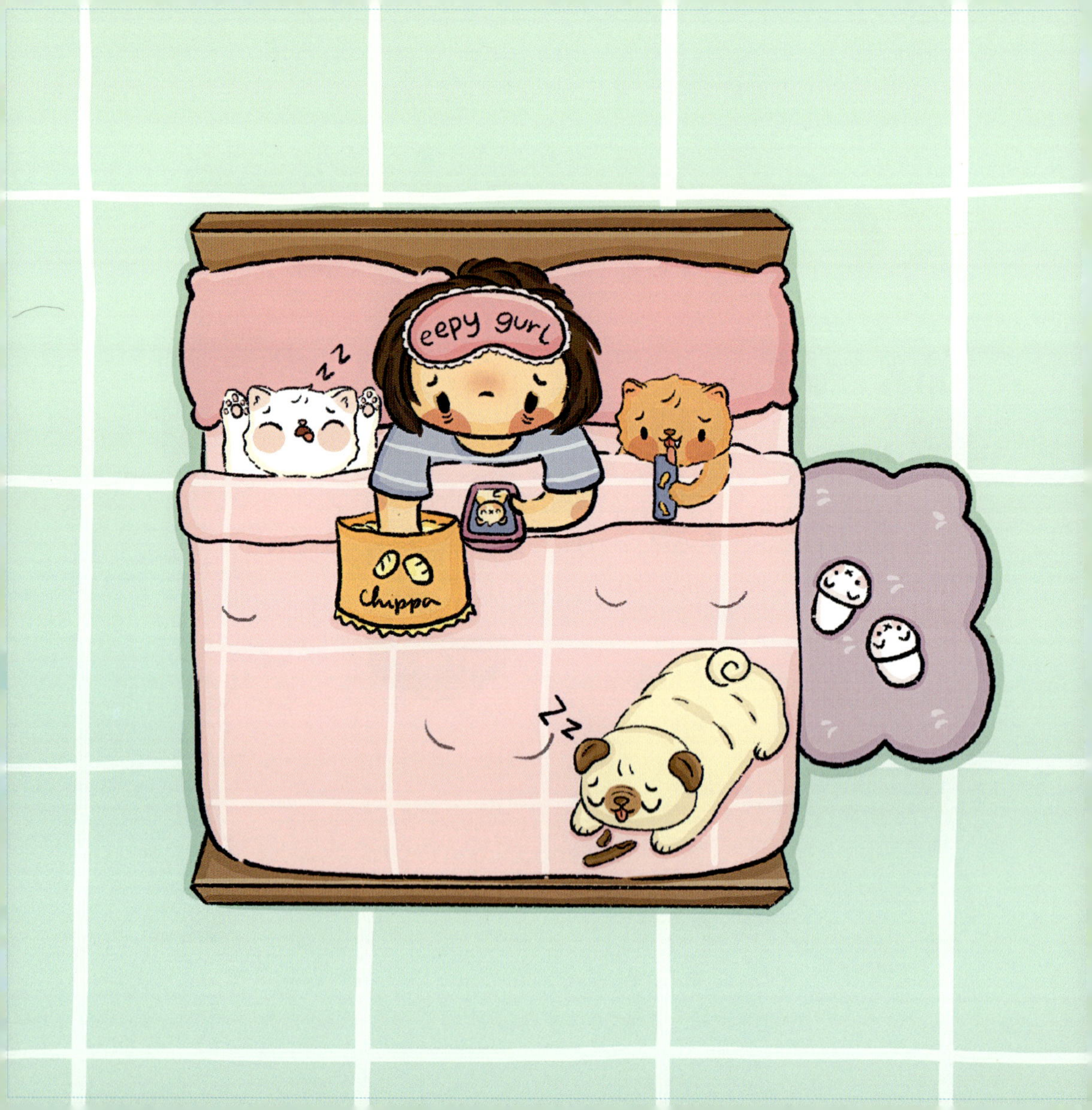
eepy gurl
Chippa

1

adulting sucks

Becoming an adult can be kinda scary. You're all on your own and you're somehow supposed to figure out everything by yourself. There's no manual or seminar on how to do things, but somehow everyone else is good at it. Like how do they know these things? Most of the time, I don't ask for help because what if they think I'm dumb? Okay, maybe I am dumb! It's okay to not know everything. There's no shame in that. But I would rather take a seven-day course on fixing my washing machine than ask for help because I feel like such a burden.

I need 20 chicken nuggets & a large coke!
eepy gurl

Suddenly, you're expected to do adult things, like go to the doctor's clinic ALONE or find a CA and do taxes, whatever that means. You also have to make money and manage that money and not spend it on things like a giant 3-feet Hello Kitty plushie. You also need to cook real food . . . like your adult body can't survive on nuggets and soda any more. AND take care of the chores . . . like there's not enough time in a day to do all of this. I spend three-fourth of the day wondering how I'm going to do any of these and it's already time for bed and I realize I have a work deadline for tomorrow.

~Who I wanna be~

colours hair every month

glasses that make me look smarter

buys expensive coffee every day

Piercings

Super confident

artsy vibe & smells fruity

Wears whatever she wants

tattoos everywhere

fancy tote with flowers

gets pink cocktails with friends

travels a lot

New shoes

☆(super successful artist)☆

~ Who I am right now ~

acne & greasy hair

Spending problem

scrunchie my bestie left behind

Mentally ill

a t-shirt I stole from my mom

bloated from PCOS

two kids I have to feed

half-shaven legs

disintegrating flip-flops

Big Boi Dino

(just does bare minimum to get by)

In a parallel universe I'd like to be

a cat with a beret, living in Paris

a smart surgeon

a hacker who bullies cyberbullies

a fortune teller + occasional scammer

a rich girlie with a tulip field

froggo boi on a lily pad

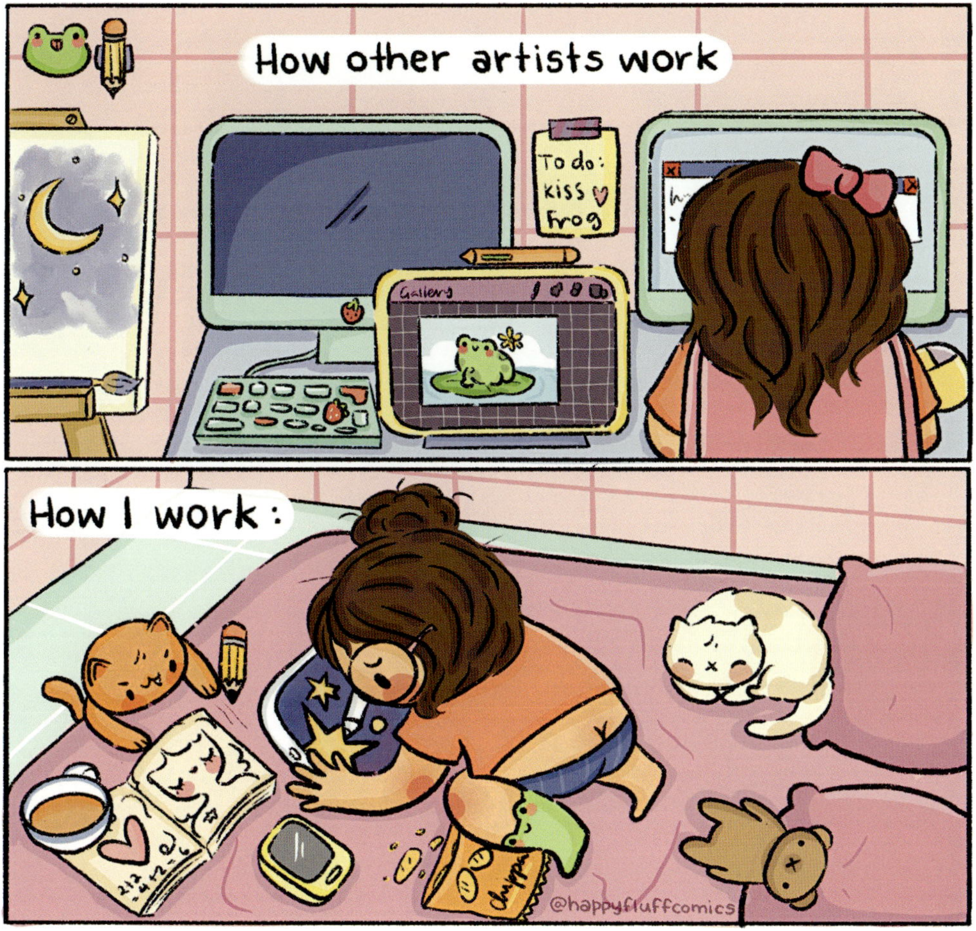
How other artists work
To do:
kiss ♡
Frog
How I work:
@happyfluffcomics

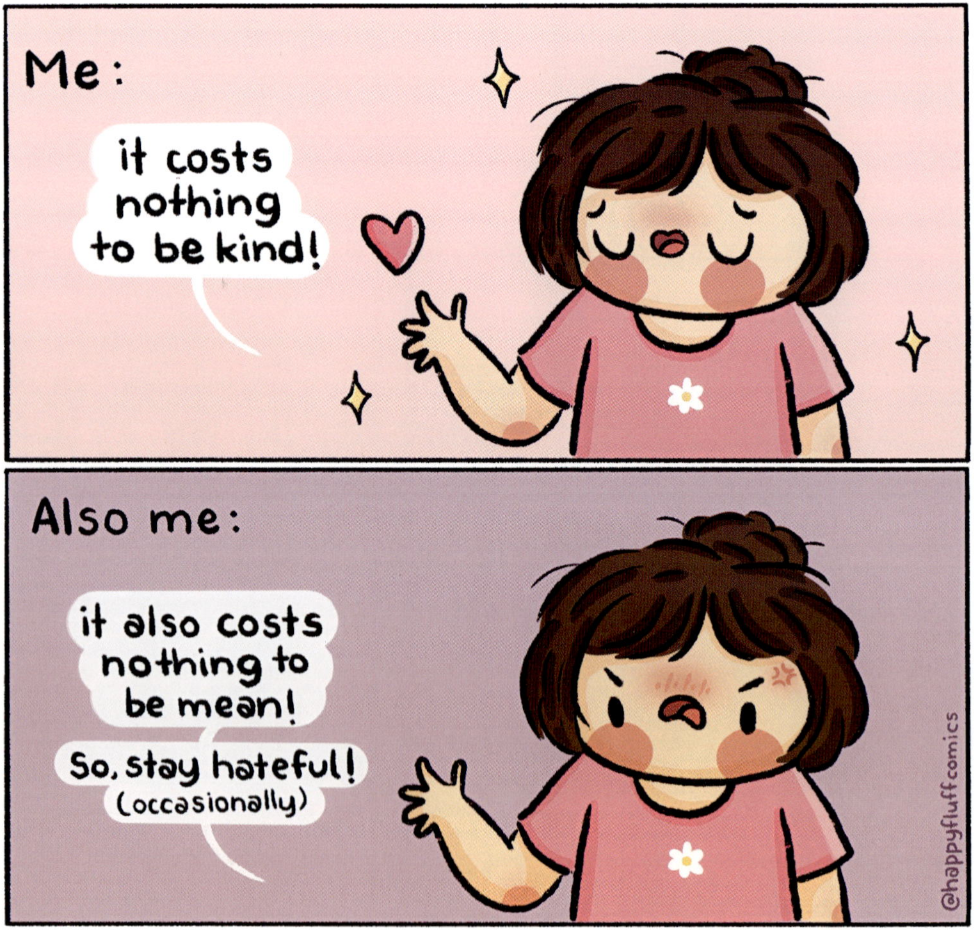
Me:
it costs nothing to be kind!
Also me:
it also costs nothing to be mean!
So, stay hateful!
(occasionally)
@happyfluffcomics

Sometimes I need to

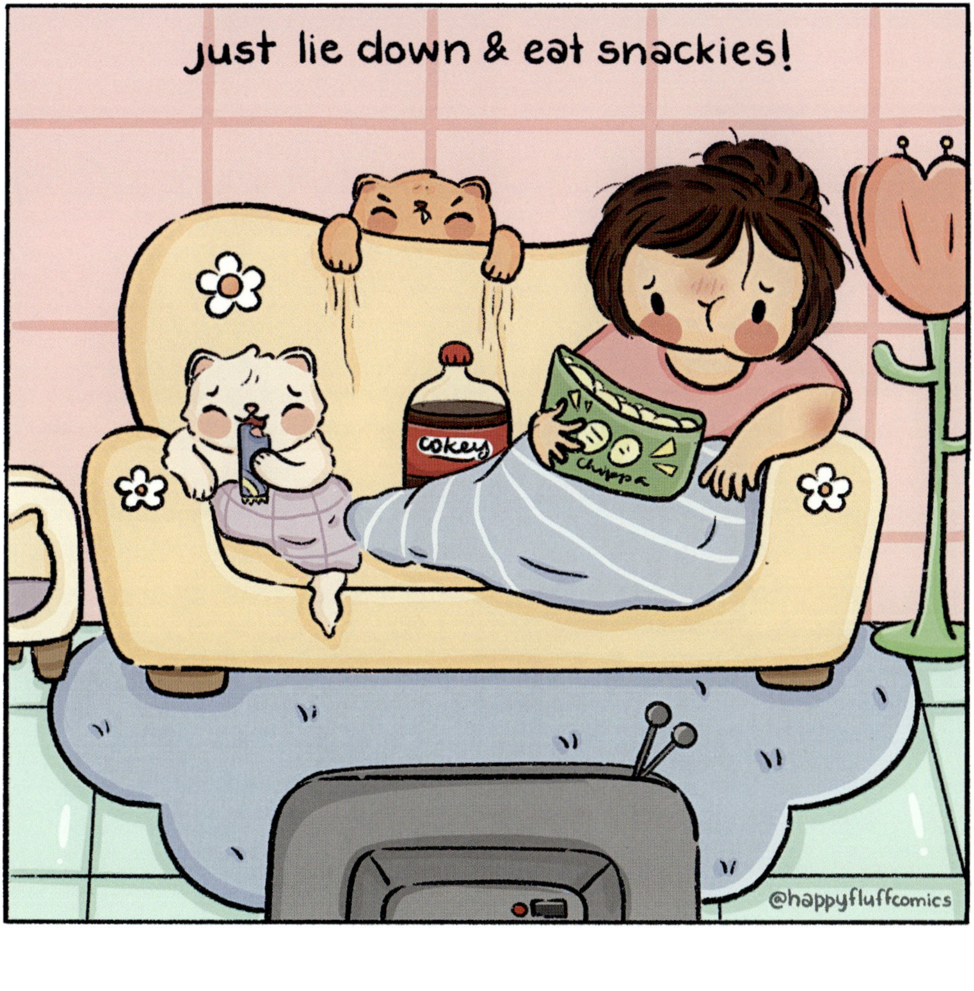
just lie down & eat snackies!
cokey
Chippa
@happyfluffcomics

home decor

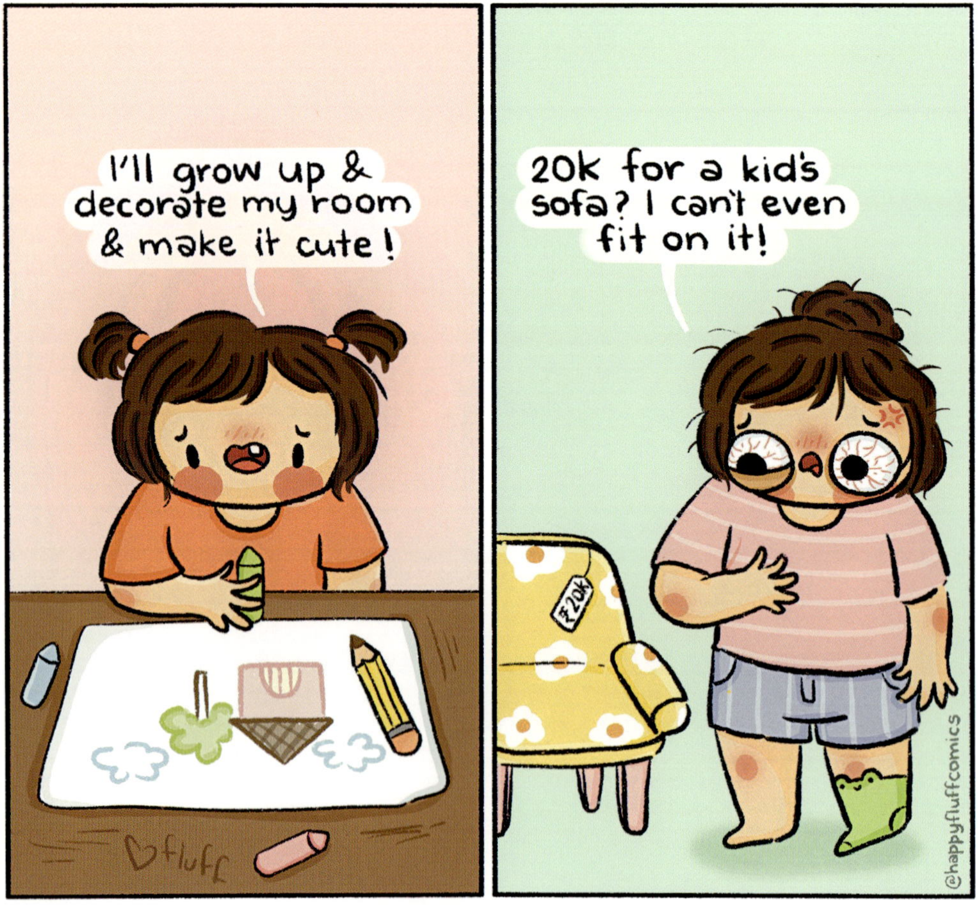
I'll grow up & decorate my room & make it cute!
20k for a kid's sofa? I can't even fit on it!
₹20k
fluff
@happyfluffcomics

house plants

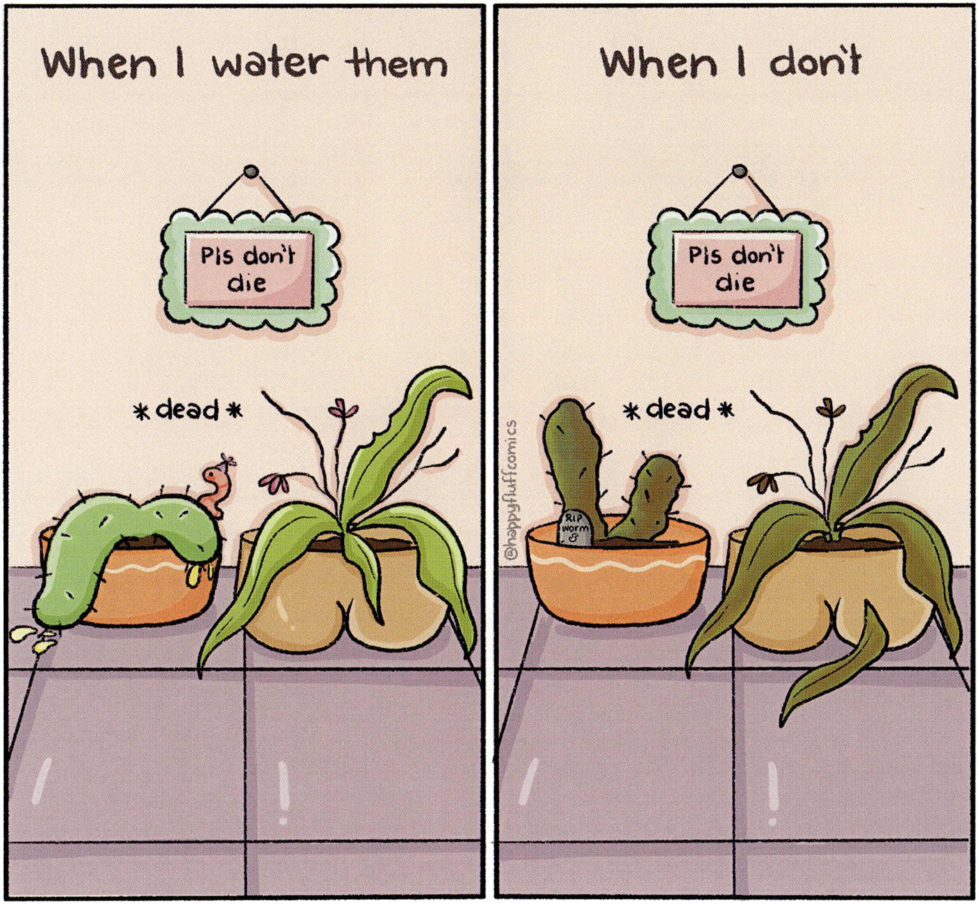

When I water them
Pls don't die
dead
When I don't
Pls don't die
dead
RIP worm
@happyfluffcomics

a guide to perfect sleep

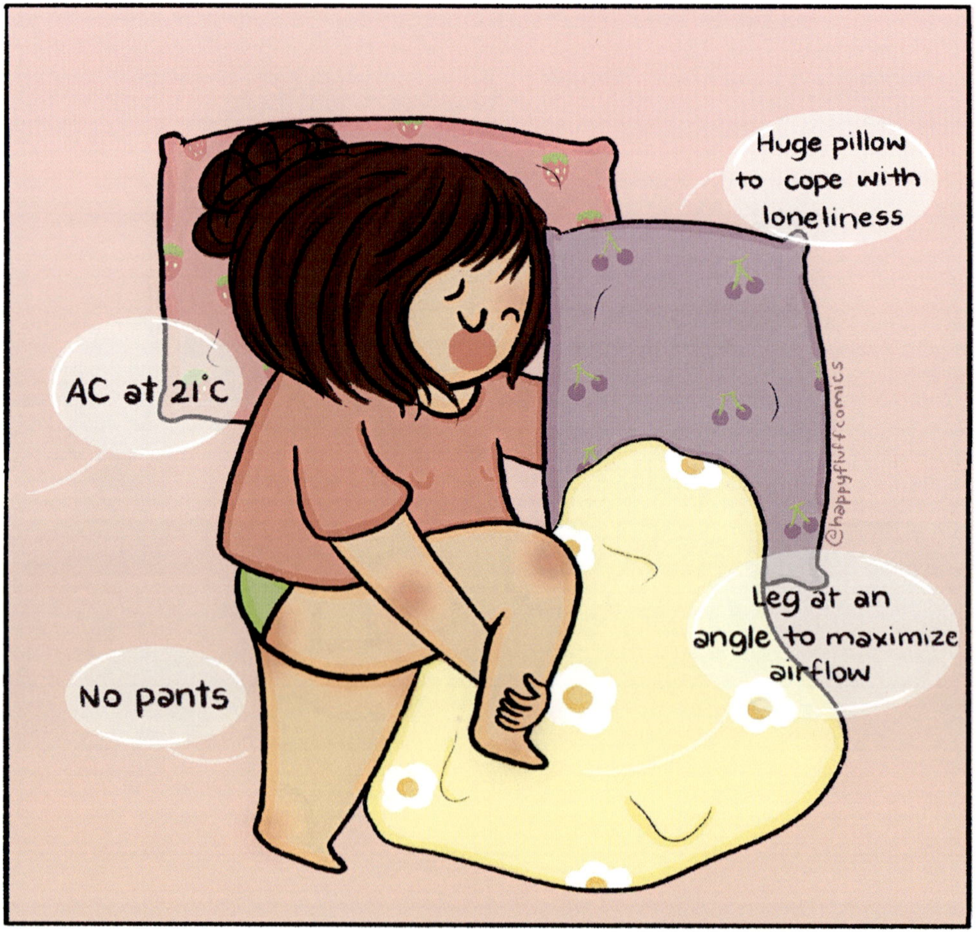
Huge pillow to cope with loneliness
AC at 21°C
Leg at an angle to maximize airflow
No pants
@happyfluffcomics

When you leave things for tomorrow

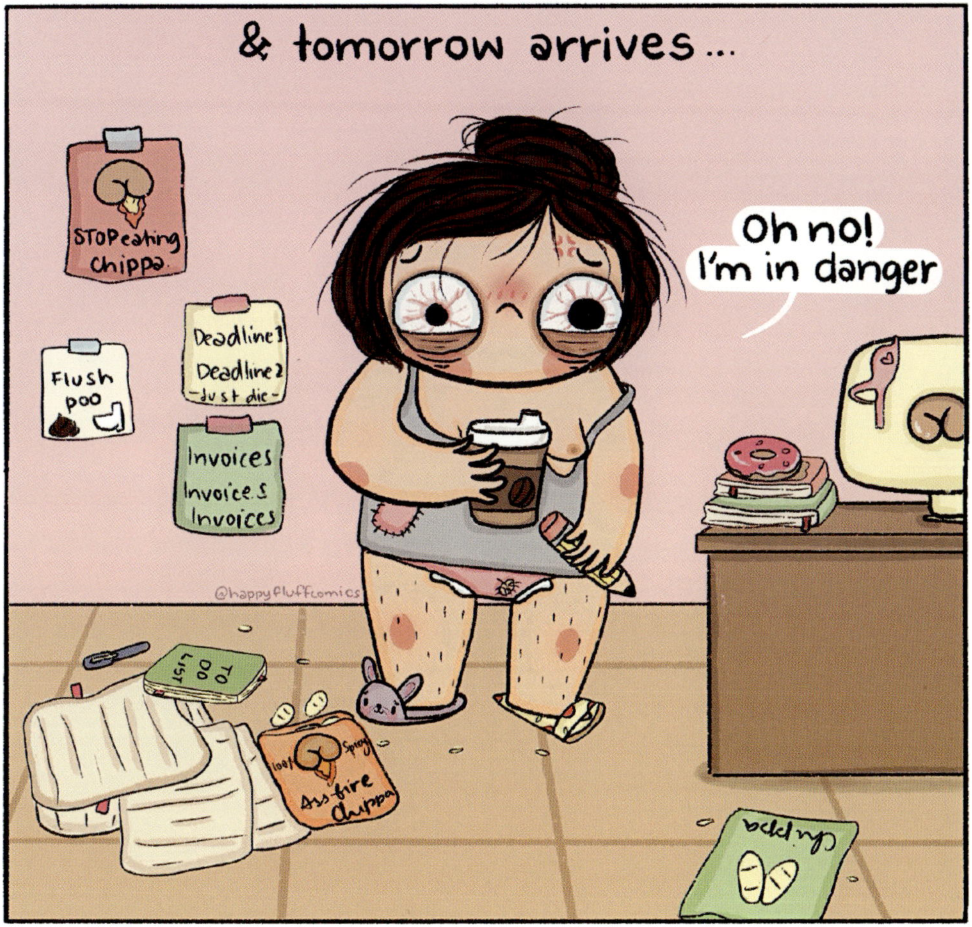
& tomorrow arrives...
Oh no!
I'm in danger
STOP eating Chippa.
Flush poo
Deadline 1
Deadline 2
-Just die-
Invoices
Invoices
Invoices
@happyfluffcomics
TO DO LIST
100% Spicy
Ass-fire Chippa
Chippa

Me at 3a.m.

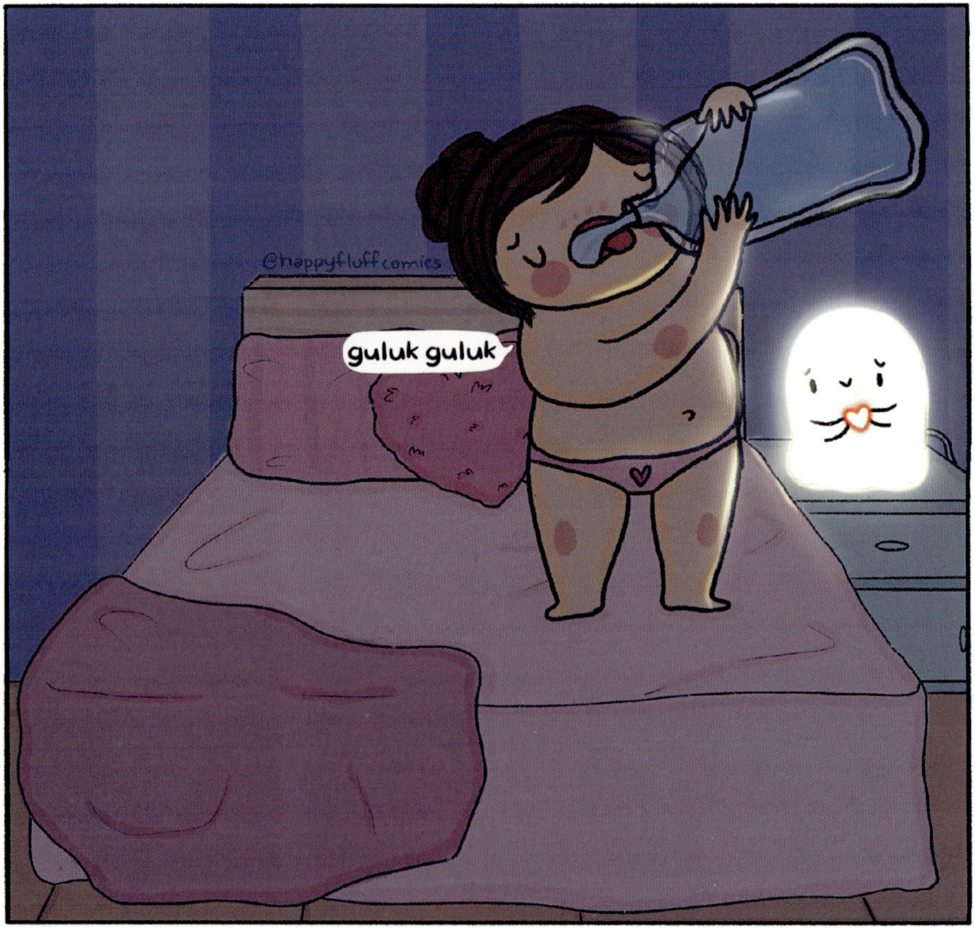
@happyfluffcomics
guluk guluk

Before starting work

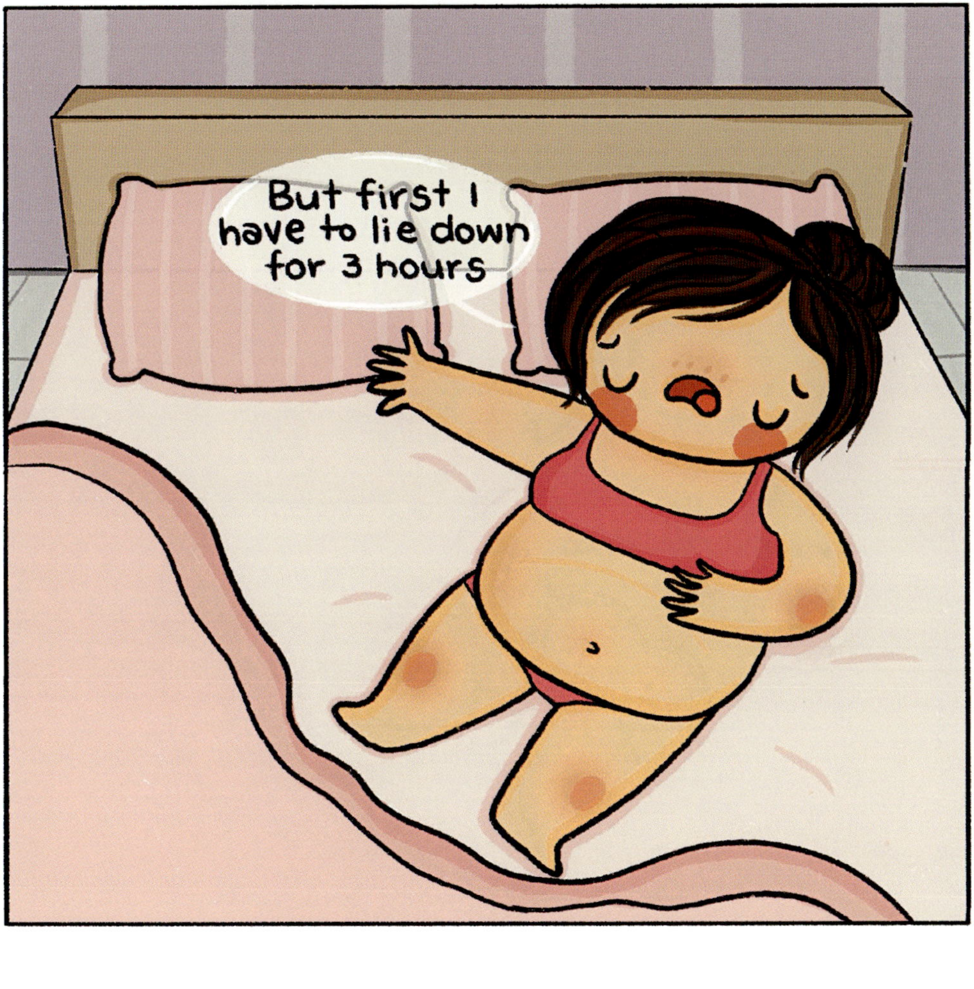
But first I have to lie down for 3 hours

growing up is realizing...

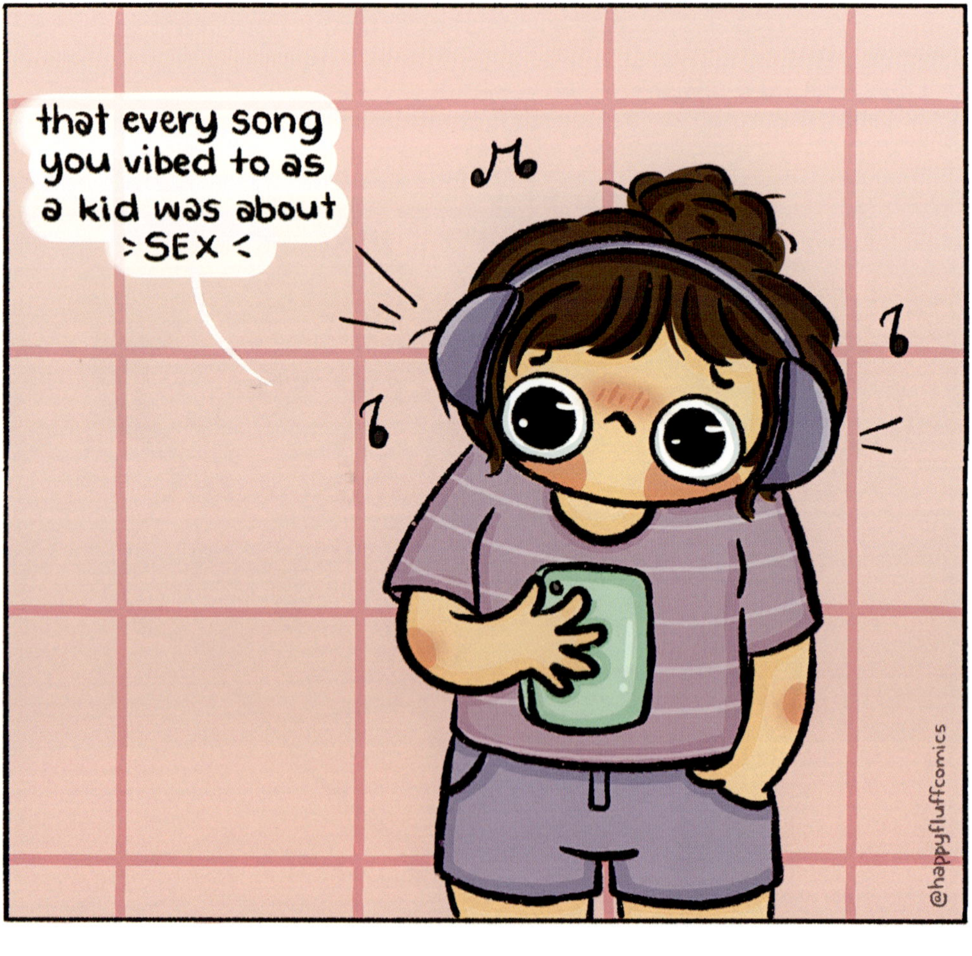
that every song you vibed to as a kid was about >SEX<
@happyfluffcomics

Sometimes you need to sit in a towel for... ever

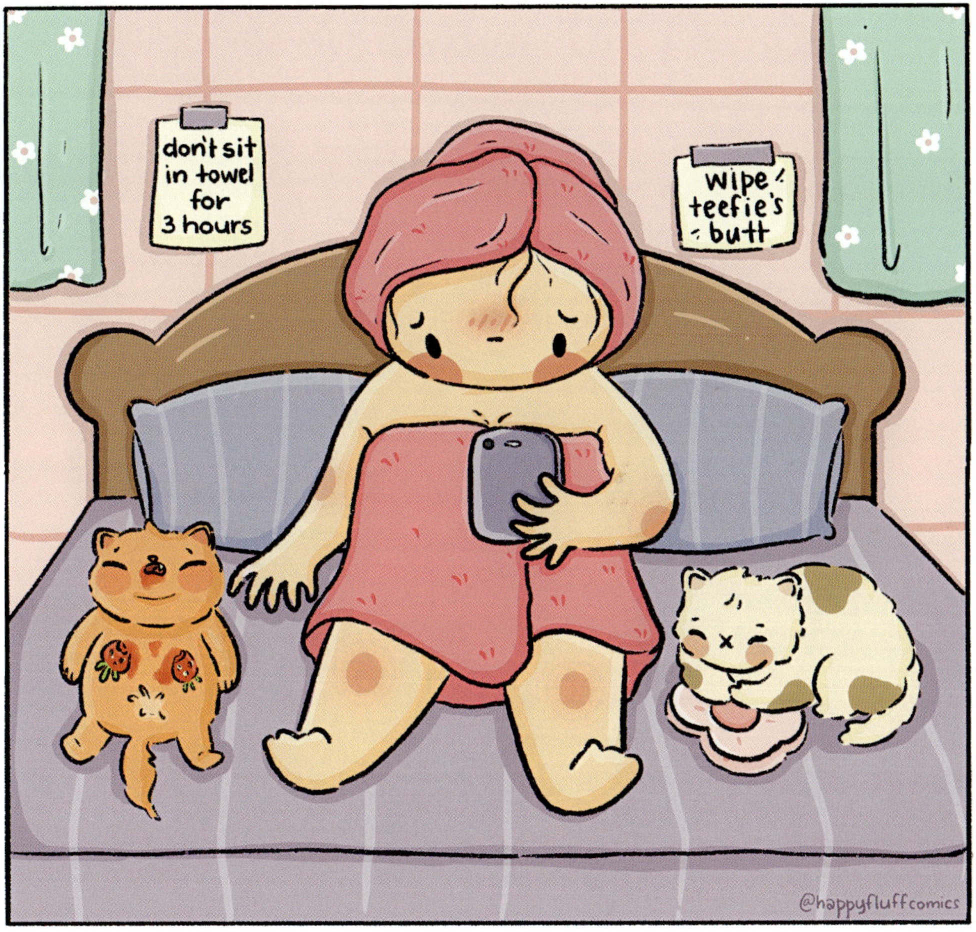

don't sit in towel for 3 hours
wipe teefie's butt
@happyfluffcomics

Zoning out mid-conversation

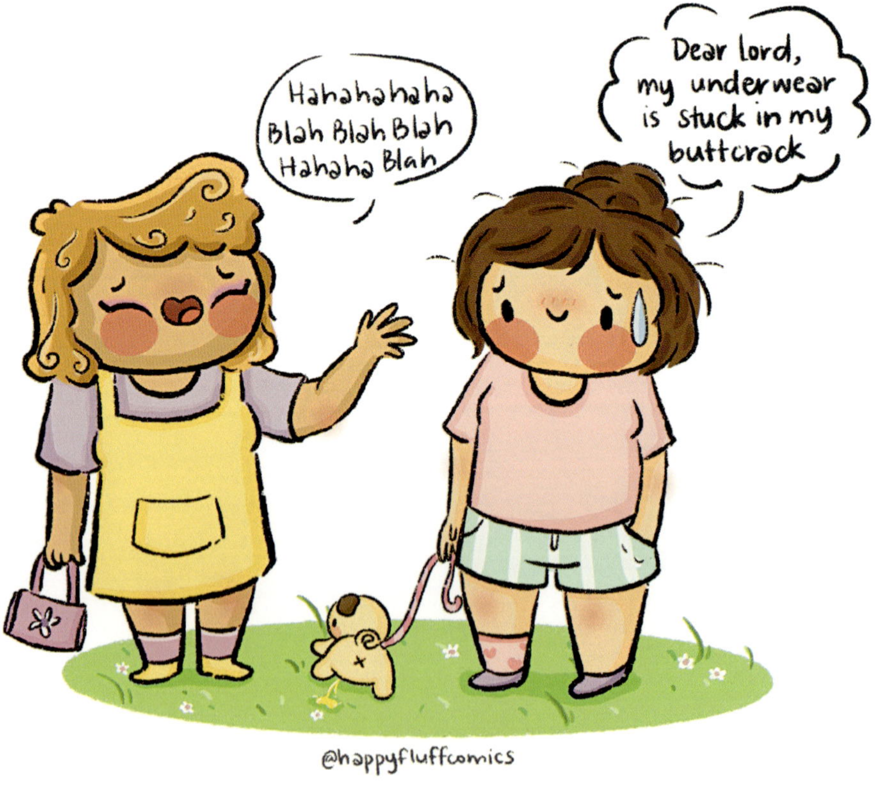
Hahahahahaha
Blah Blah Blah
Hahaha Blah
Dear lord, my underwear is stuck in my buttcrack
@happyfluffcomics

things that shouldn't exist :(

Banana-flavoured
candy—cuz ew!

crocs—they're
ugly as hell

Olives—tastes
like butt

Wet slice of tomato
in a burger

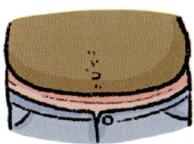

low-waist jeans

Podcasts
(you know why)

How some people sleep

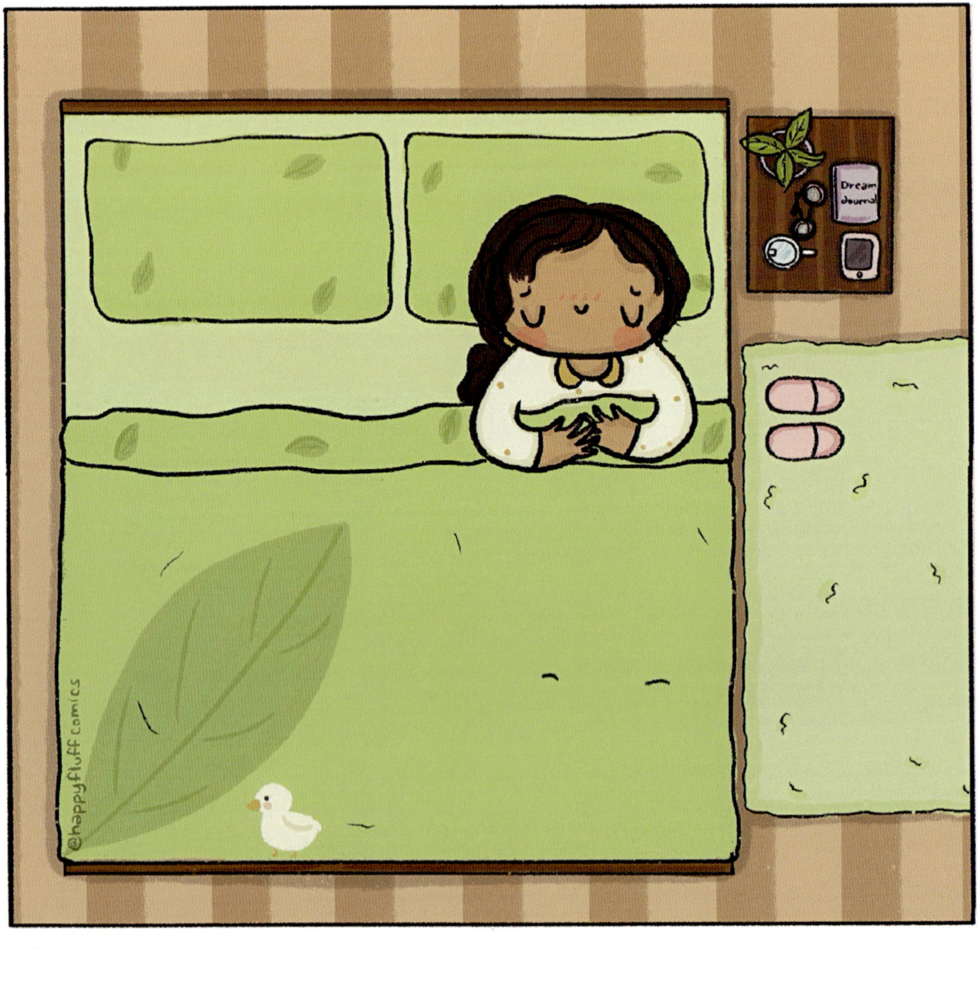
Dream Journal
@happyfluffcomics

How I sleep

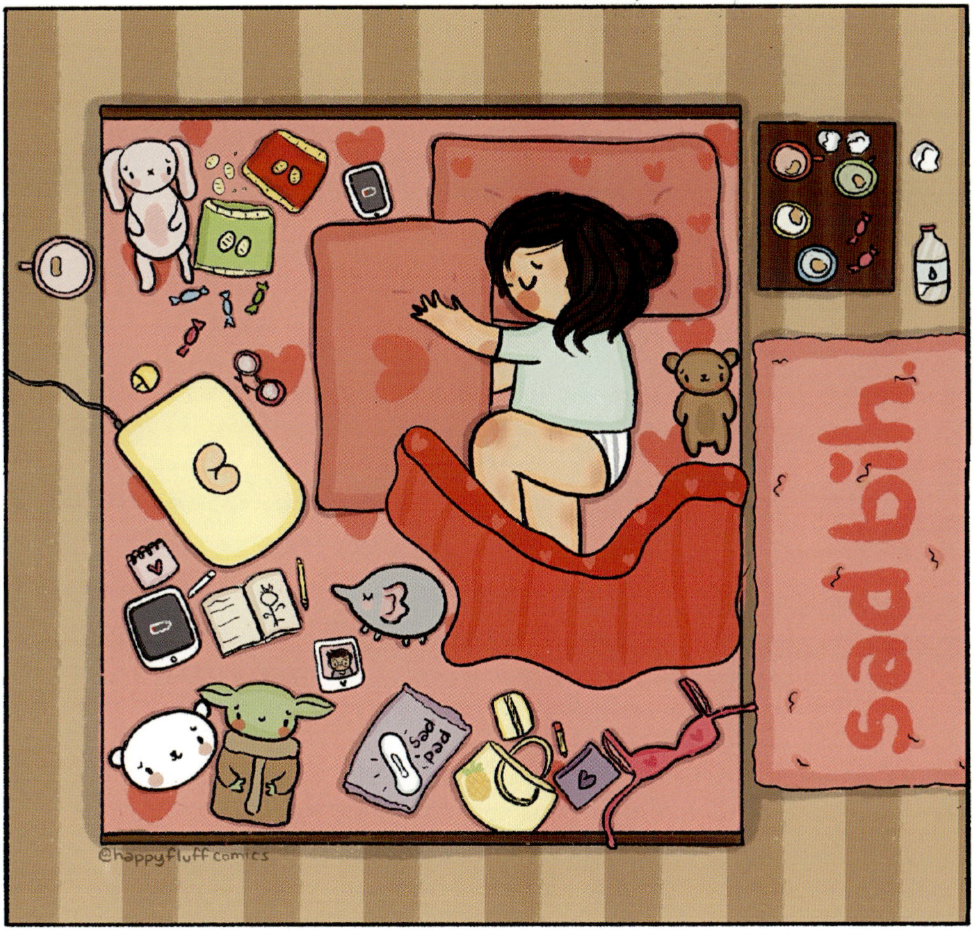
sad pad
sad bih
@happyfluffcomics

Me with everything in life

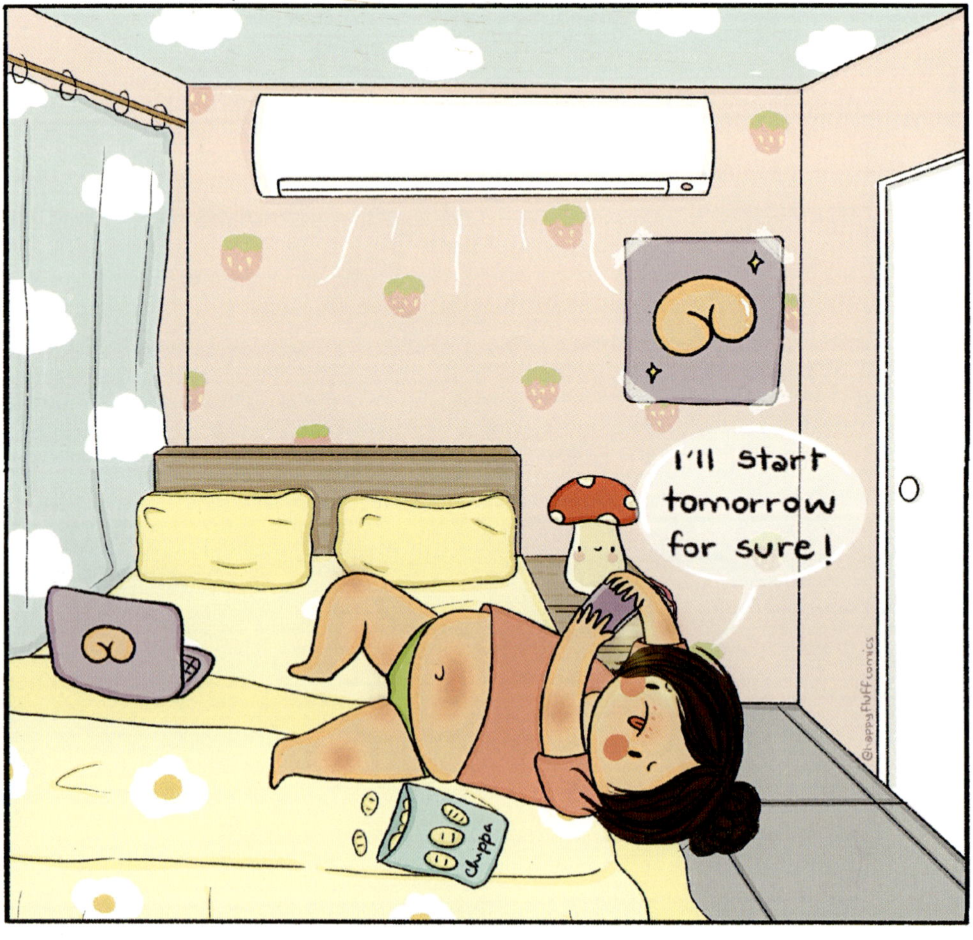
I'll start tomorrow for sure!
Chippa
@happyfluffcomics

Using a public toilet

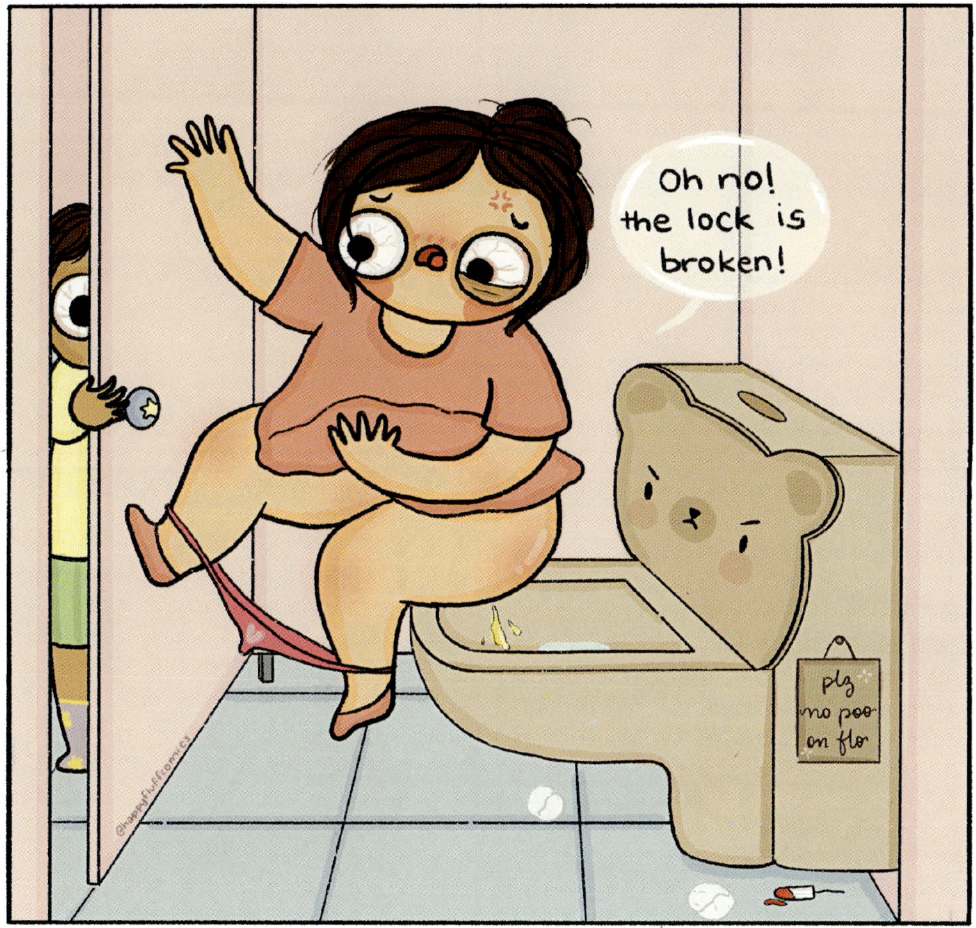
Oh no! the lock is broken!
plz no poo on flor
@happyfluffcomics

Random fears

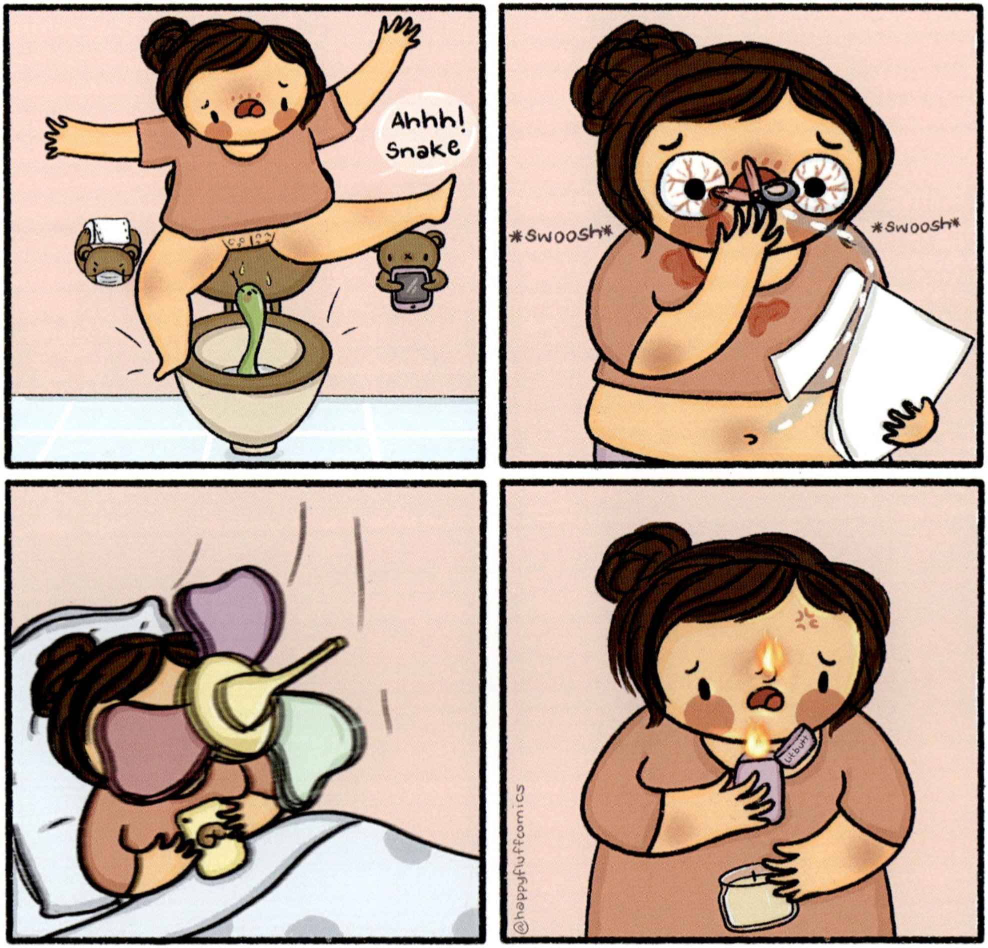
Ahhh! Snake
swoosh
swoosh
@happyfluffcomics

Weird dreams

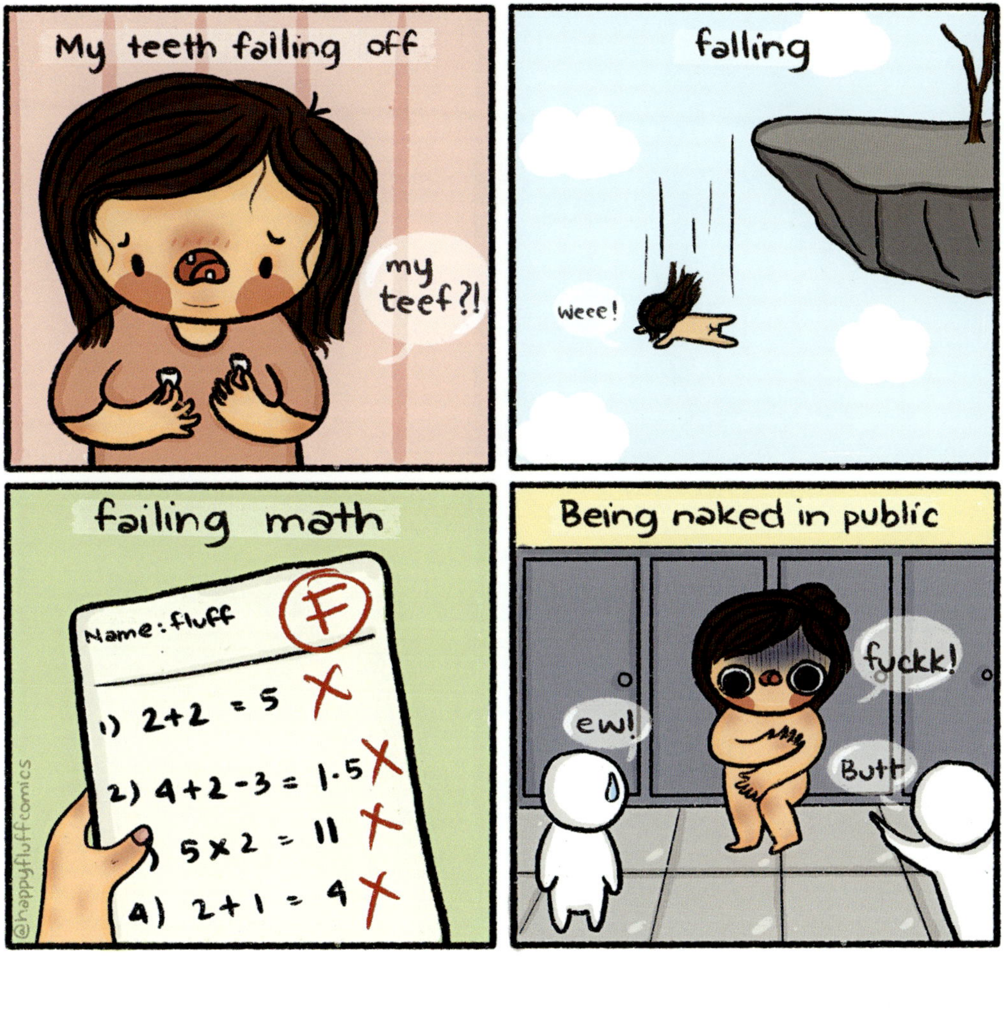
My teeth falling off
my teef?!
falling
weee!
failing math
Name: fluff
F
1) 2+2 = 5
2) 4+2-3 = 1.5
5x2 = 11
4) 2+1 = 4
@happyfluffcomics
Being naked in public
fuckk!
ew!
Butt

Pooping

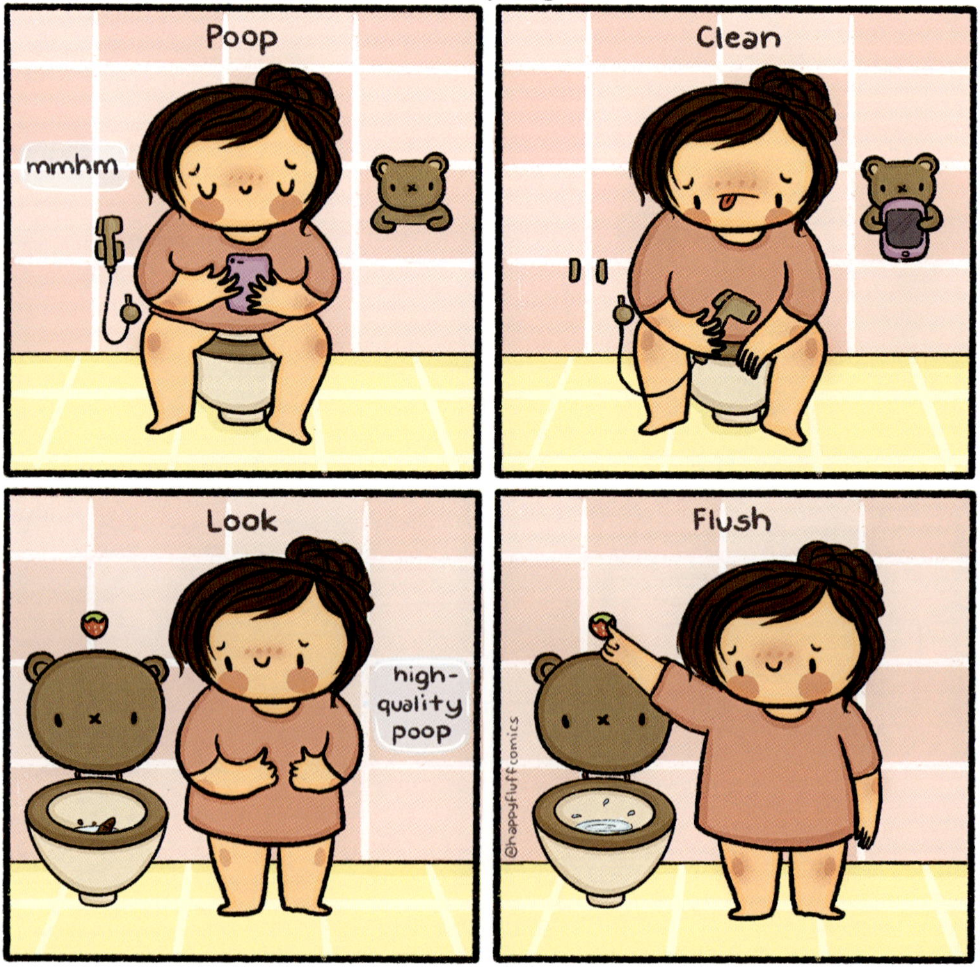
Poop
mmhm
Clean
Look
high-quality poop
@happyfluffcomics
Flush

What I mean when I say I have plans

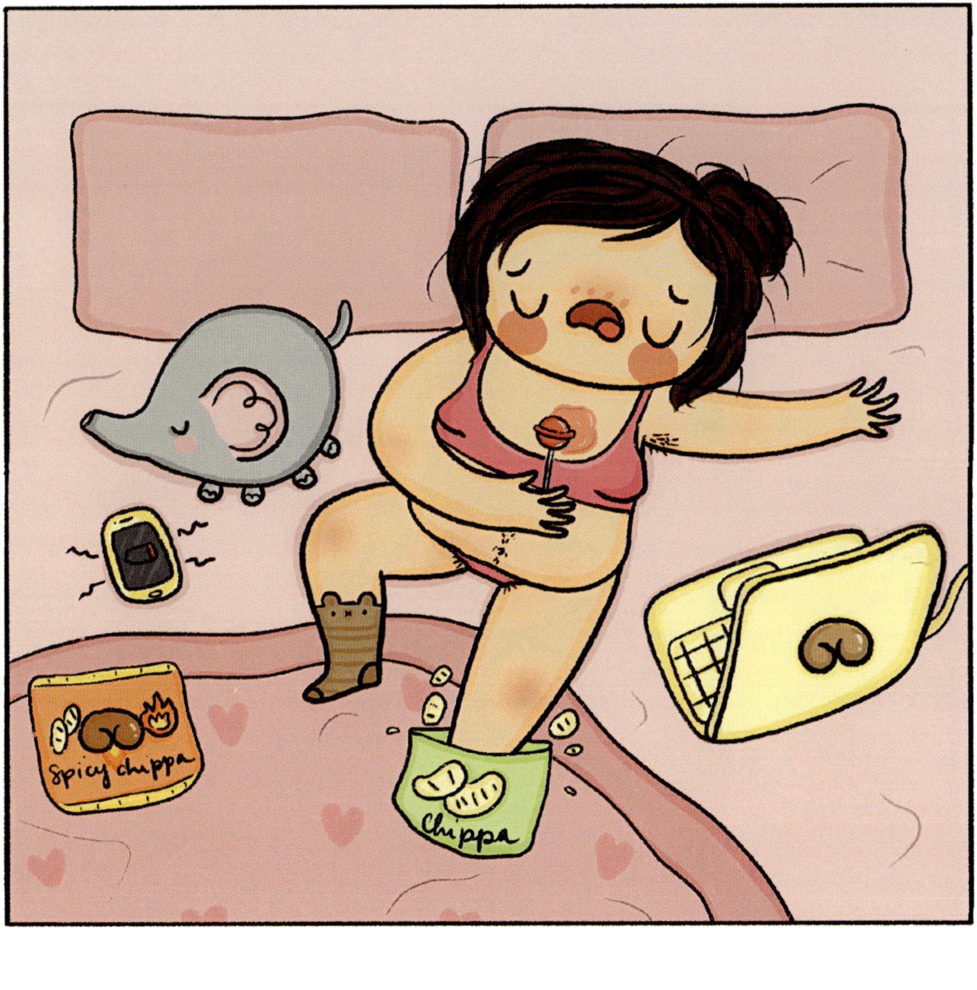
spicy chippa
Chippa

When you just got comfy and -

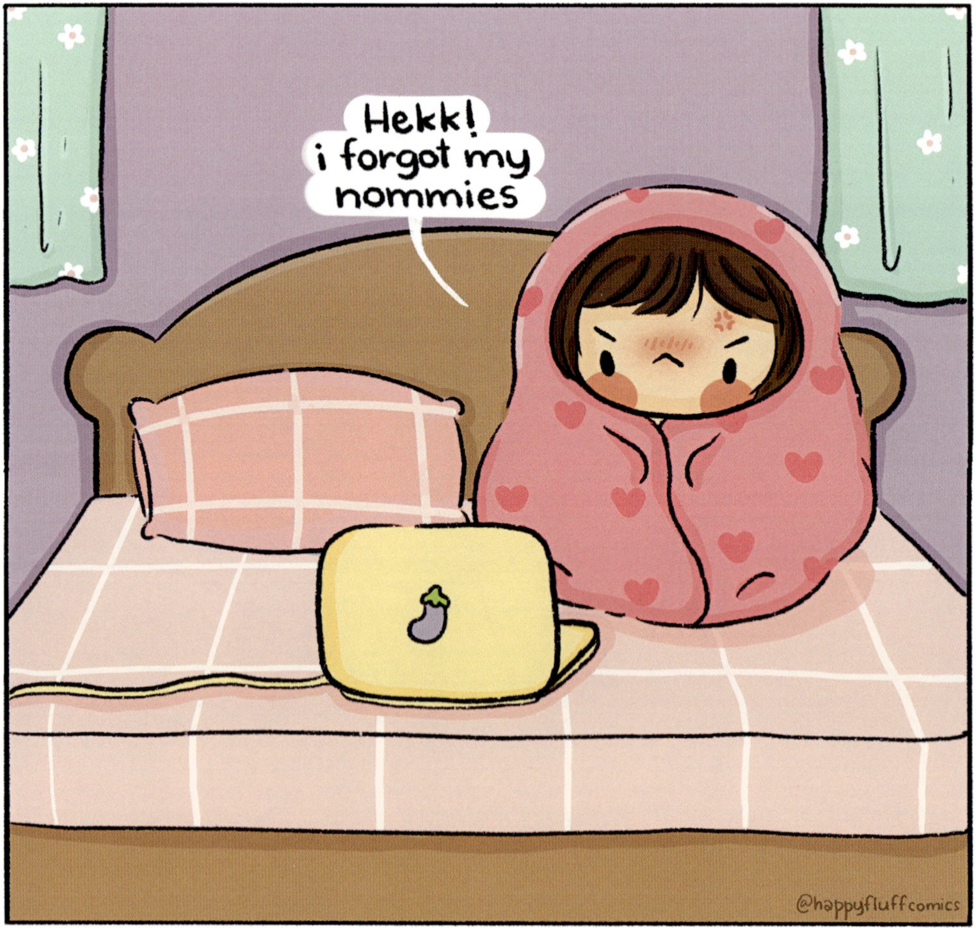
Hekk!
i forgot my
nommies
@happyfluffcomics

Playing with barbies as a kid

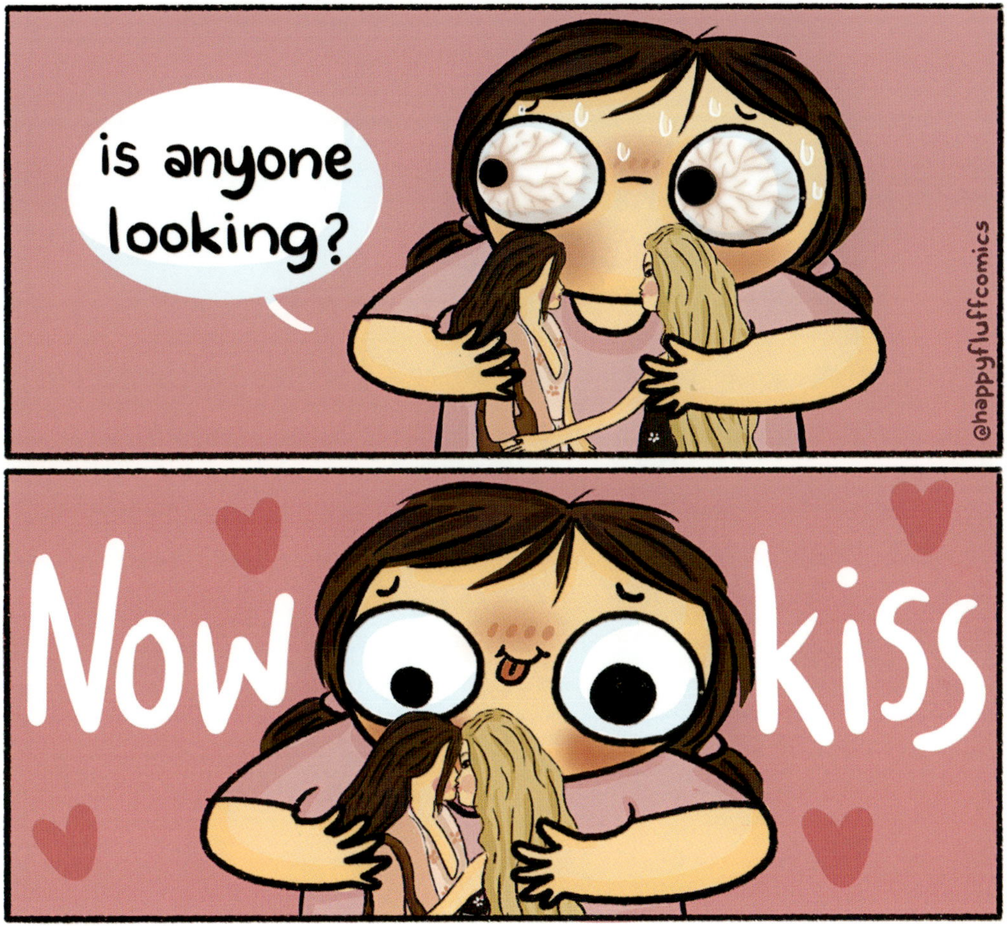

Hot-girl summer

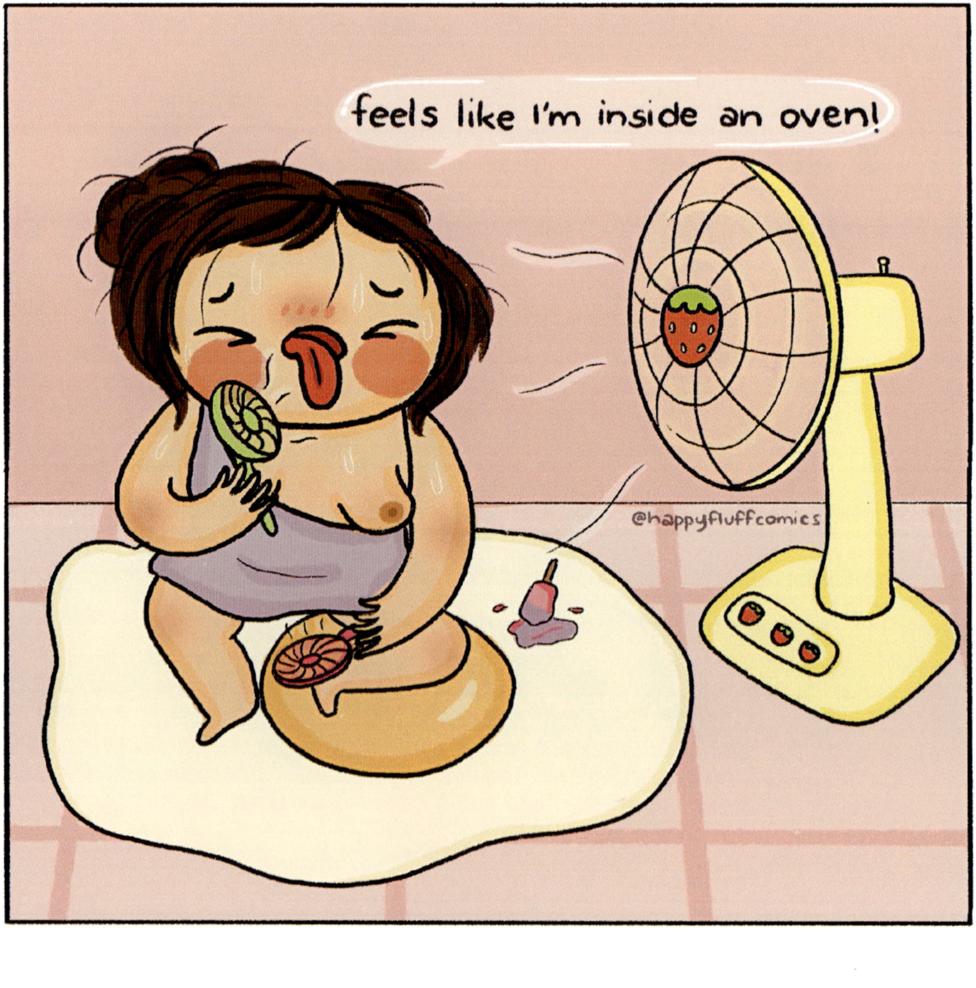
feels like I'm inside an oven!
@happyfluffcomics

trying to make a phone call

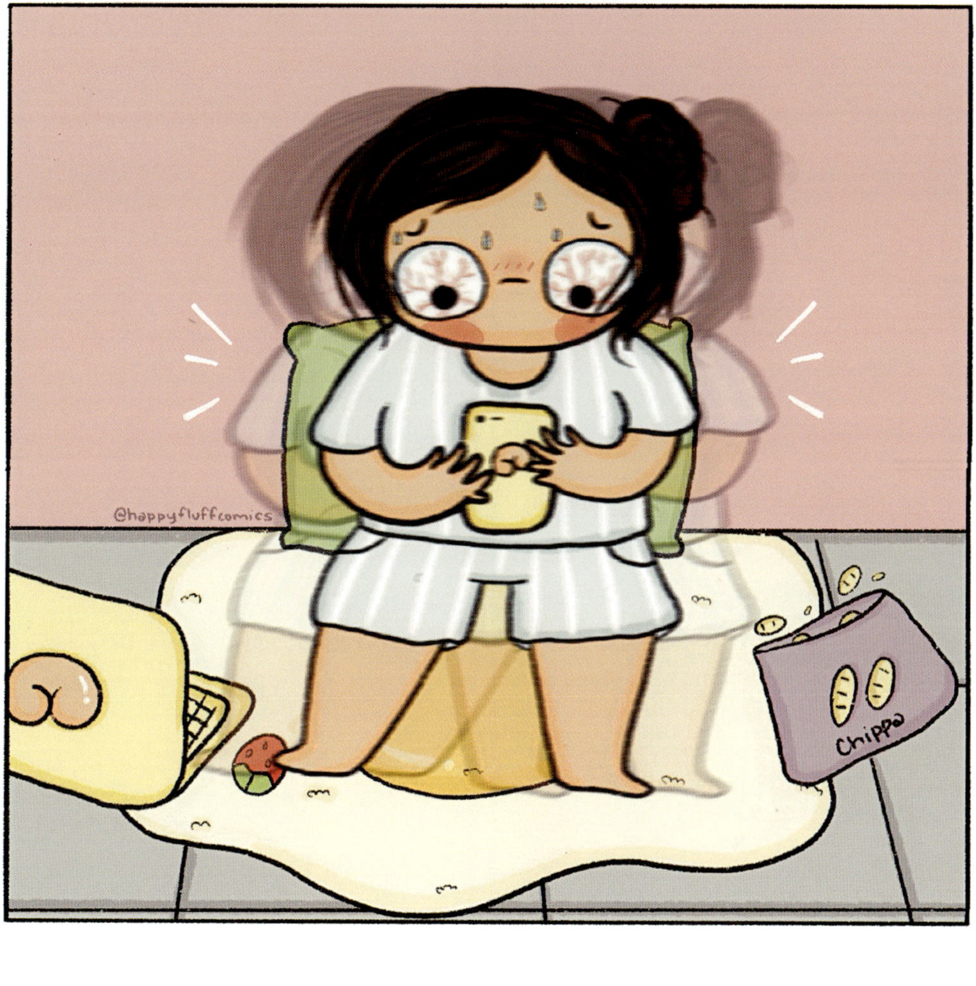
@happyfluffcomics
Chippa

I love the rain but...

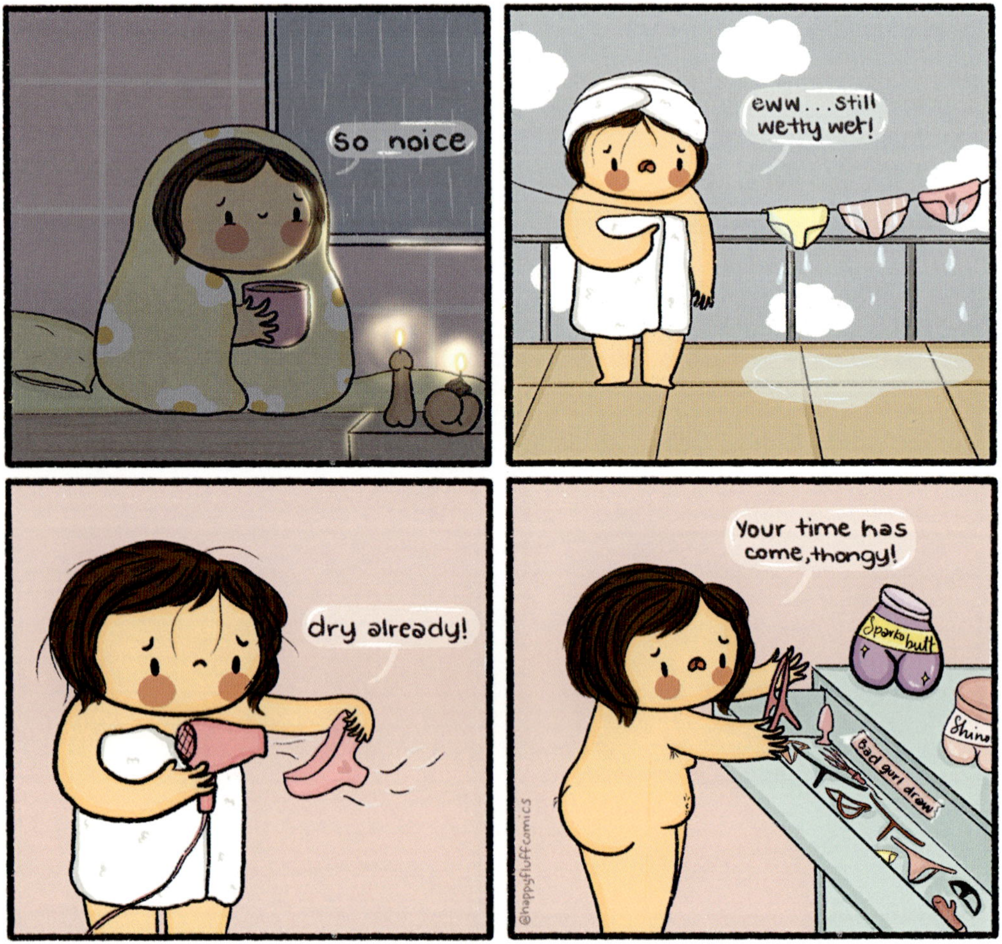

so noice
eww...still wetty wet!
dry already!
Your time has come, thongy!
Sparko butt
Shino
Bad gurl draw
@happyfluffcomics

Dreaming

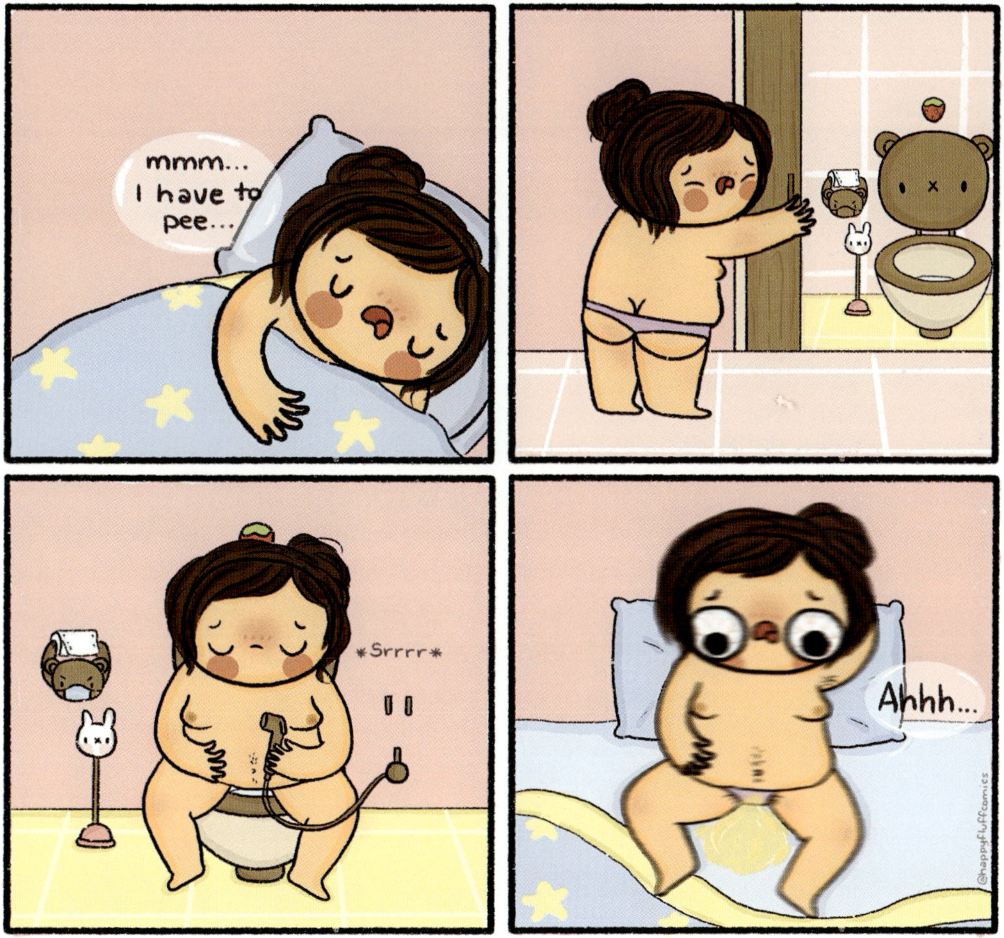
mmm... I have to pee...
Srrrr
Ahhh...
@happyfluffcomics

living alone

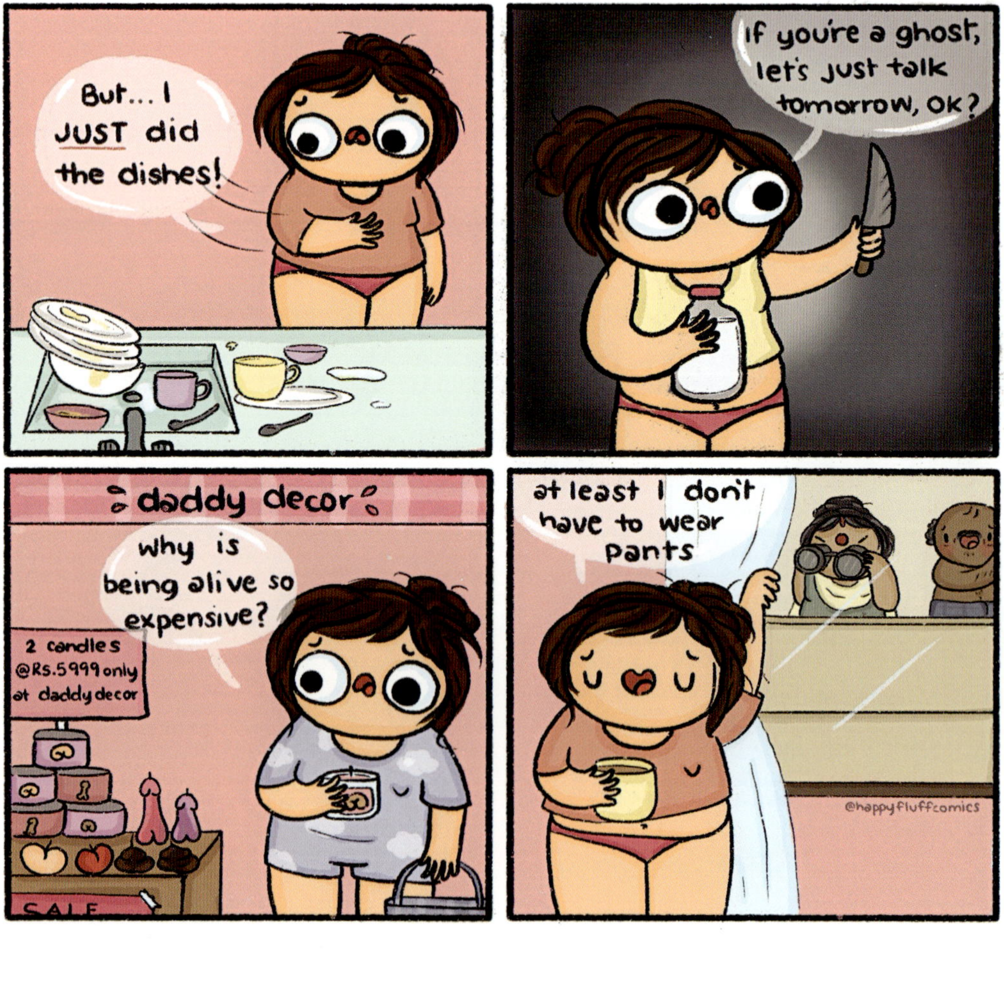
But... I JUST did the dishes!
If you're a ghost, let's just talk tomorrow, OK?
daddy decor
why is being alive so expensive?
2 candles @RS.5999 only at daddy decor
SALE
at least I don't have to wear pants
@happyfluffcomics

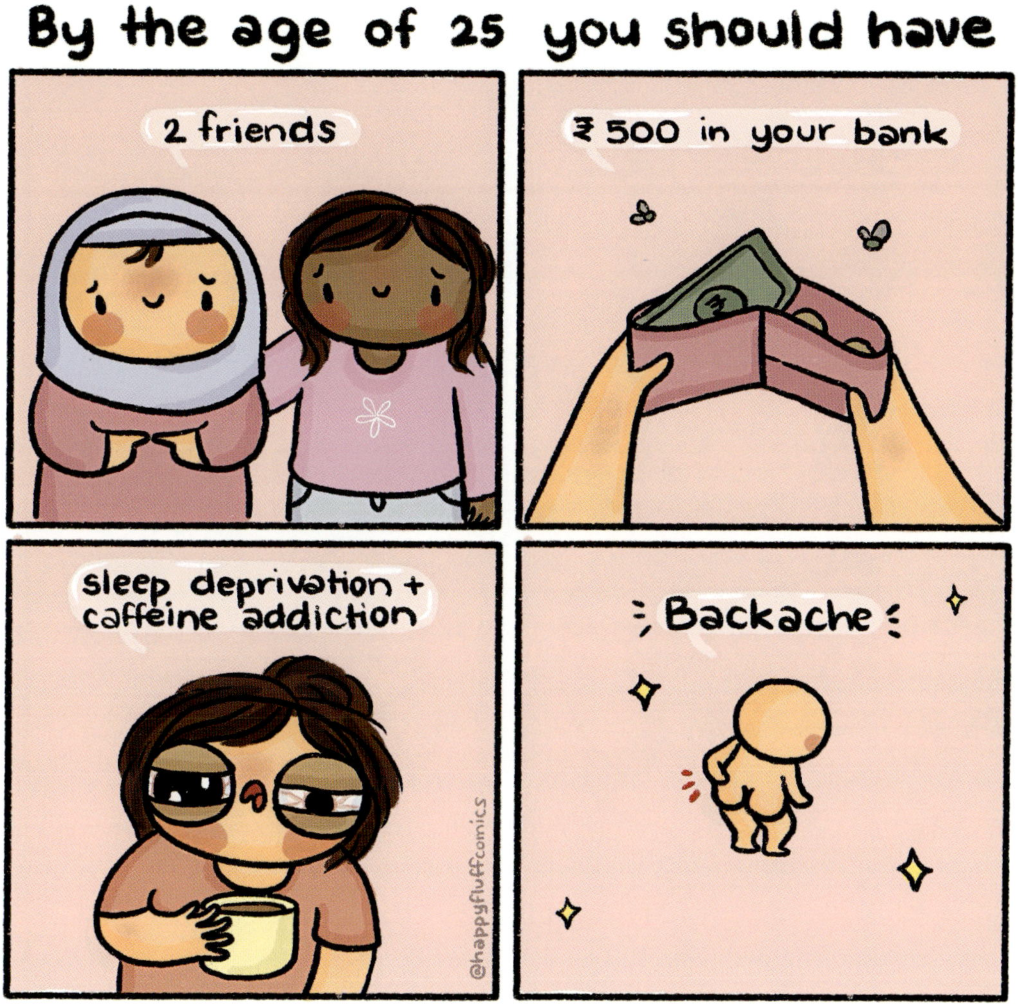
By the age of 25 you should have
2 friends
₹500 in your bank
sleep deprivation + caffeine addiction
Backache
@happyfluffcomics

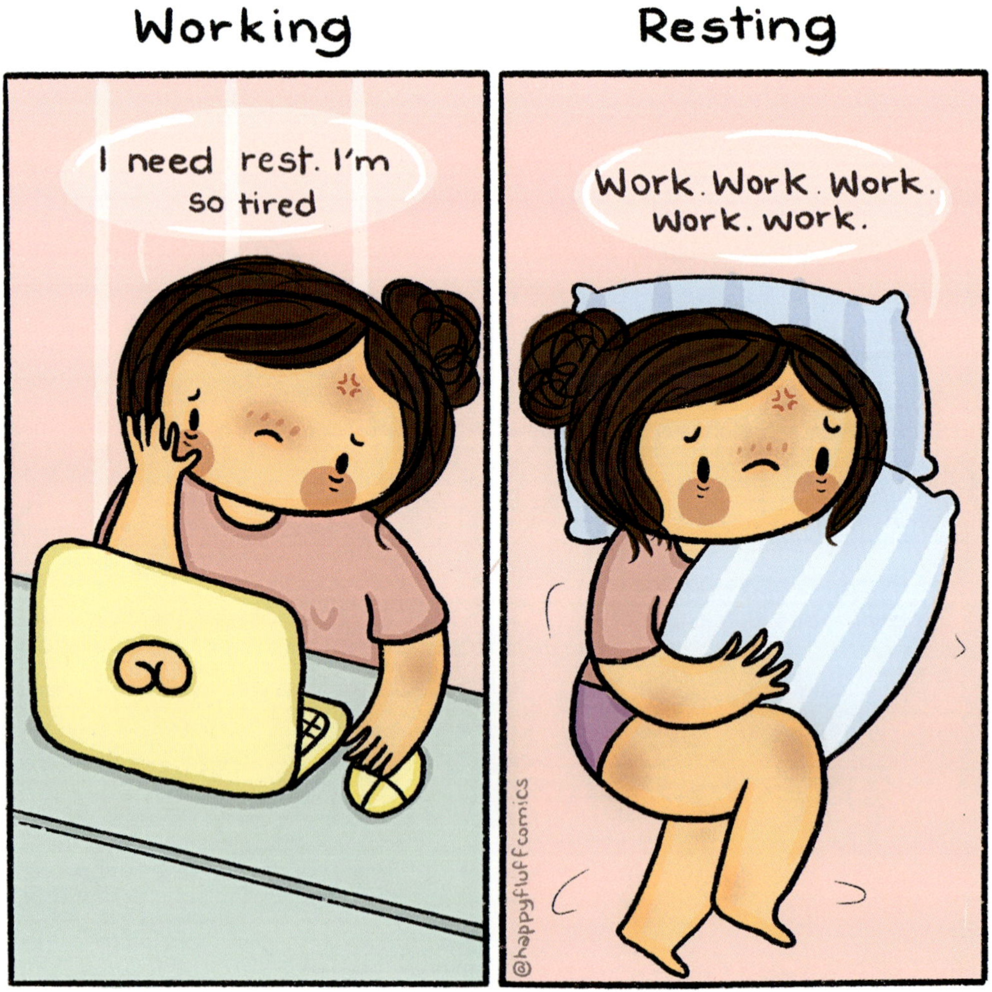
Working
Resting
I need rest. I'm so tired
Work. Work. Work. Work. work.
@happyfluffcomics

Trying to be productive

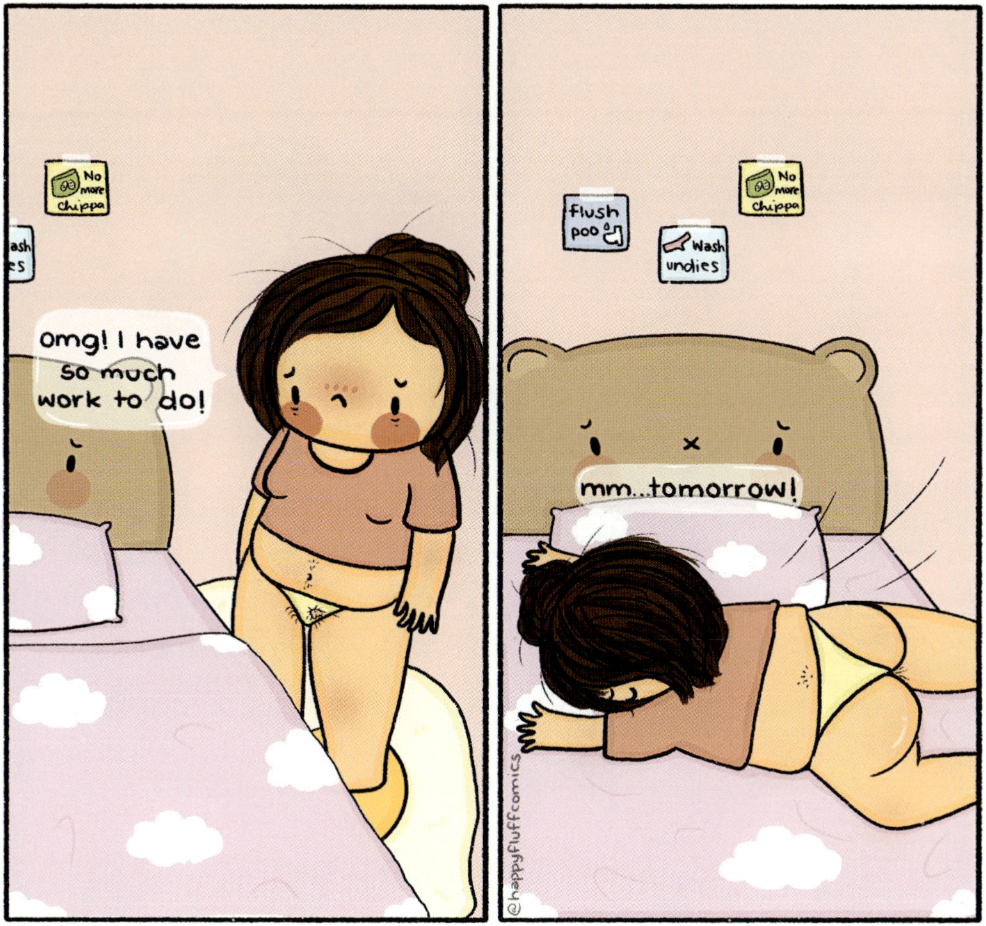
No more Chippa
omg! I have so much work to do!
flush poo
Wash undies
No more Chippa
mm...tomorrow!
@happyfluffcomics

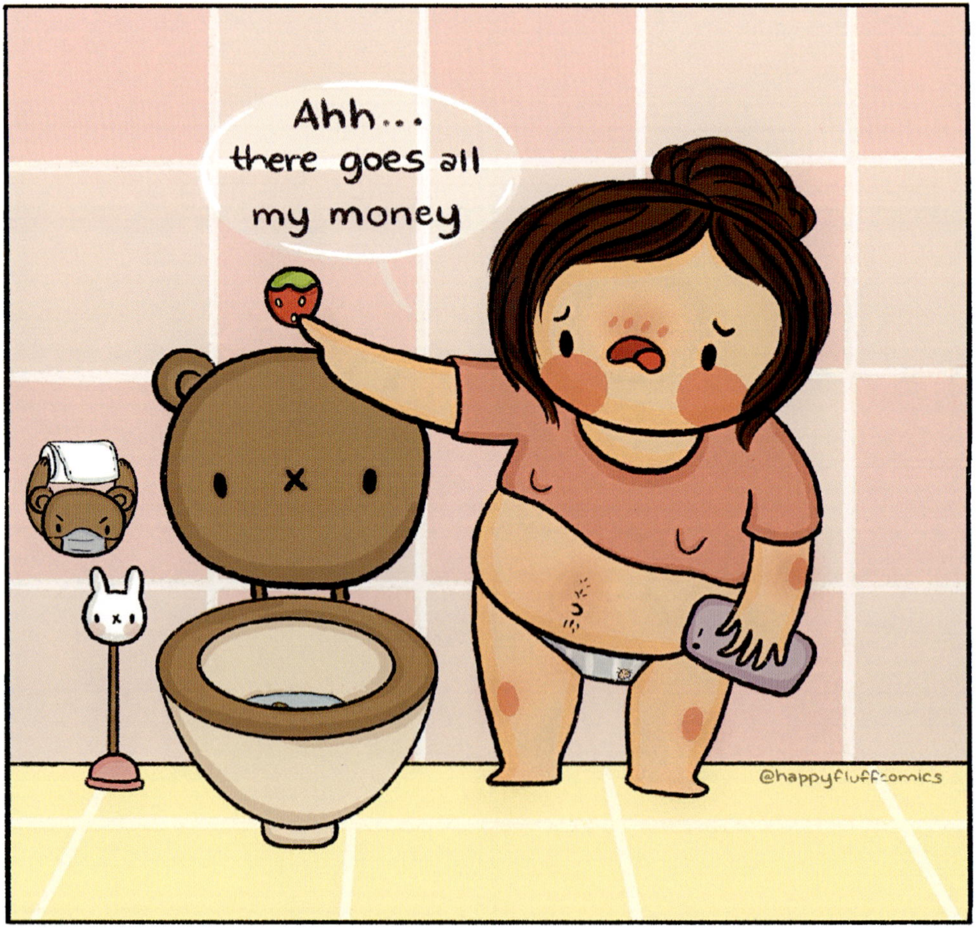
Ahh...
there goes all
my money
@happyfluffcomics

Unpacking after a trip

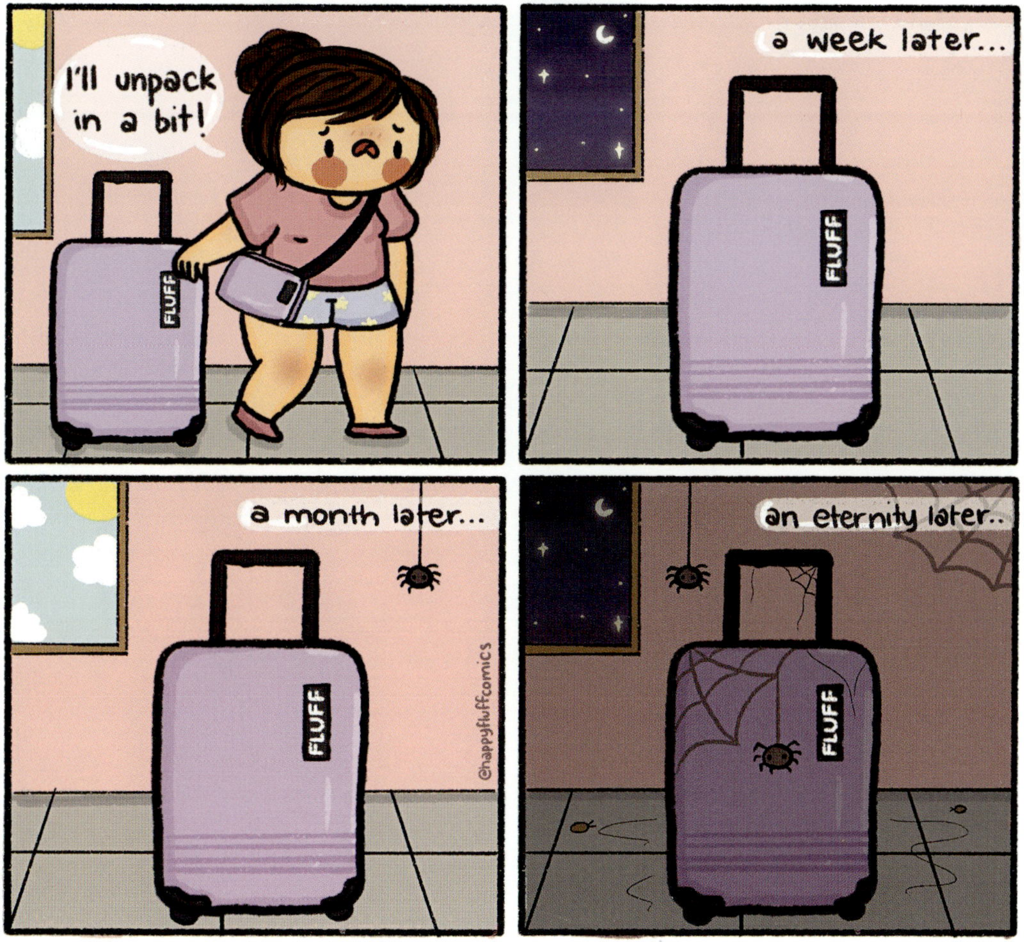
I'll unpack in a bit!
FLUFF
a week later...
FLUFF
a month later...
FLUFF
@happyfluffcomics
an eternity later..
FLUFF

When you try to turn the tap on!

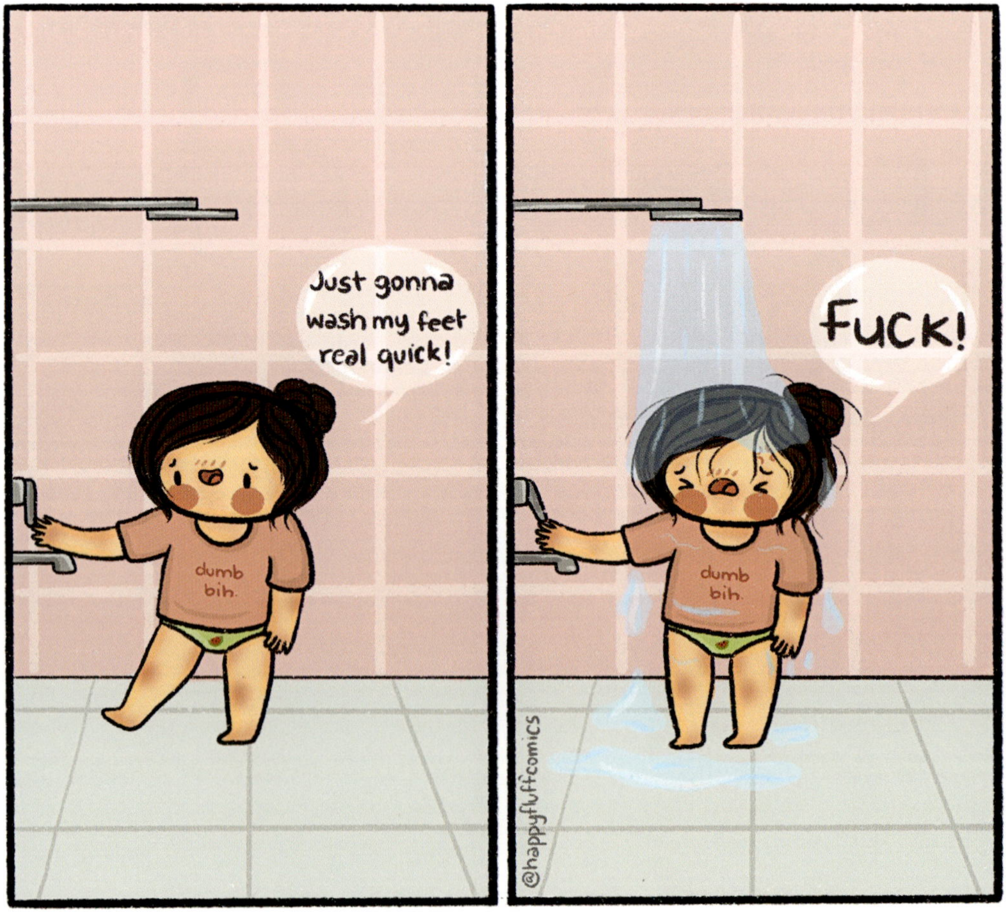
Just gonna wash my feet real quick!
dumb bih.
dumb bih.
FUCK!
@happyfluffcomics

How I work

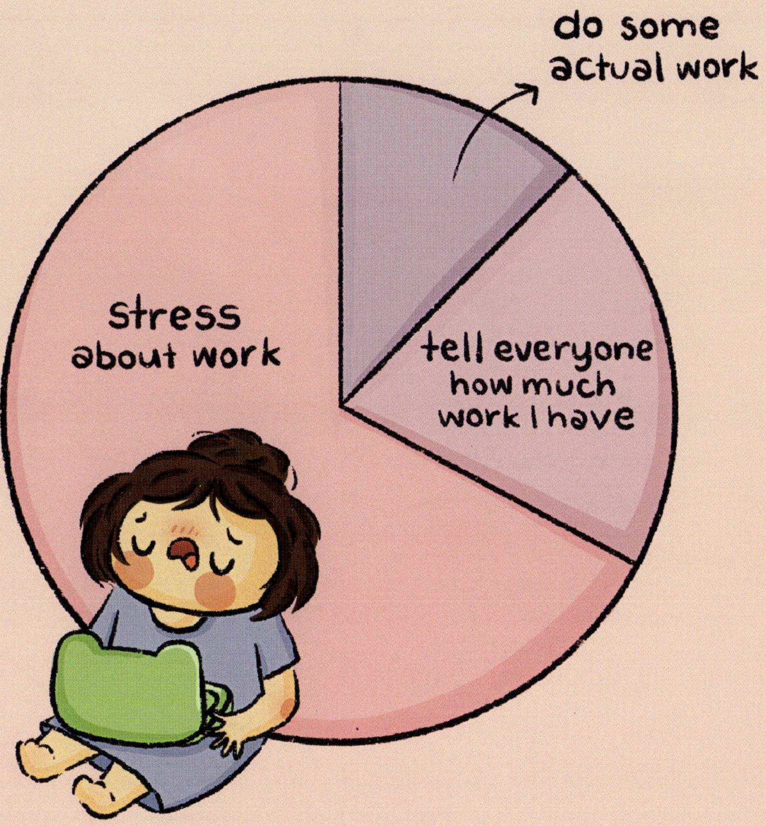
do some actual work
stress about work
tell everyone how much work I have

Me at 3 a.m. | Me the next day

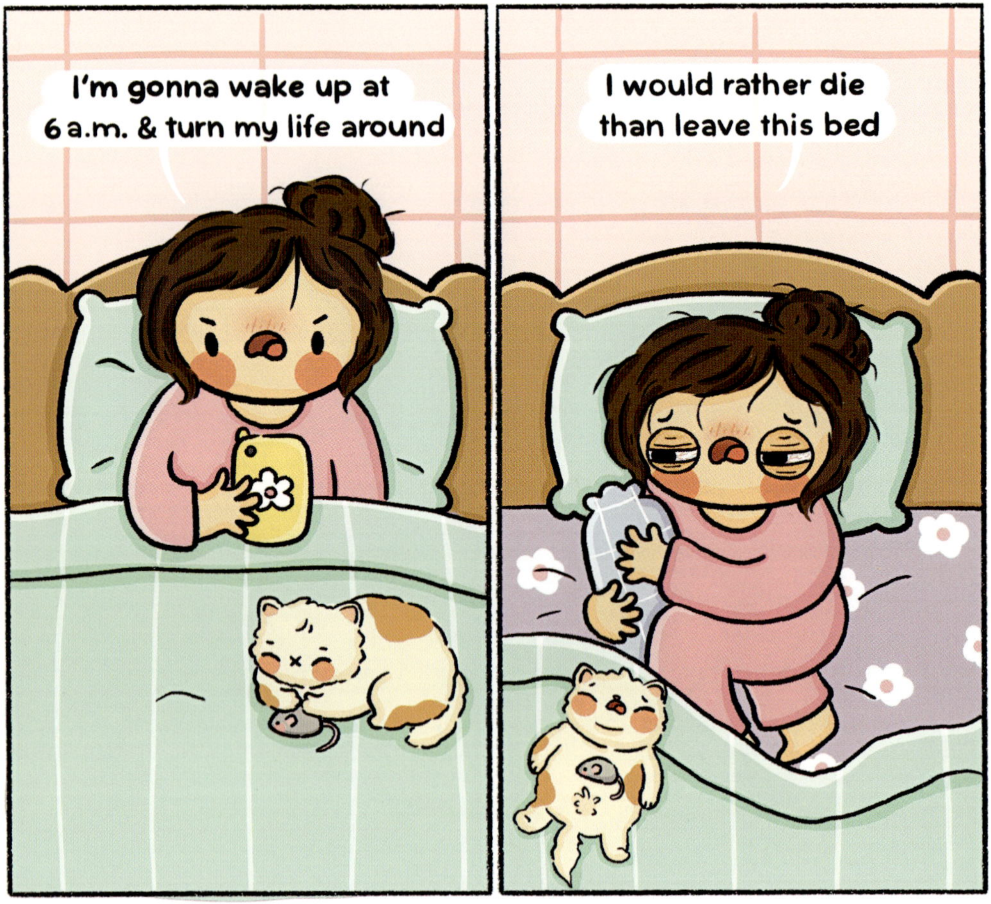
I'm gonna wake up at 6 a.m. & turn my life around
I would rather die than leave this bed

Headaches

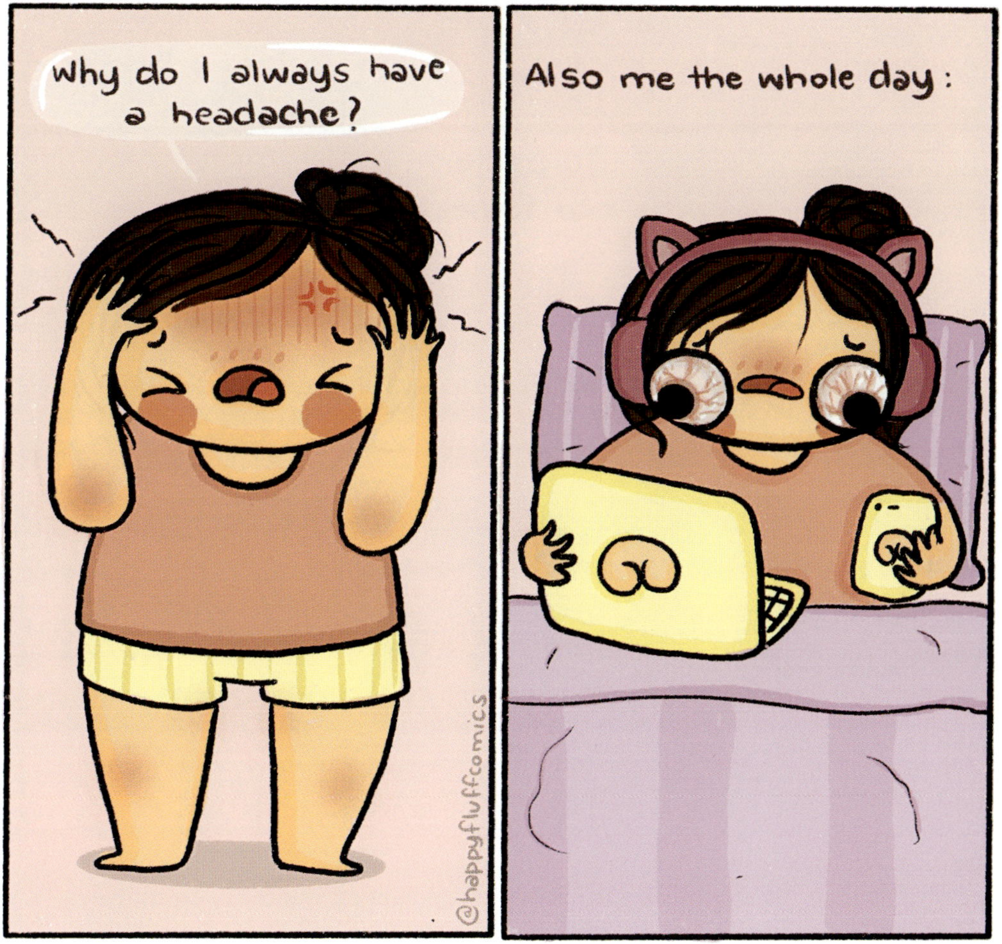

Why do I always have a headache?
Also me the whole day:
@happyfluffcomics

When I finally get comfortable in bed

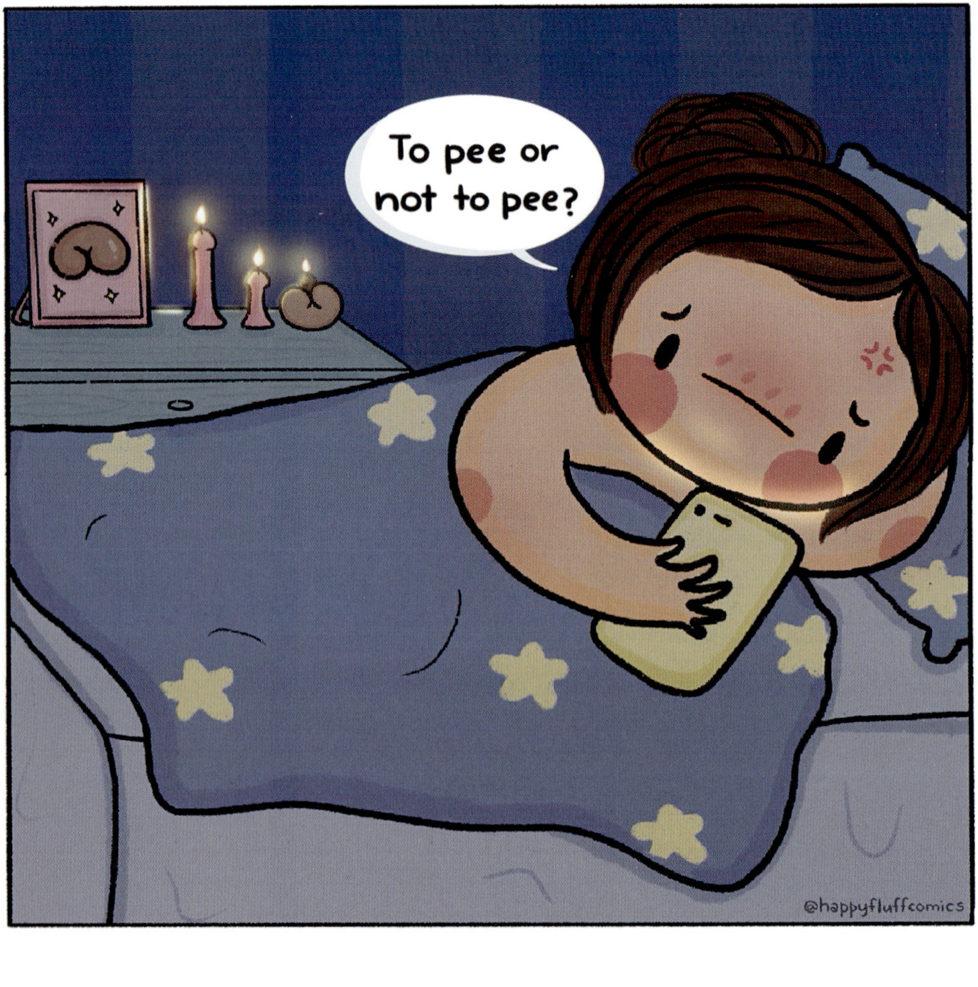
To pee or not to pee?
@happyfluffcomics

When you drop a massive turd

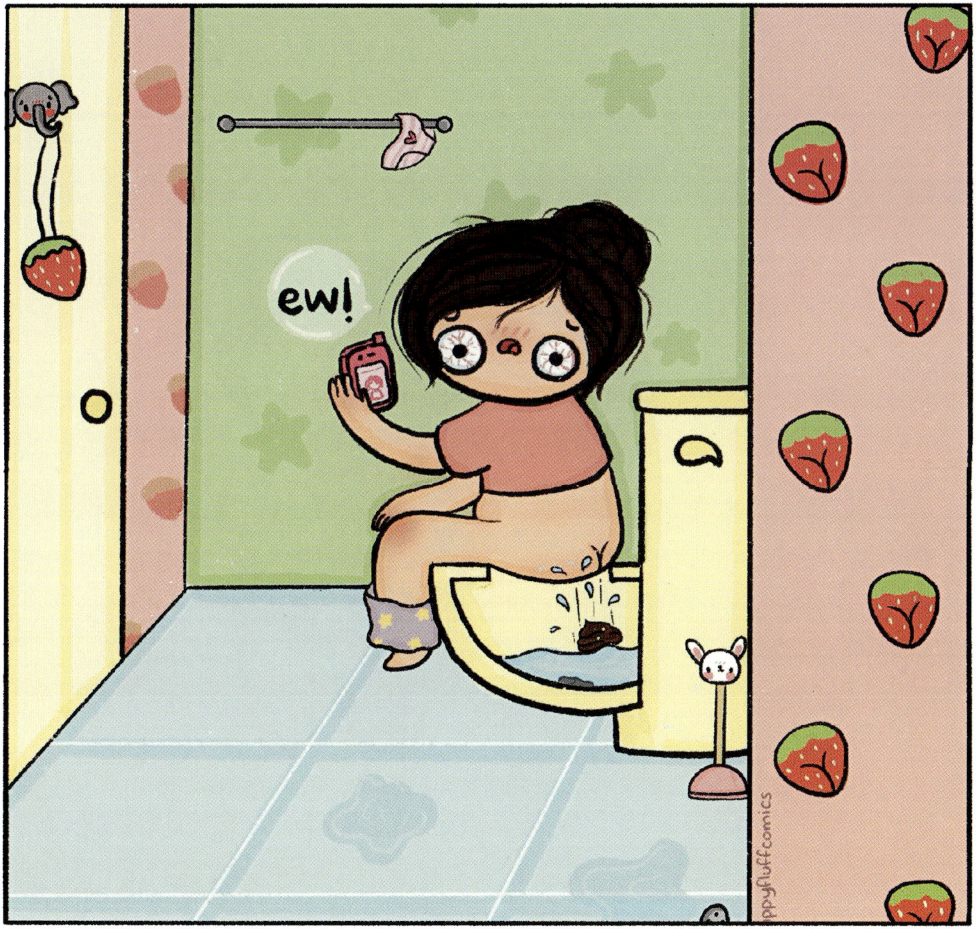
ew!
ppyfluffcomics

Me making a three-course meal at 3a.m.

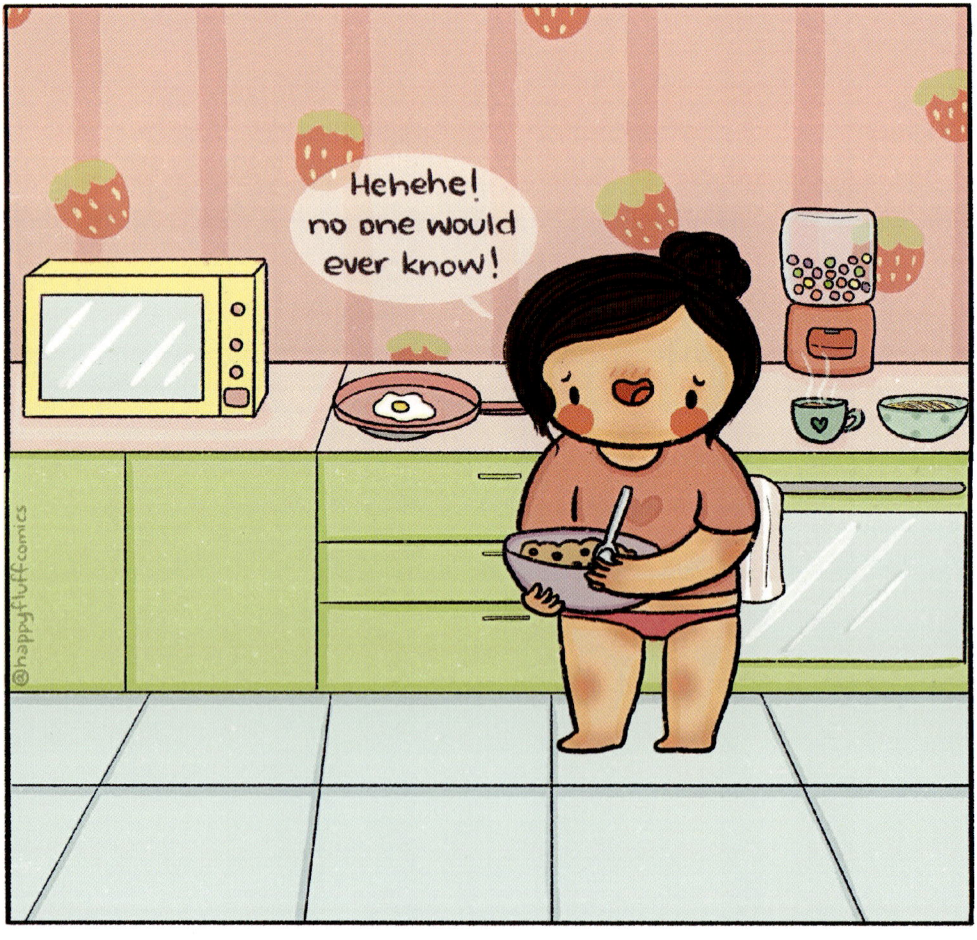
Hehehe! no one would ever know!
@happyfluffcomics

Me trying to be productive

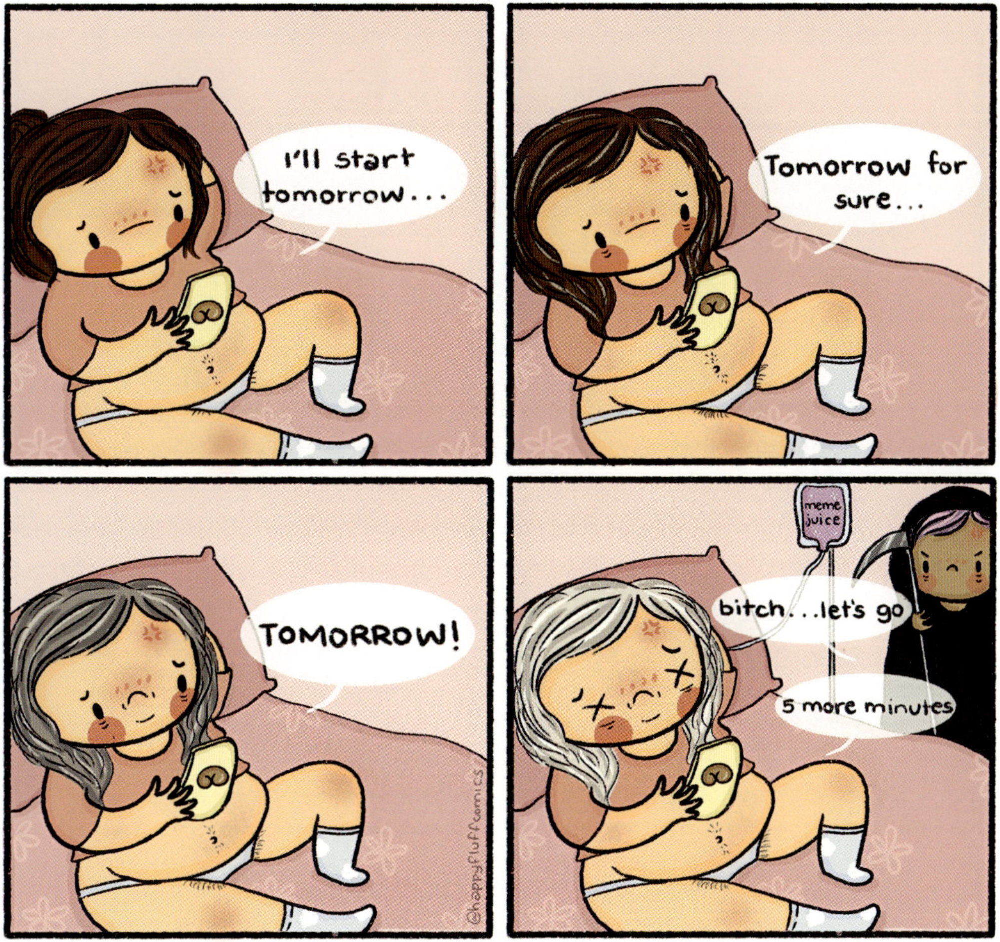
I'll start tomorrow...
Tomorrow for sure...
TOMORROW!
@happyfluffcomics
meme juice
bitch...let's go
5 more minutes

Living with pets

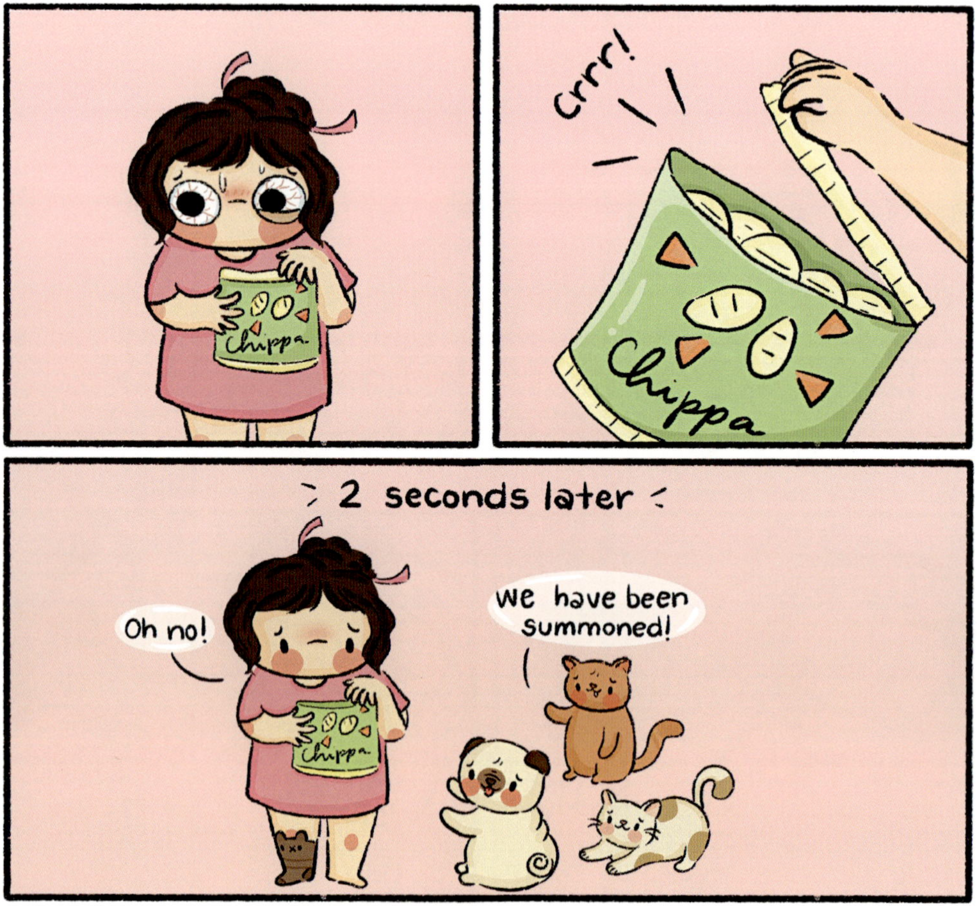
Chippa
Crrr!
Chippa
2 seconds later
Oh no!
We have been summoned!
Chippa

When your palm is itchy

itchie-itch!
there's only one solution
big chompa!

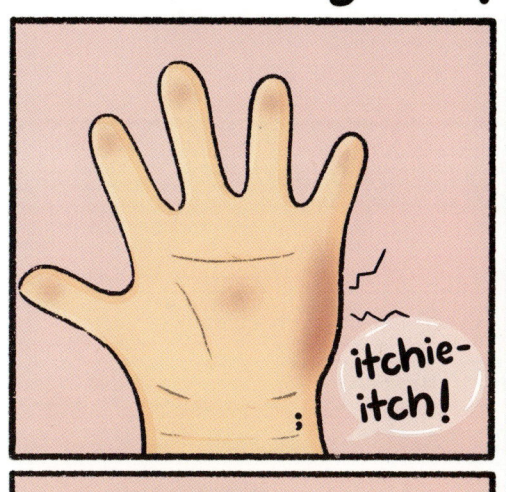

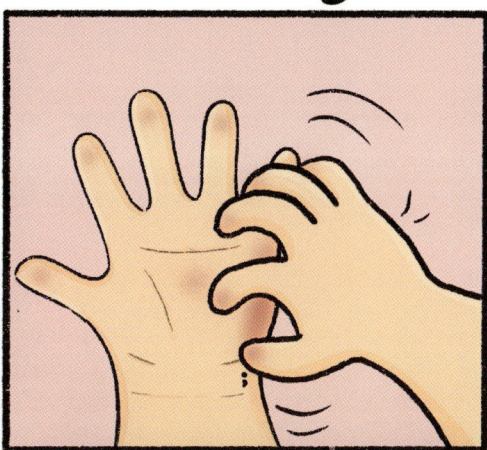

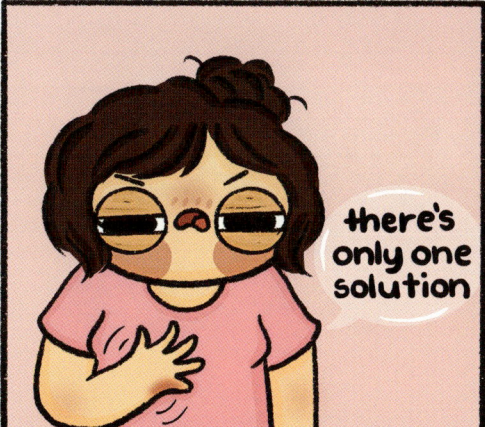

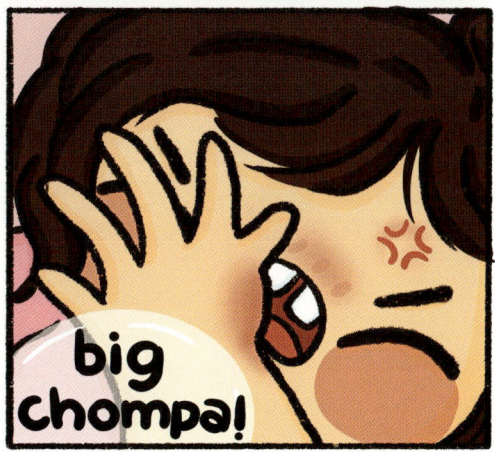

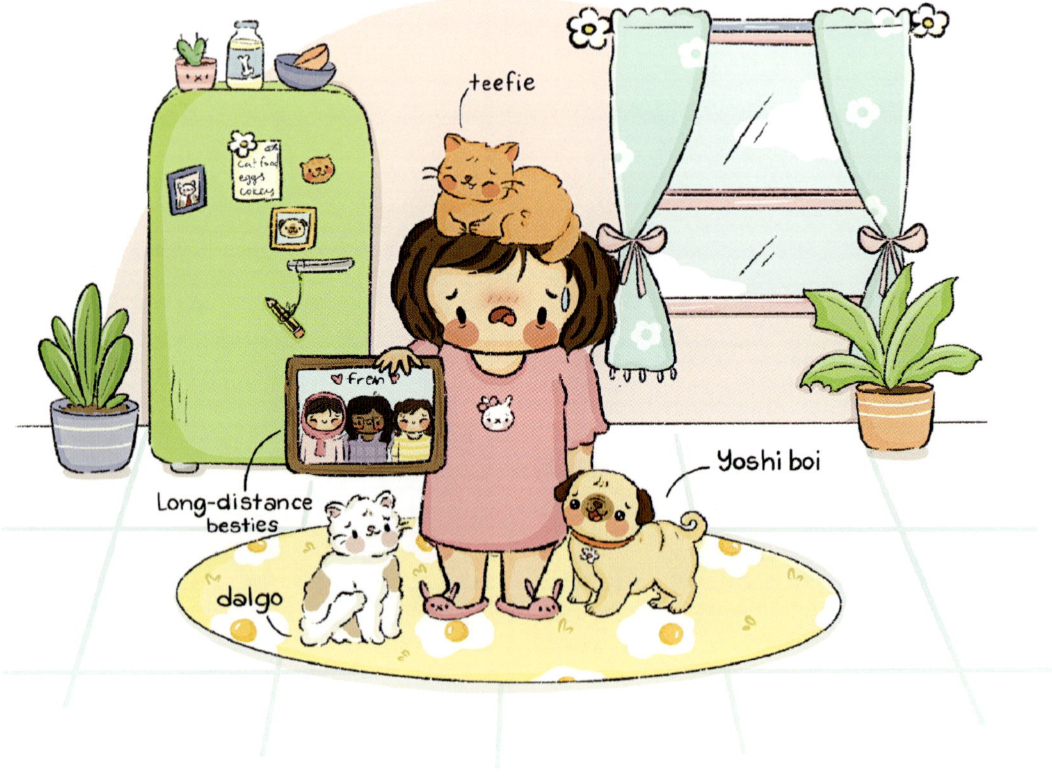

teefie
cat food
eggs
cokey
fren
Long-distance besties
Yoshi boi
dalgo

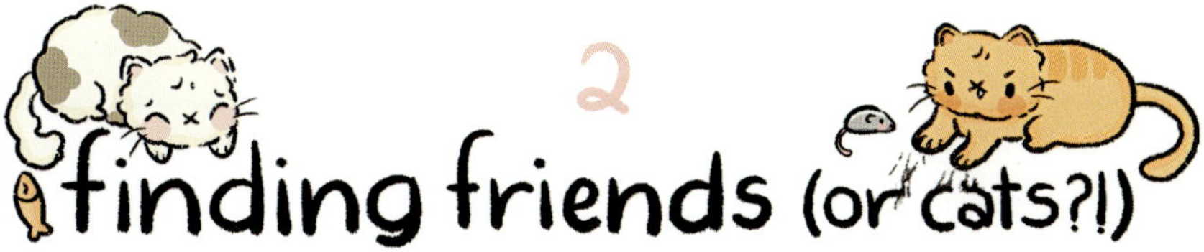

2

finding friends (or cats?!)

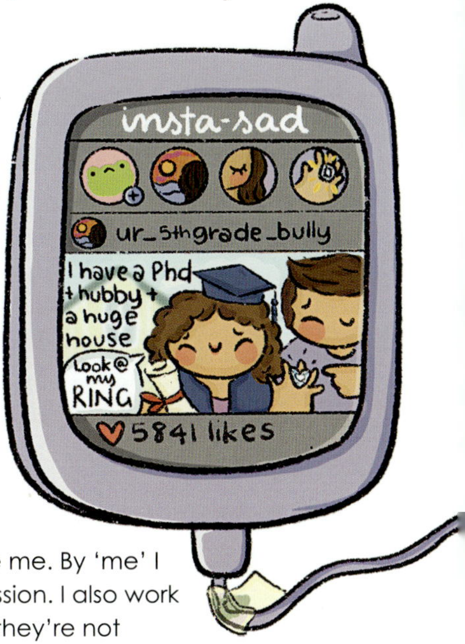

insta-sad
ur_5thgrade_bully
I have a Phd + hubby + a huge house
Look@ my RING
5841 likes

So, I open Instagram to look at cat memes because that's the only thing that makes me happy. 'Oh God . . . why did I do this?' Everyone's doing better than me. They all have fancy jobs, everyone's moving to the UK for some reason and a lot of them are married . . . some even have kids . . . how did this even happen?

All my friends are at different points in their life, which is so strange because until yesterday, we had the same priorities like submitting our design sheets or stalking our celebrity crush or . . . eating cake. And now suddenly, everyone's so grown up. All of them are either married or getting married and moving abroad. I don't know how it happened but . . . I just got left behind.

It's so hard to find friends as an adult. Especially if you're me. By 'me' I mean someone with crippling social anxiety and depression. I also work from home, so the only people I meet are my cats and they're not even 'people'.

So you try to socialize . . . but somehow everyone already has a group of friends and wants nothing to do with you. You can't walk into a café and sit next to a stranger. They're there alone because they want to be left alone. So you try and you try some more and finally accept your defeat.

Bffs

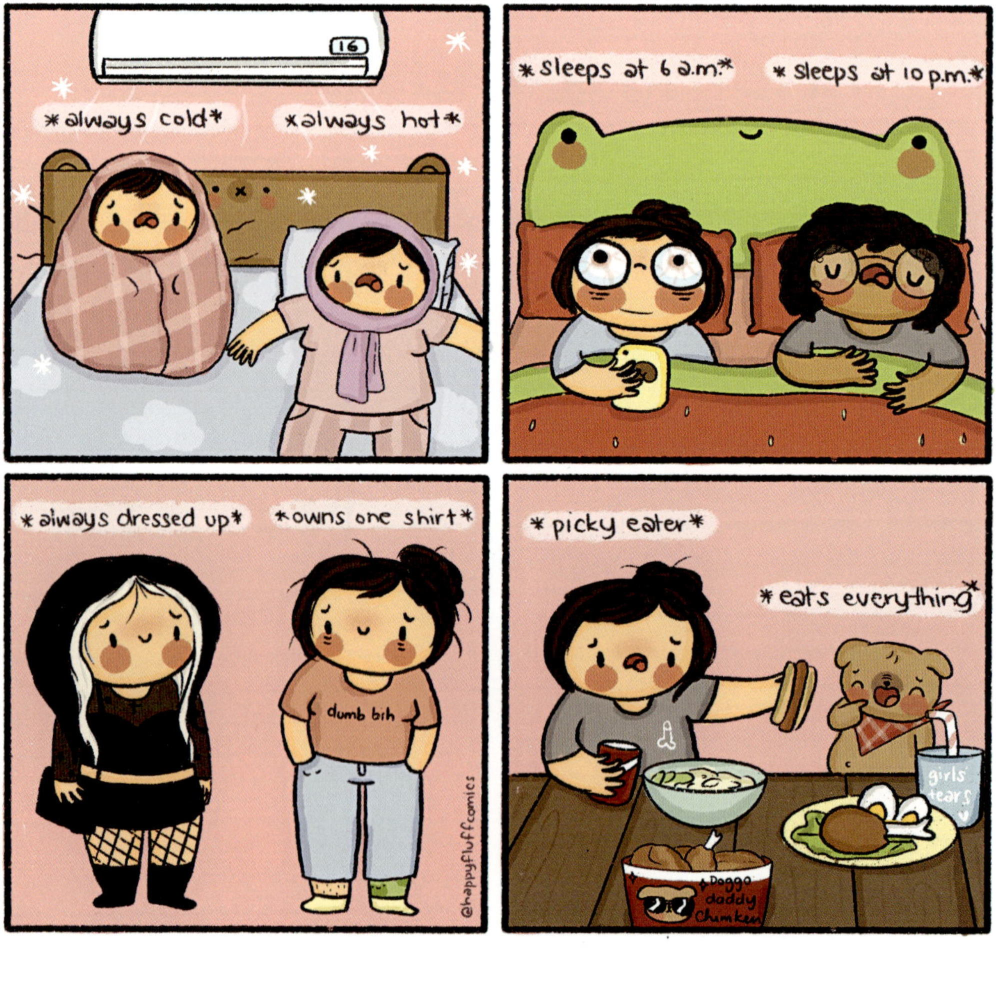
16
always cold
always hot
sleeps at 6 a.m.
sleeps at 10 p.m.
always dressed up
owns one shirt
dumb bih
@happyfluffcomics
picky eater
eats everything
girls' tears
Doggo daddy Chimken

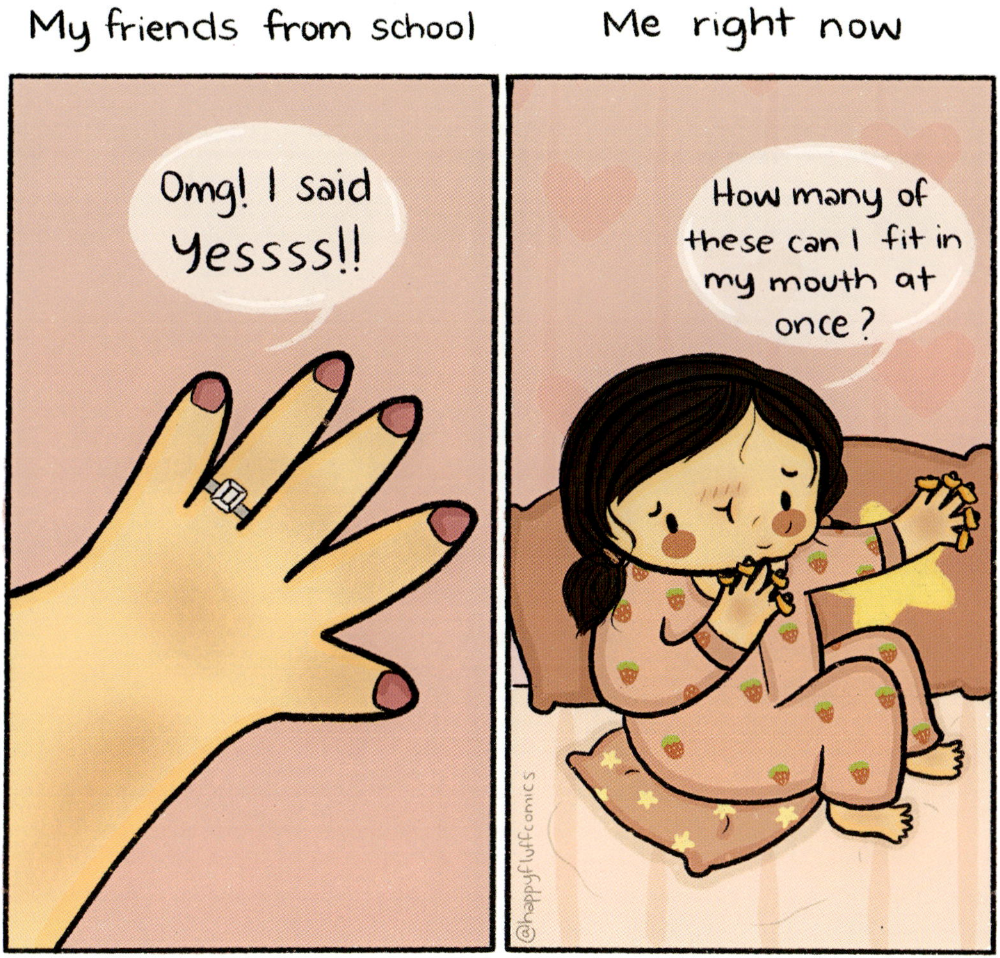
My friends from school
Me right now
Omg! I said Yessss!!
How many of these can I fit in my mouth at once?
@happyfluffcomics

Me after every phone call

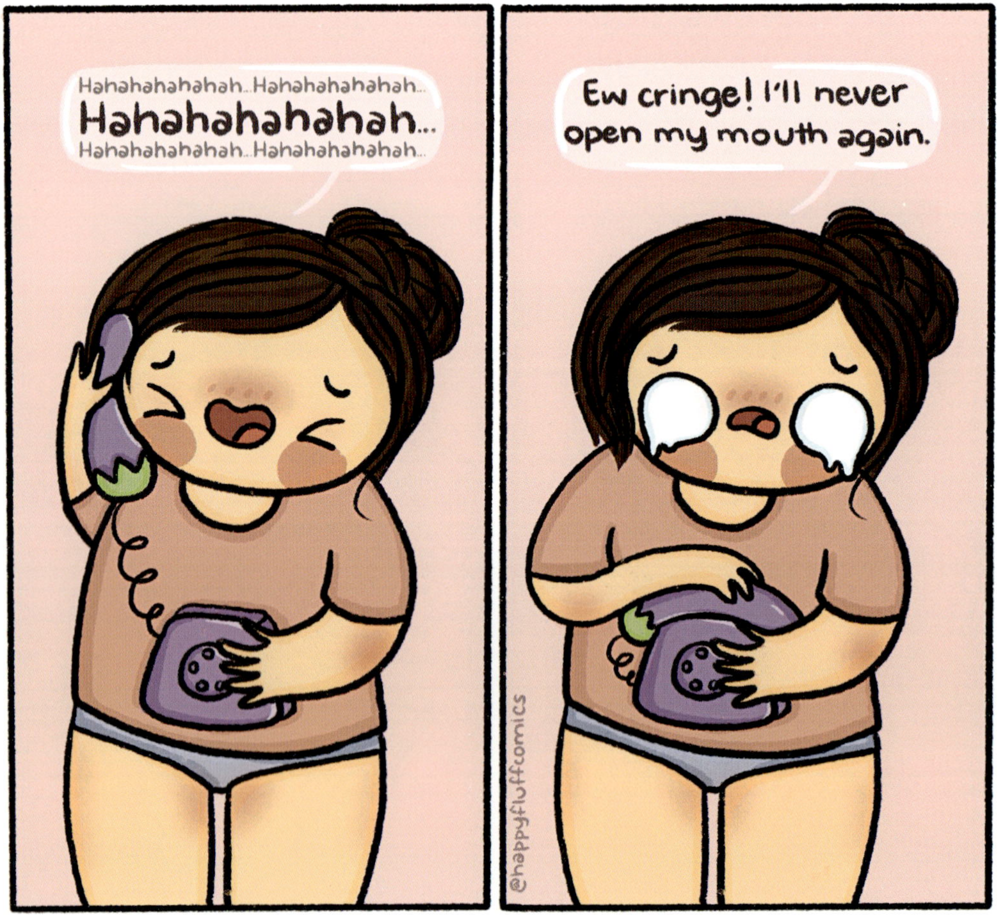

Hahahahahahah... Hahahahahahah...
Hahahahahahah...
Hahahahahahah... Hahahahahahah...
Ew cringe! I'll never open my mouth again.
@happyfluffcomics

Me after watching Masterchef

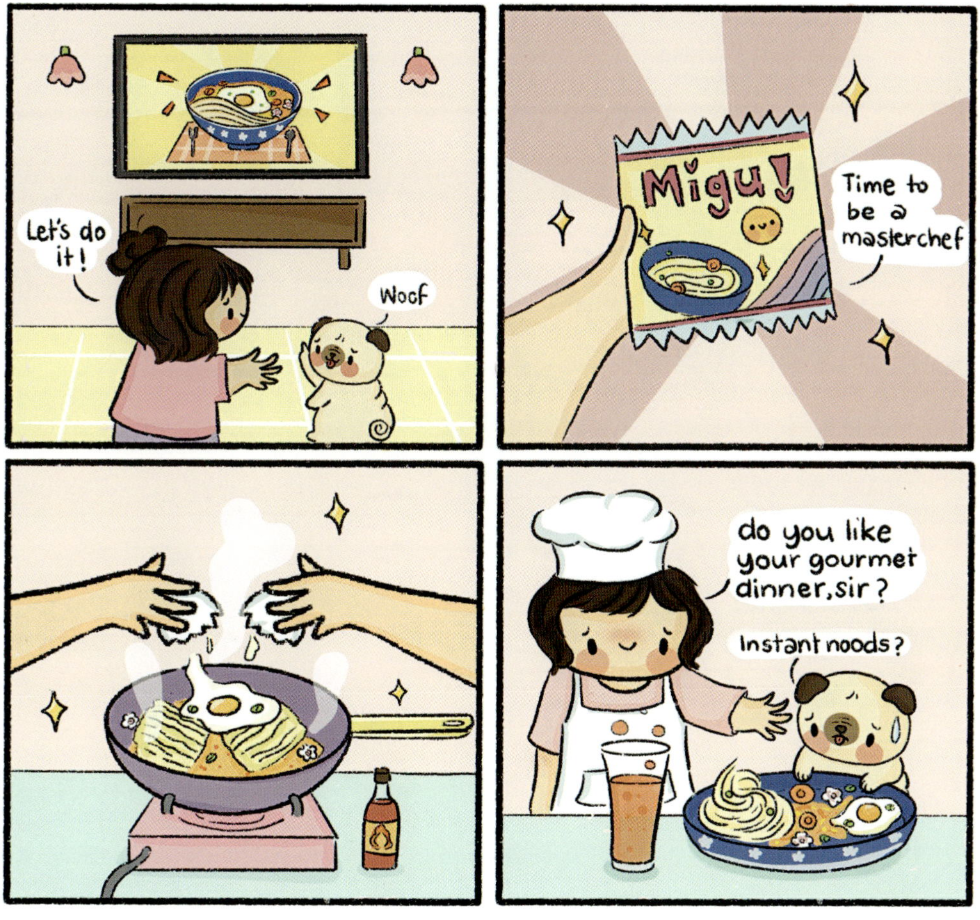
Let's do it!
Woof
Migu!
Time to be a masterchef
do you like your gourmet dinner, sir?
Instant noods?

When your best friend shows you a new song

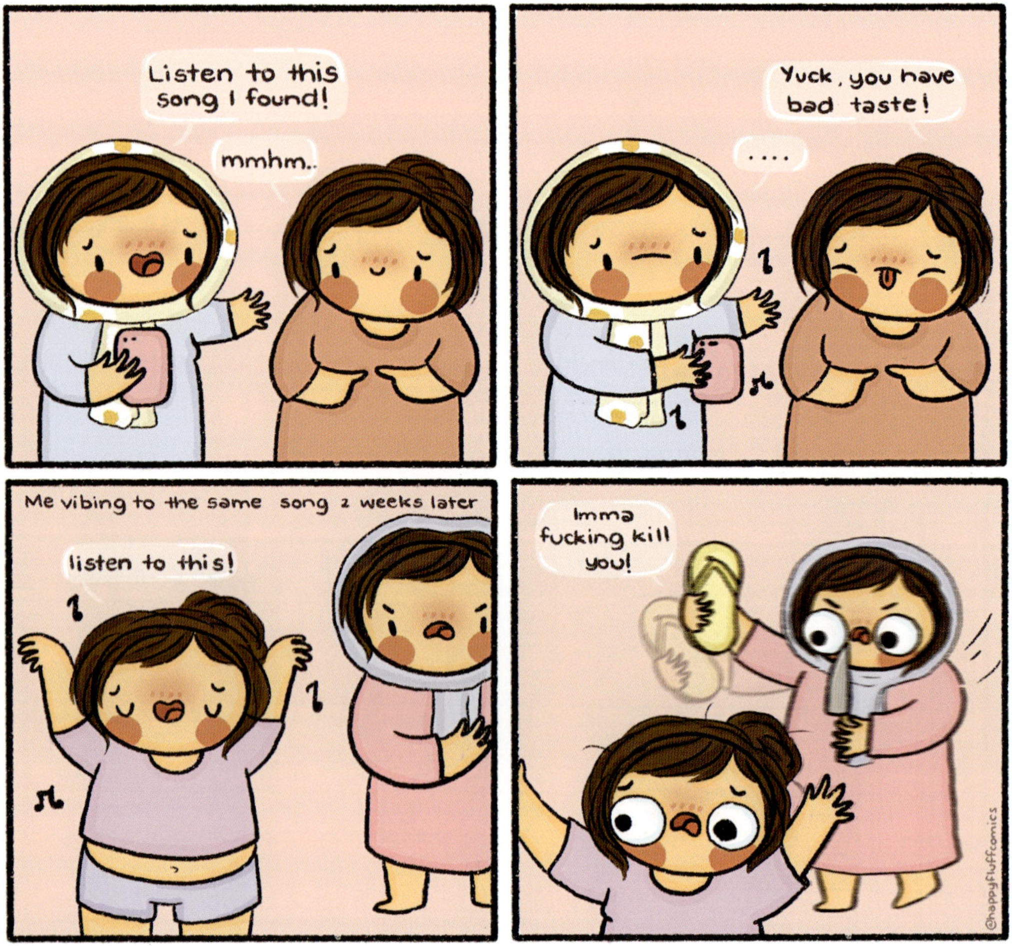
Listen to this song I found!
mmhm..
Yuck, you have bad taste!
....
Me vibing to the same song 2 weeks later
listen to this!
Imma fucking kill you!
@happyfluffcomics

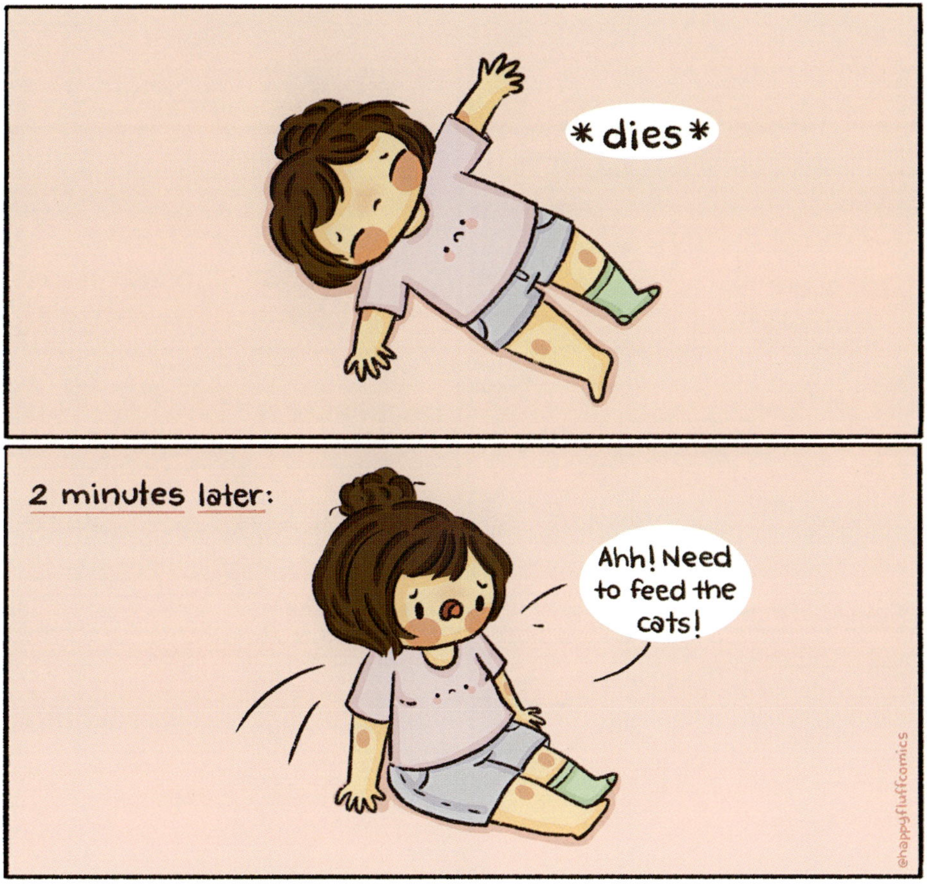
dies
2 minutes later:
Ahh! Need to feed the cats!
@happyfluffcomics

Buying your cattos stuff

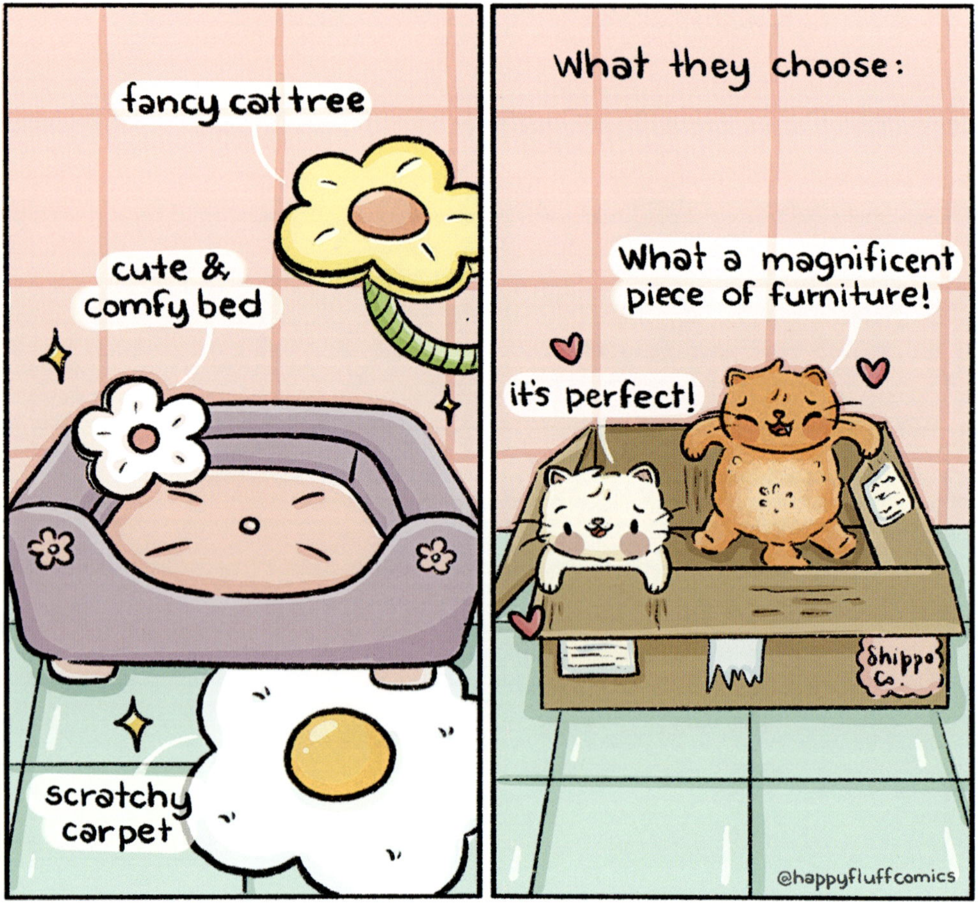

fancy cat tree
cute & comfy bed
scratchy carpet
What they choose:
What a magnificent piece of furniture!
it's perfect!
Shippo Co.
@happyfluffcomics

'You let your dog sleep on your bed?'

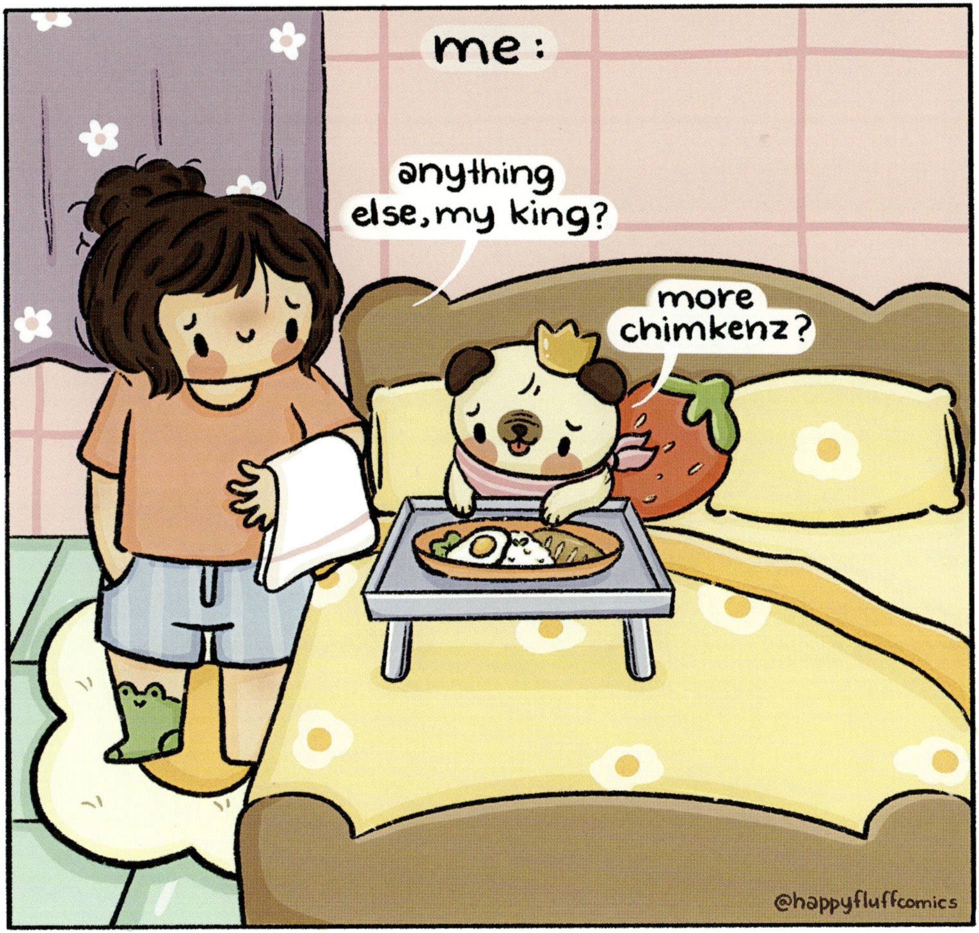
me:
anything else, my king?
more chimkenz?
@happyfluffcomics

my cat at the crack of dawn

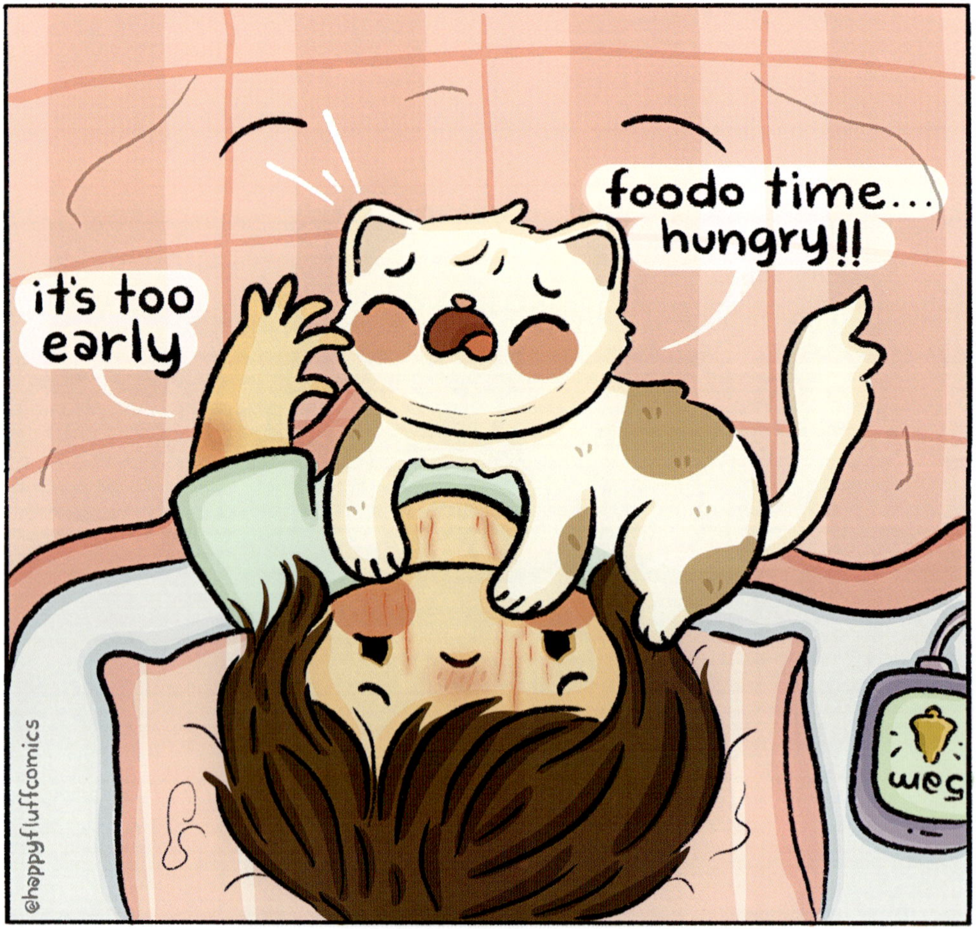
it's too early
foodo time... hungry!!
5am
@happyfluffcomics

Sharing the bed with pets

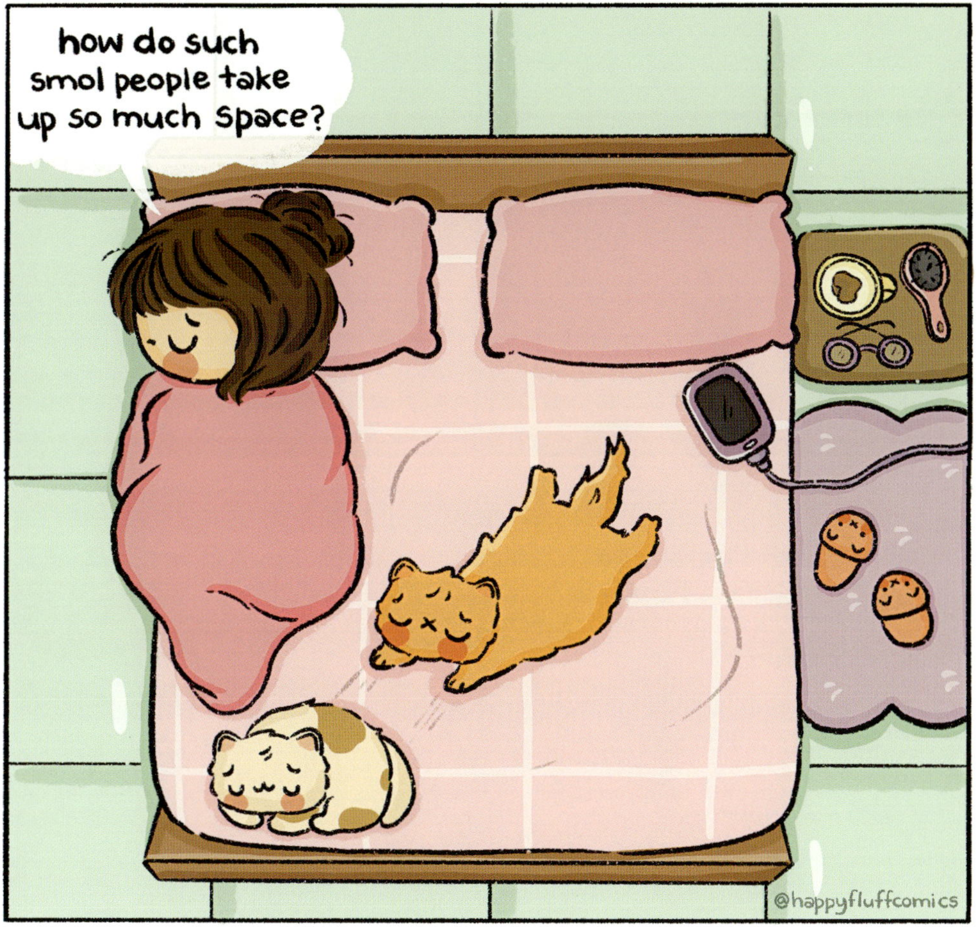
how do such smol people take up so much space?
@happyfluffcomics

feeling pukey
omg, hurry!
@happyfluffcomics
thank God! Made it to the carpet on time!

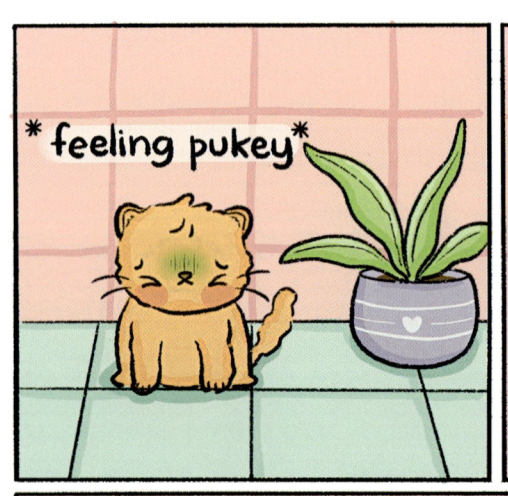

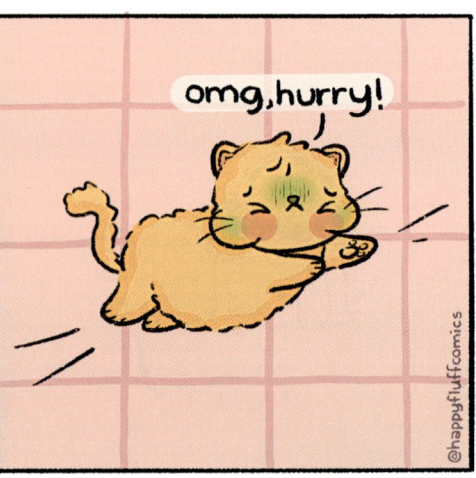

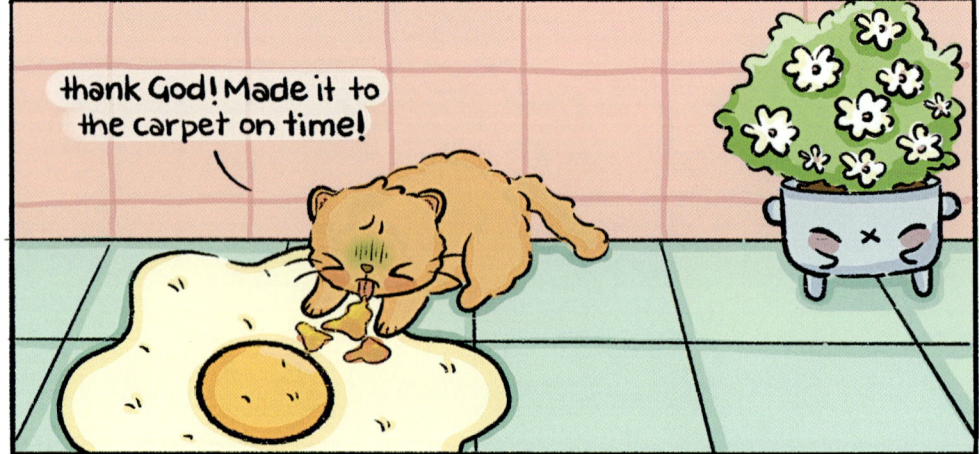

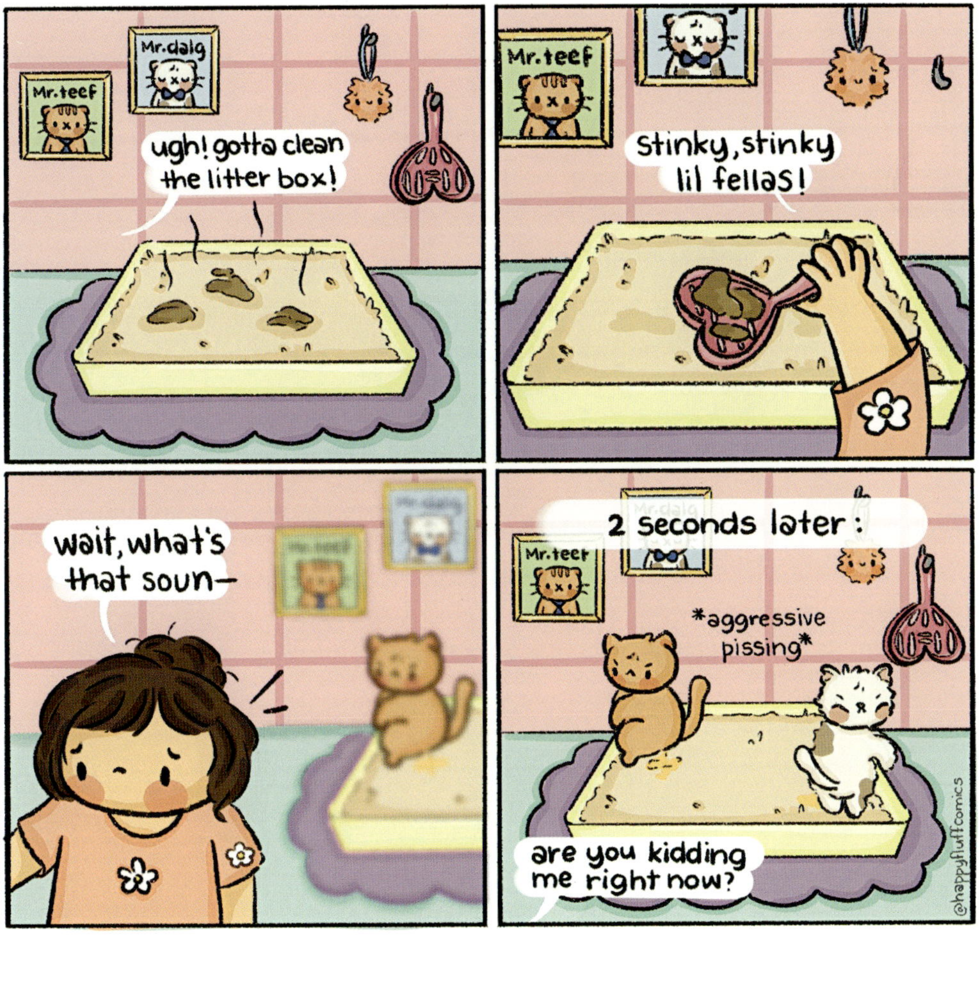
Mr.dalg
Mr.teef
ugh! gotta clean the litter box!
Mr.teef
stinky, stinky lil fellas!
wait, what's that soun–
2 seconds later:
Mr.teef
aggressive pissing
are you kidding me right now?
@happyfluffcomics

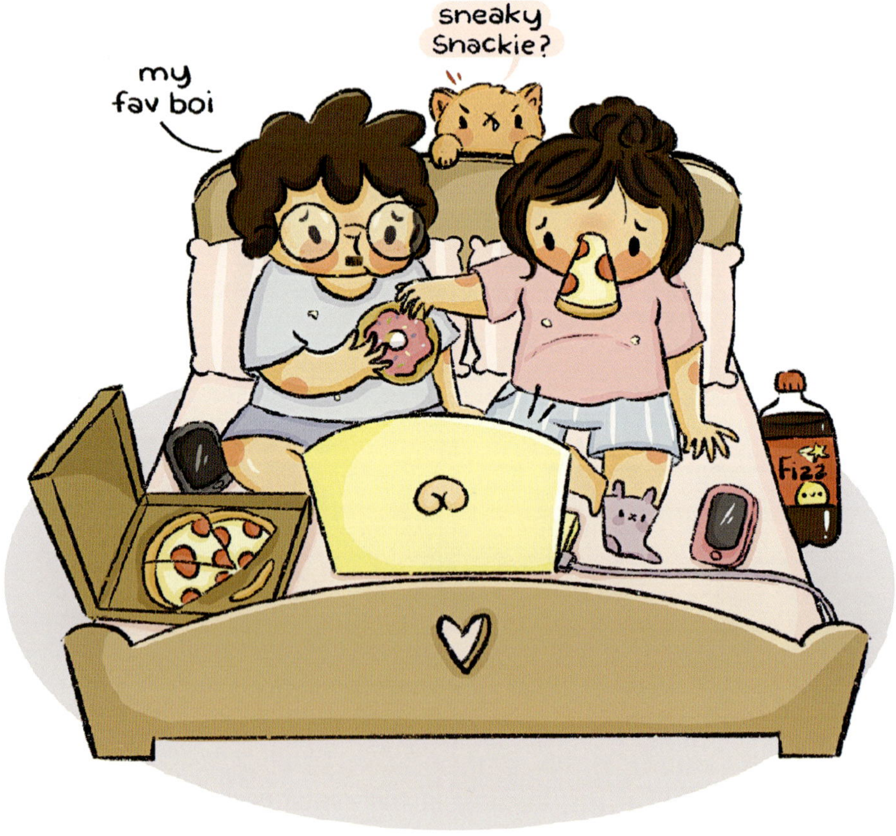
my fav boi
sneaky snackie?
Fizz

dating & stuff

Miss you ♥   ♥ Miss you

So, you sign up on a dating app to seek some validation from strangers so you don't hate yourself any more than you already do. You go on a few dates because you're lonely and at this point, you'd take any crumb of attention you can find. Some go well and some . . . send you a playlist of 100 loud songs that give you a migraine. You kinda get fed up of asking people what their favourite colour is after the first few failed dates.

I finally matched with someone nice when I was at the verge of deleting the app. He had glasses, and if you know me, you know I love glasses (not in a creepy kind of way or anything though).

We talked and I realized that he's from a different city. I wasn't looking for anything serious because of my extreme abandonment issues and depression. But the banter was great and I kept it going for months until we ended up being in a two-year-long serious long-distance relationship. How did I manage to find yet another long-distance relationship when every other relationship in my life right now is long distance?

Well, I'm back to where I started. I need to find friends . . . Again.

my Dream Boi @ 16

(Never dated before)

Nice voice

good looking

funny

Nice to my friends

Romantic + writes me letters

Speaks my language

fluffy hair

Big Chonky glasses

No beard

fancy job

has good Style

into art (maybe)

smells good

Dream guy after 25

(after a series of horrible relationships)

Bonus:
Wears glasses

likes me

likes pets

doesn't yell
at me

Wears
deodorant
(hopefully)

bare minimum
kinda dude

responds
to texts

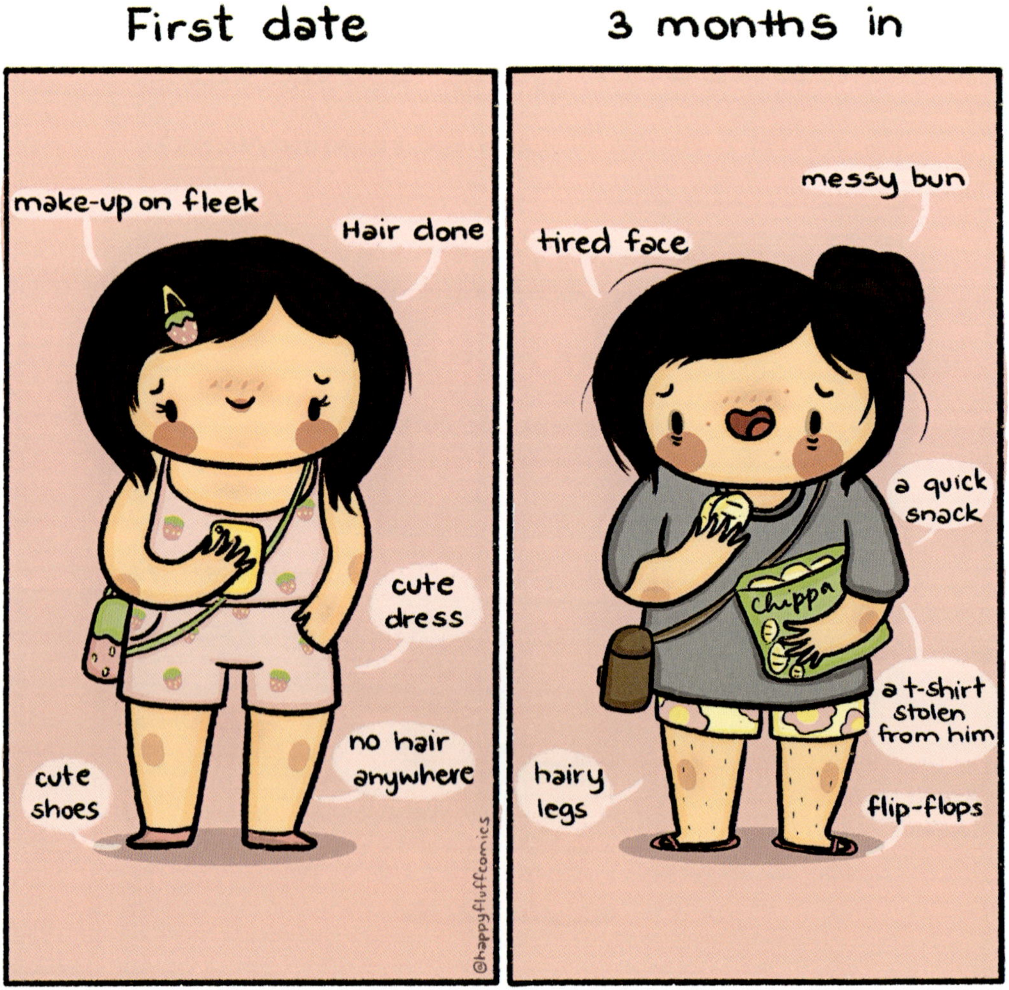
First date
3 months in
make-up on fleek
Hair done
cute dress
no hair anywhere
cute shoes
@happyfluffcomics
messy bun
tired face
a quick snack
Chippa
a t-shirt stolen from him
hairy legs
flip-flops

Valentine's day

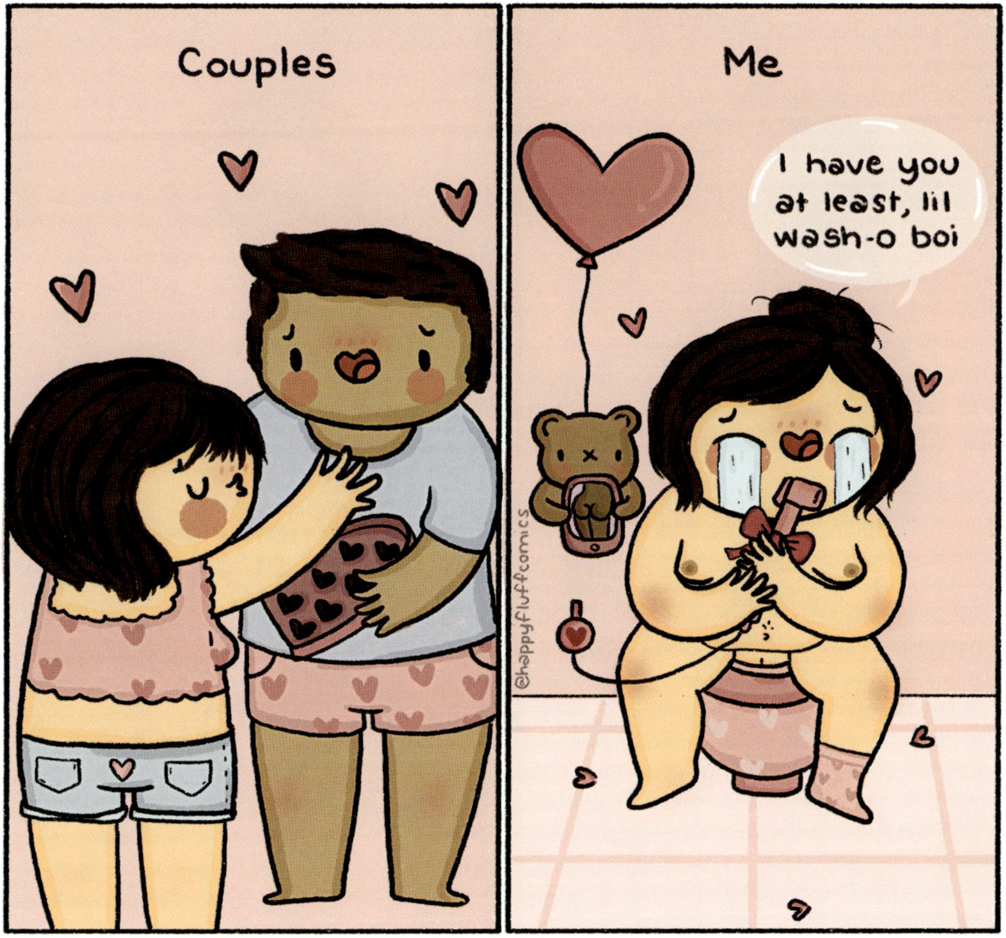
Couples
Me
I have you at least, lil wash-o boi
@happyfluffcomics

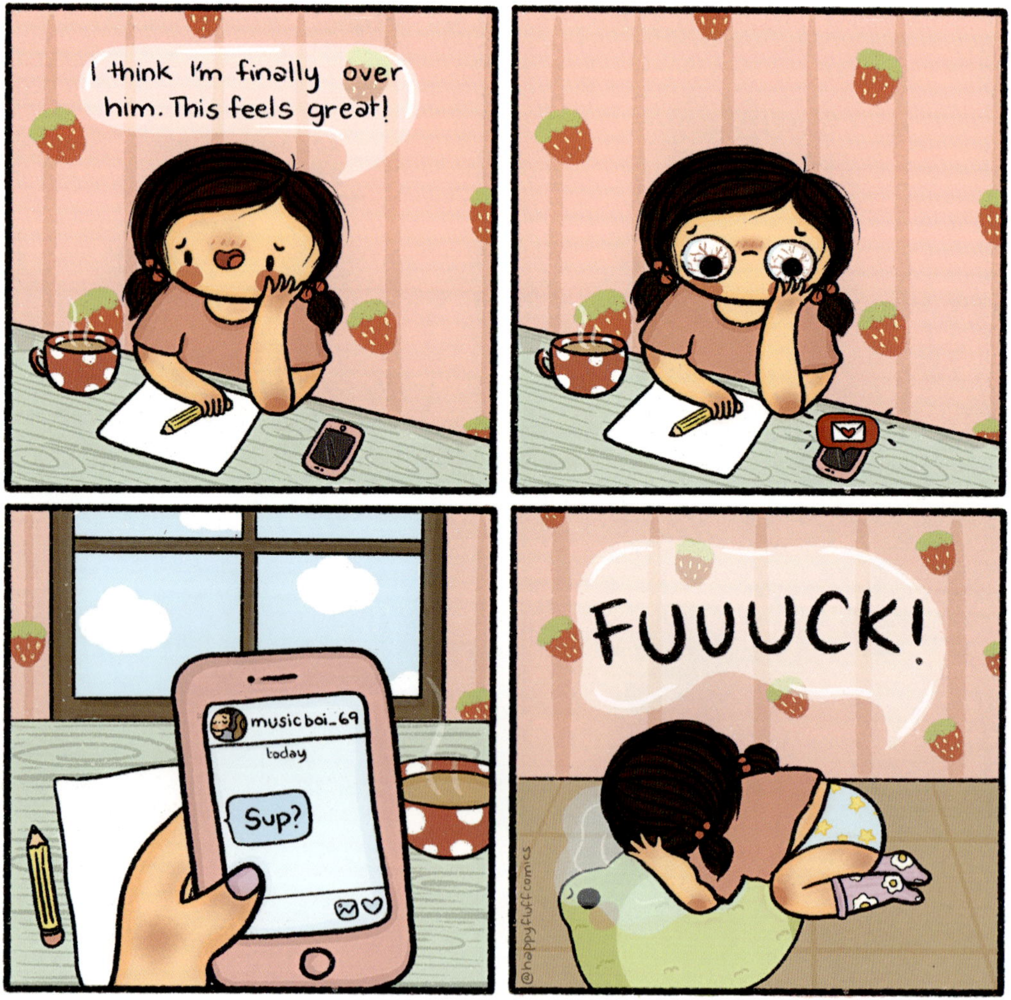
I think I'm finally over him. This feels great!
music boi_69
today
Sup?
FUUUCK!
@happyfluffcomics

When you finally get to go on a date...

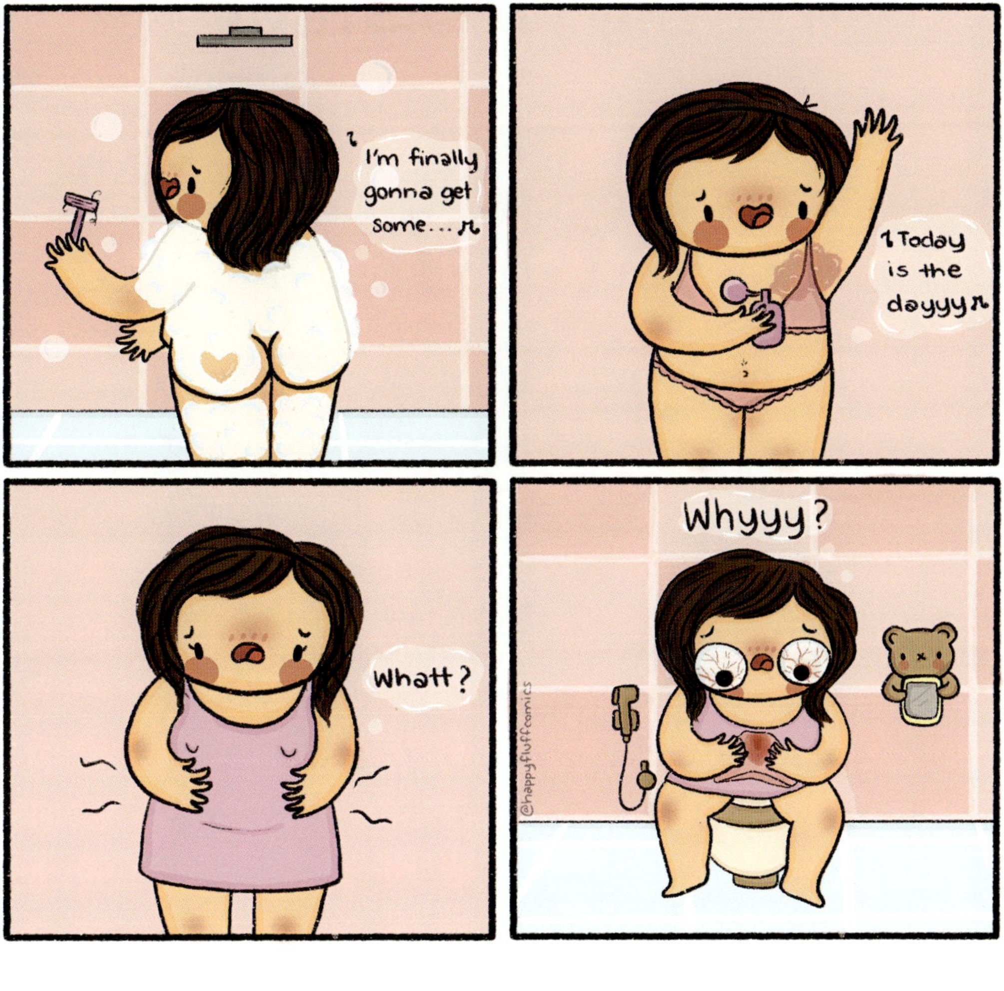

I'm finally gonna get some...
Today is the dayyy
Whatt?
Whyyy?
@happyfluffcomics

the boi who stayed

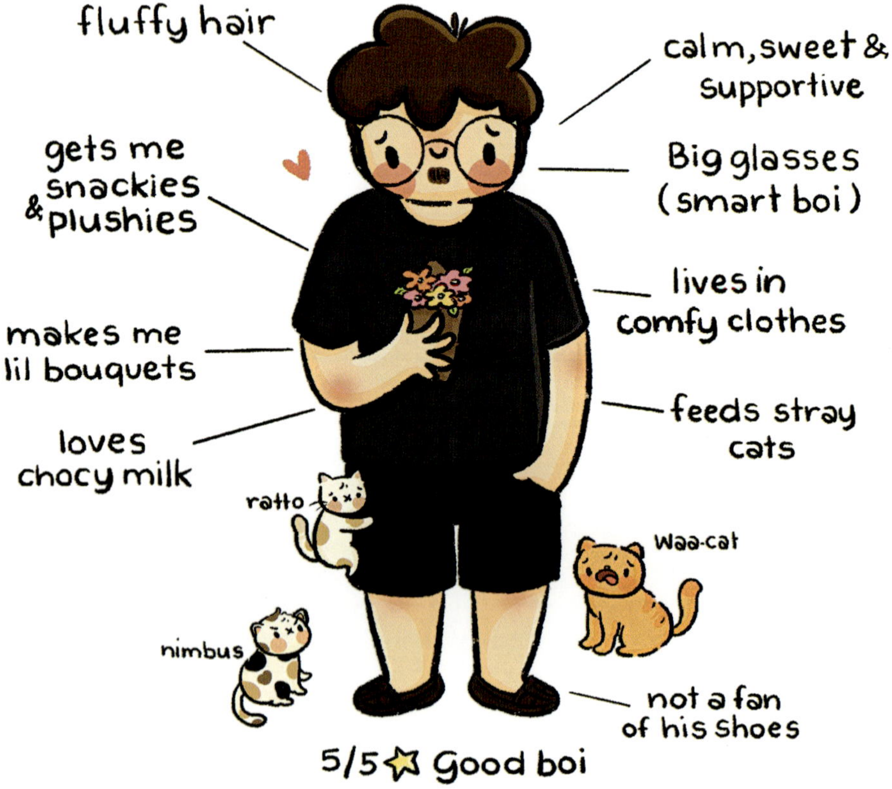
fluffy hair
calm, sweet & supportive
gets me snackies & plushies
Big glasses (smart boi)
lives in comfy clothes
makes me lil bouquets
feeds stray cats
loves chocy milk
ratto
waa-cat
nimbus
not a fan of his shoes
5/5 Good boi

Long-distance relationship things

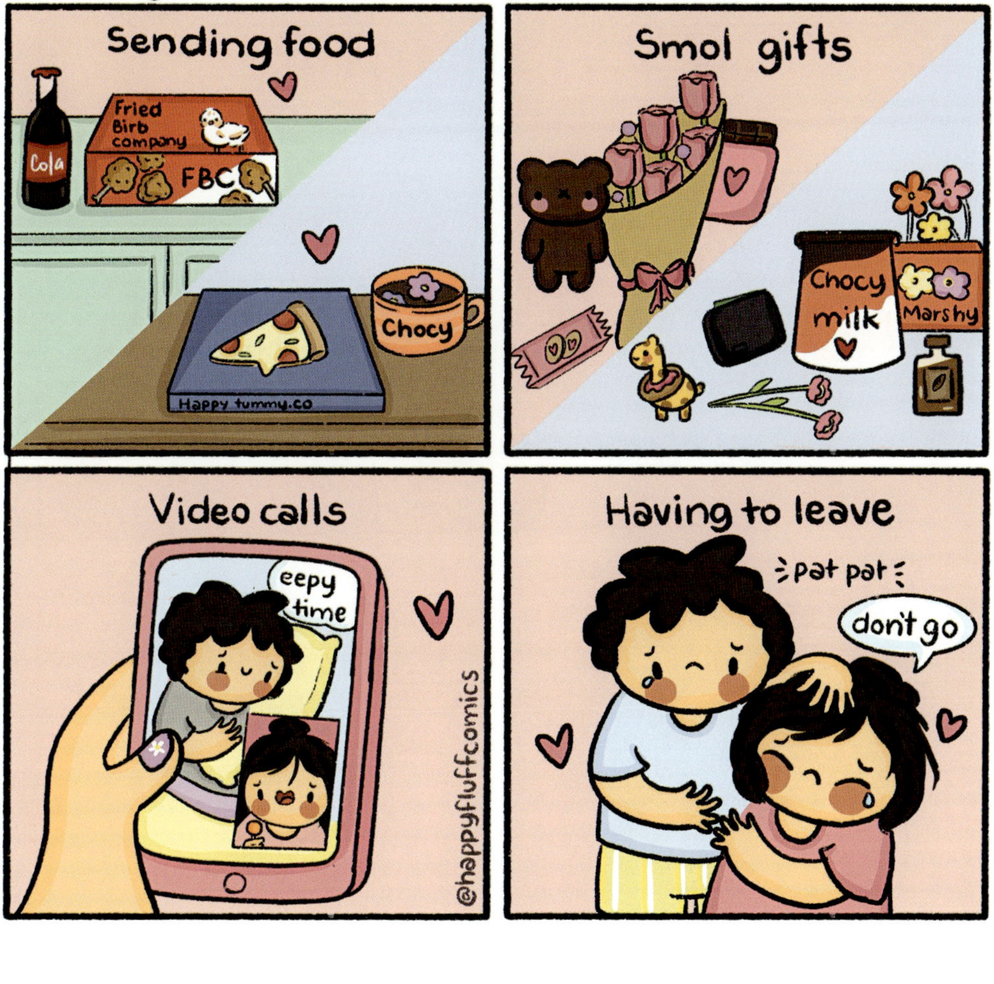

Sending food
Cola
Fried Birb company
FBC
Chocy
Happy tummy.co
Smol gifts
Chocy milk
Marshy
Video calls
eepy time
@happyfluffcomics
Having to leave
pat pat
don't go

When you're done showering &

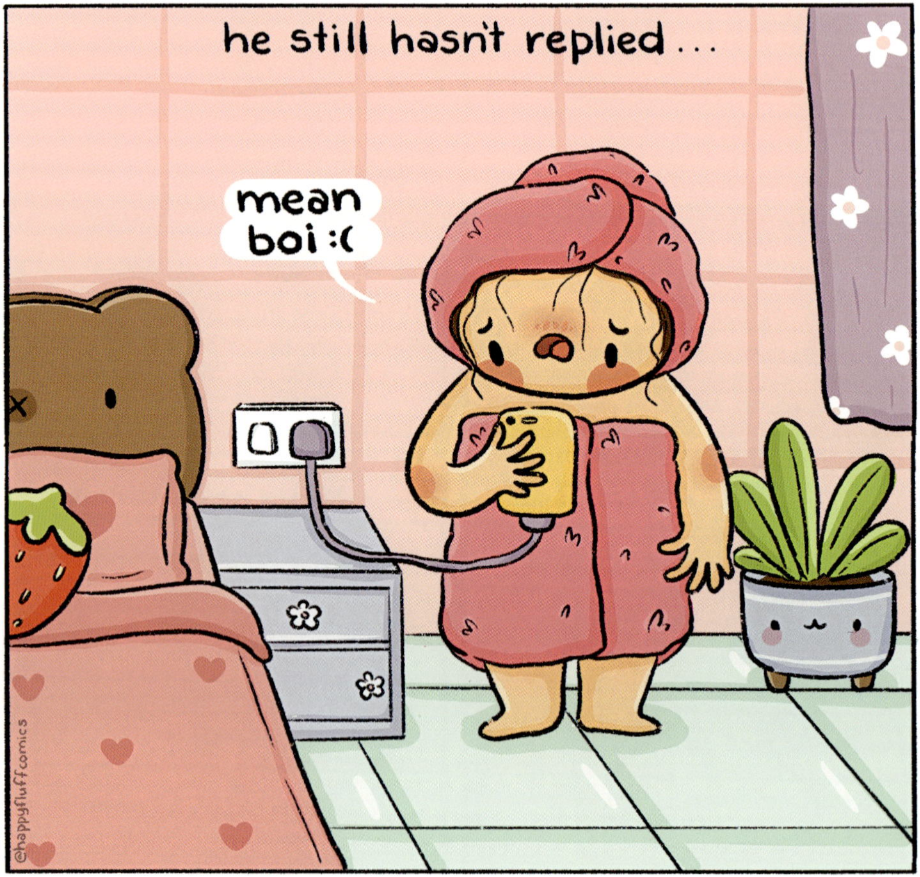
he still hasn't replied...
mean boi :(
@happyfluffcomics

talking to your boyfriend after 11p.m.

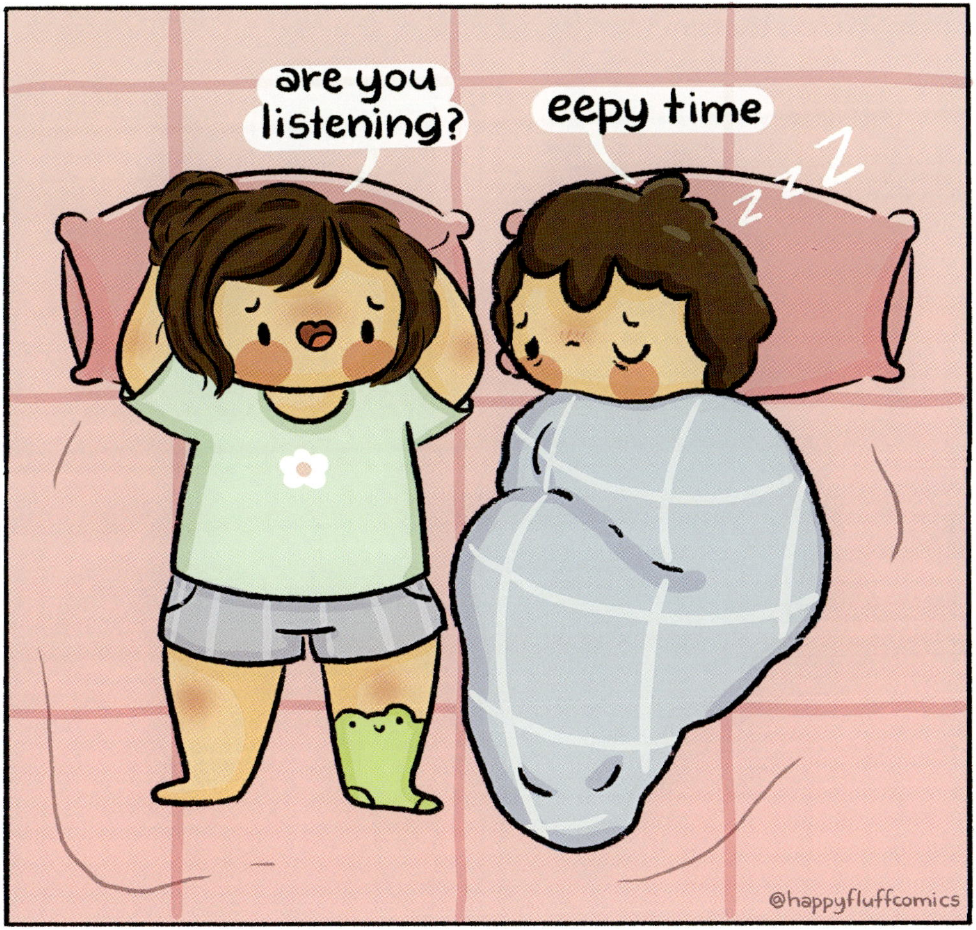
are you listening?
eepy time
z z Z
@happyfluffcomics

Cuddling in summer

bum bum BAM!

Sweaty hand'o

booty touch

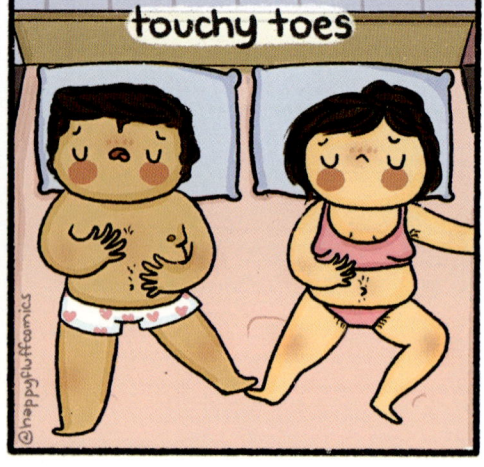

touchy toes

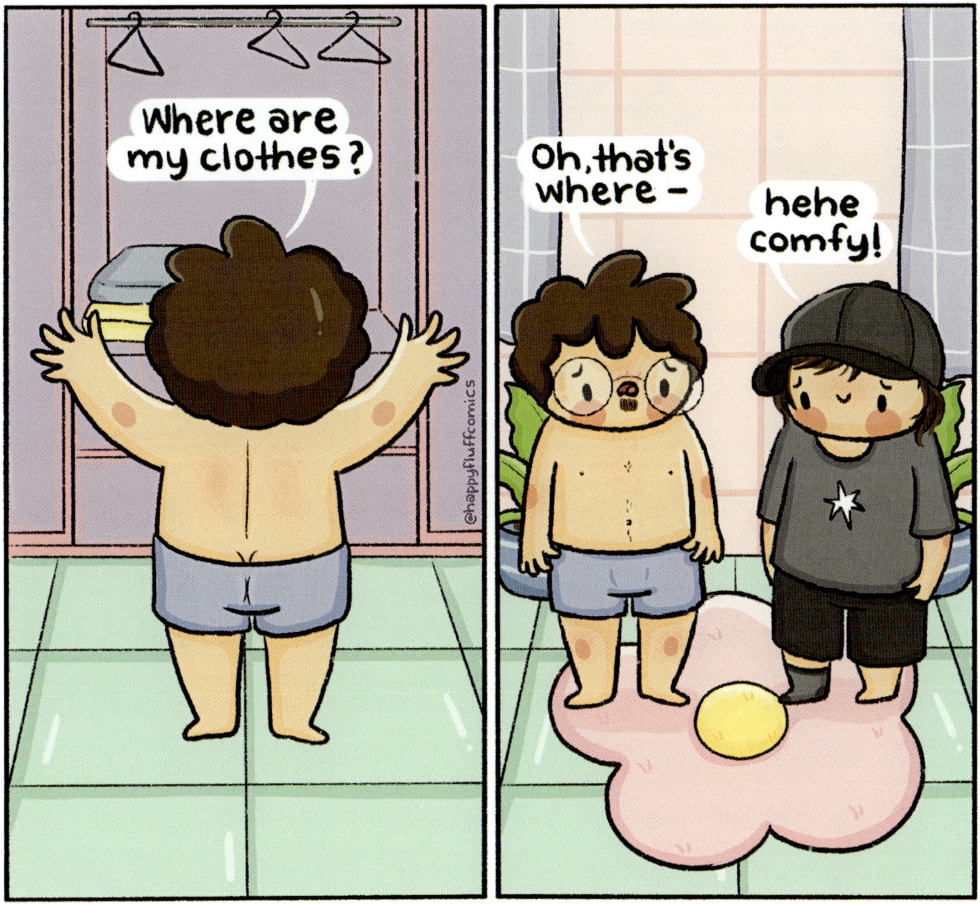
Where are my clothes?
@happyfluffcomics
Oh, that's where -
hehe comfy!

Sharing the sheets

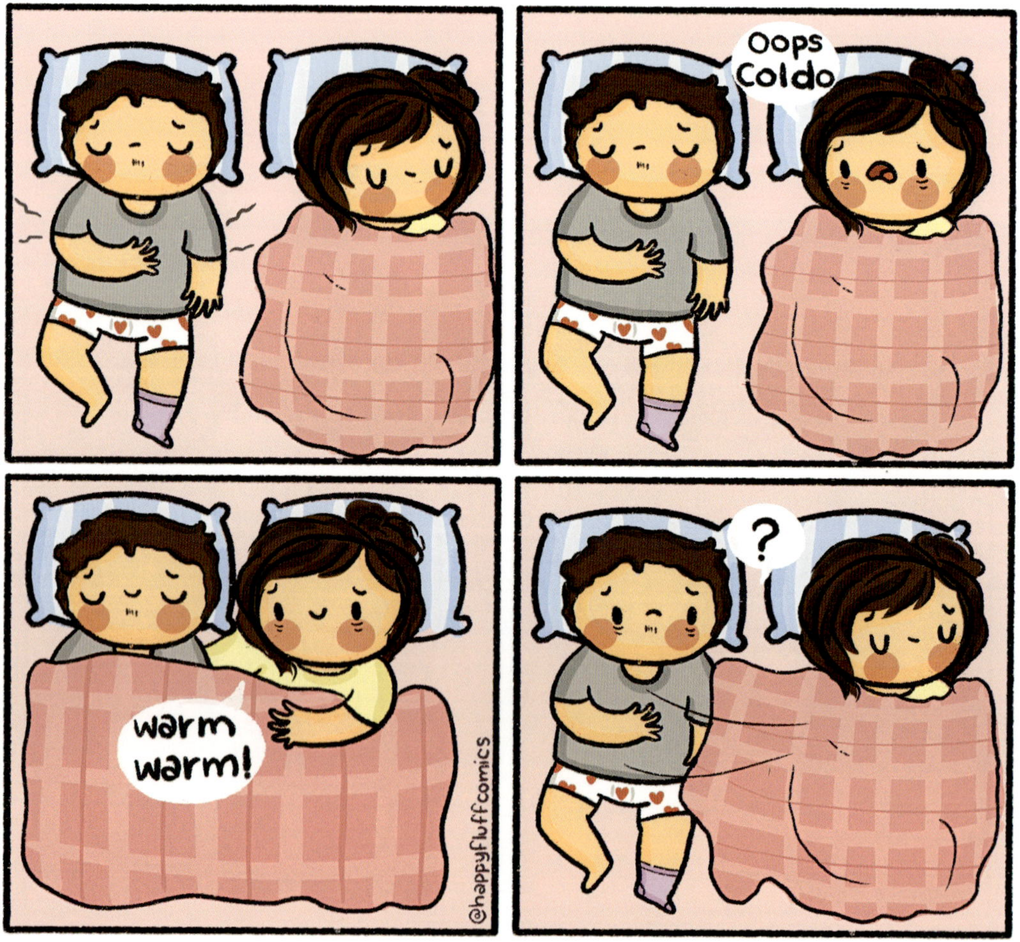
Oops
Coldo
warm
warm!
@happyfluffcomics
?

When you're both mad but love each other

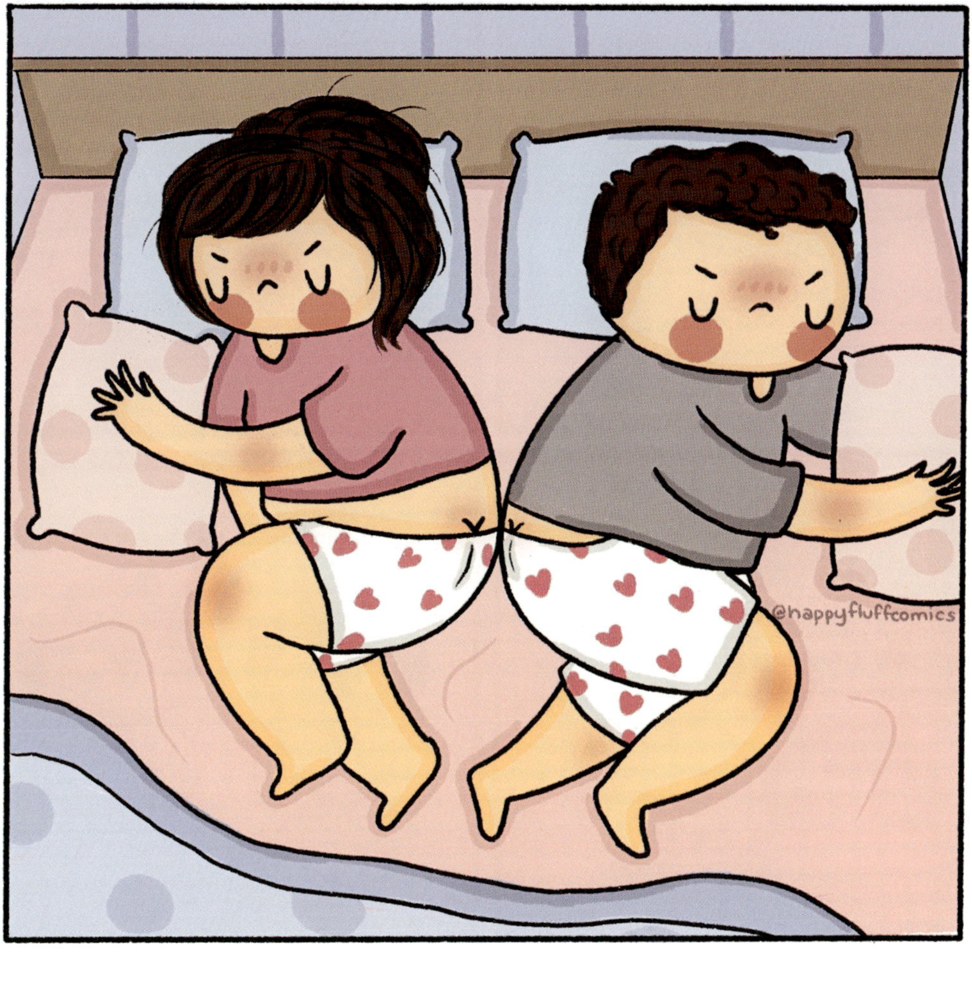
@happyfluffcomics

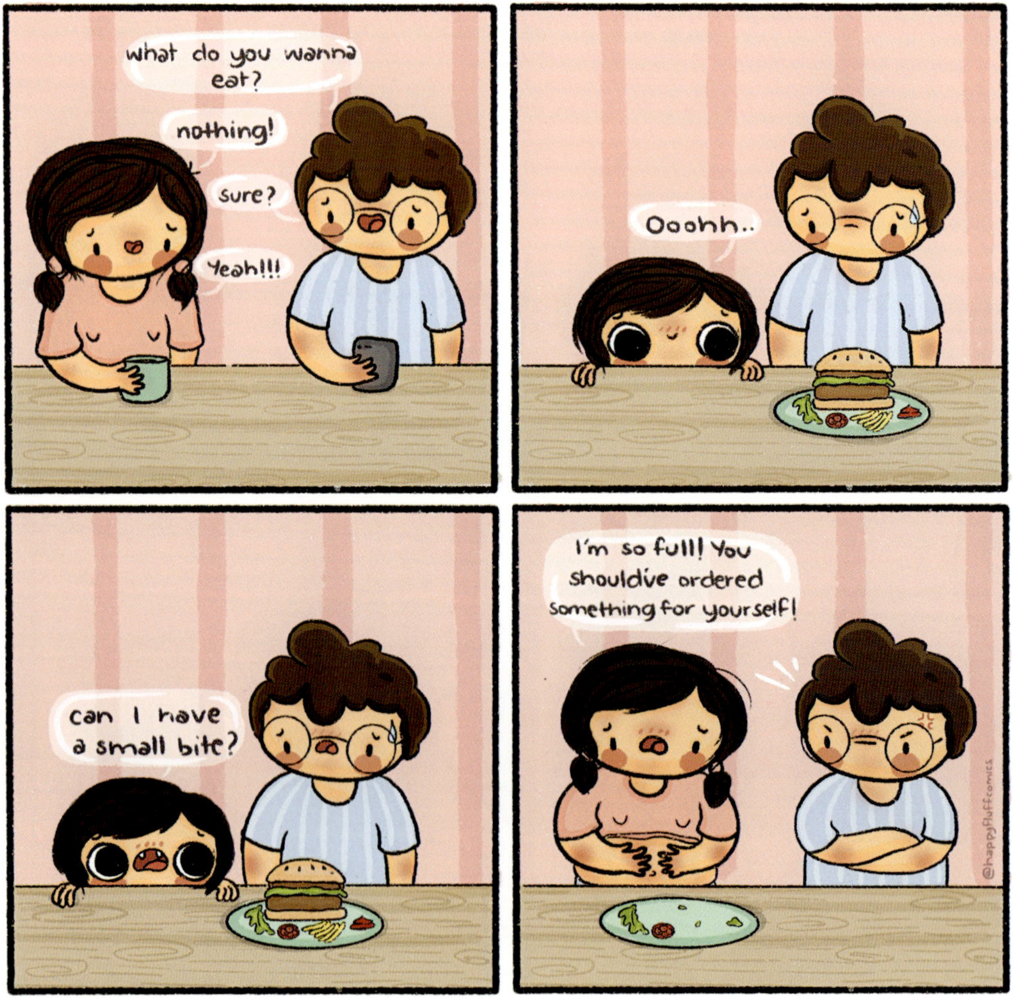
what do you wanna eat?
nothing!
sure?
Yeah!!!
Ooohh..
can I have a small bite?
I'm so full! You should've ordered something for yourself!
@happyfluffcomics

Signs that you're a panda

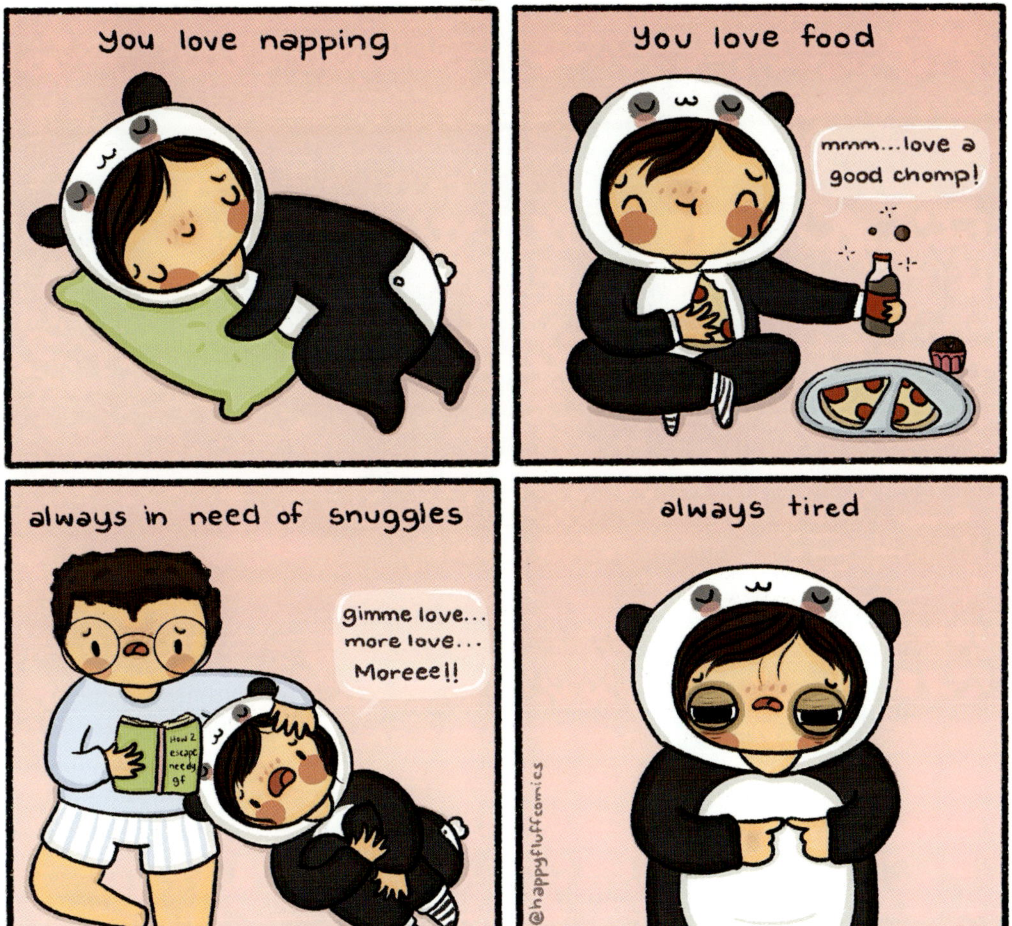

you love napping
you love food
mmm...love a good chomp!
always in need of snuggles
How 2 escape needy gf
gimme love... more love... Moreee!!
@happyfluffcomics
always tired

How to console someone

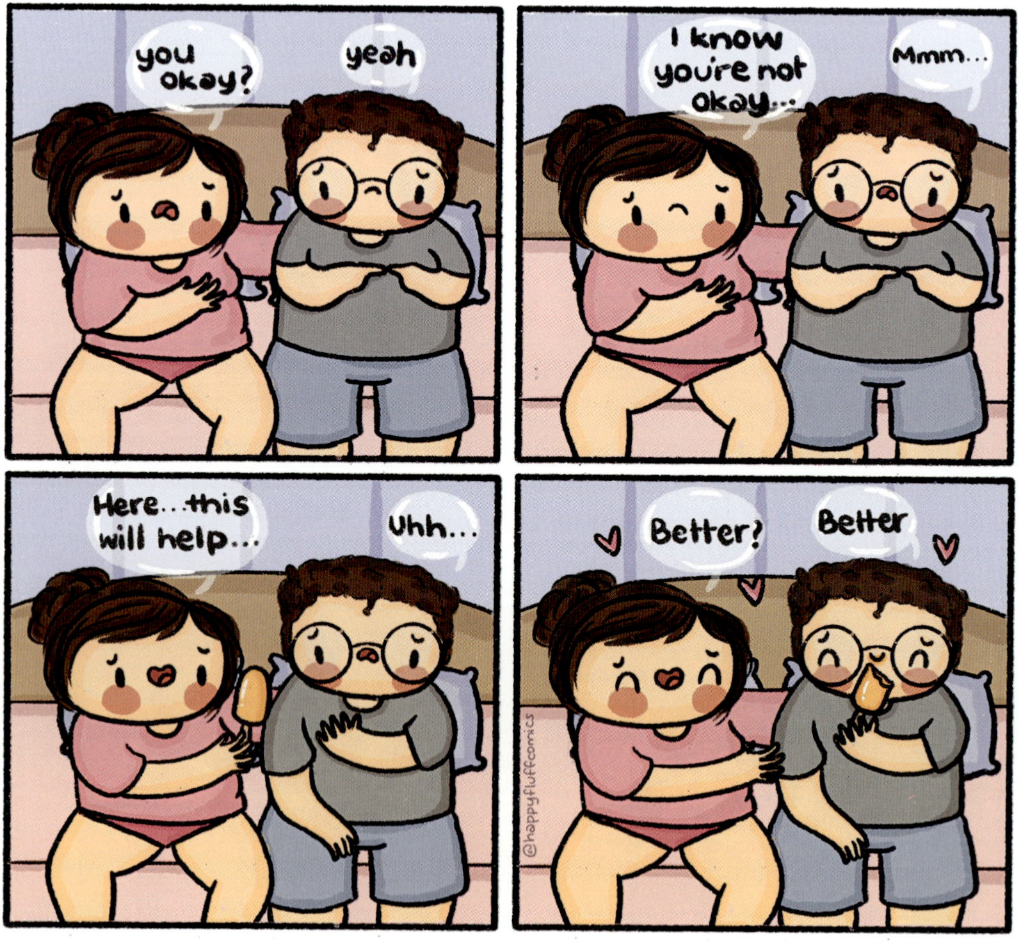
you okay?
yeah
I know you're not okay...
Mmm...
Here... this will help...
Uhh...
Better?
Better
@happyfluffcomics

How to hug

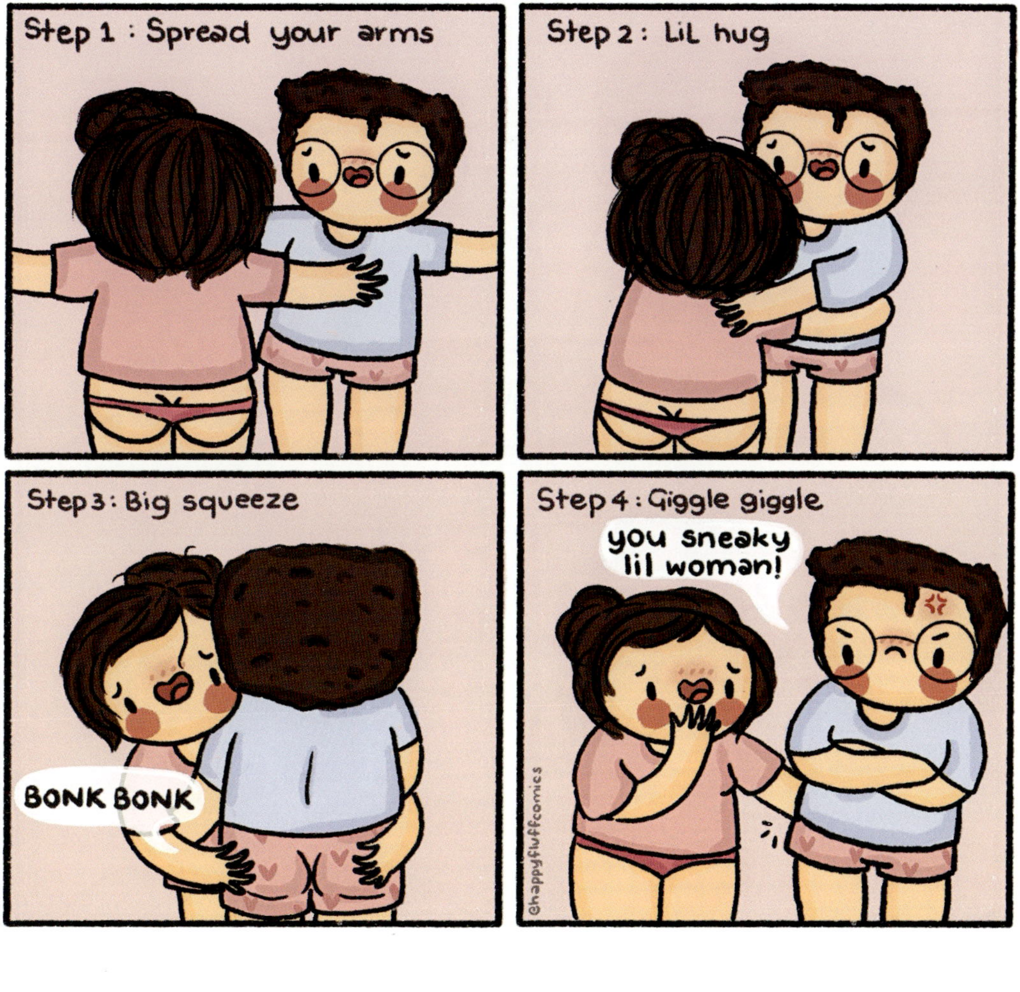
Step 1 : Spread your arms
Step 2: LiL hug
Step 3: Big squeeze
BONK BONK
Step 4: Giggle giggle
you sneaky lil woman!
@happyfluffcomics

When you have a hungry girlfriend!

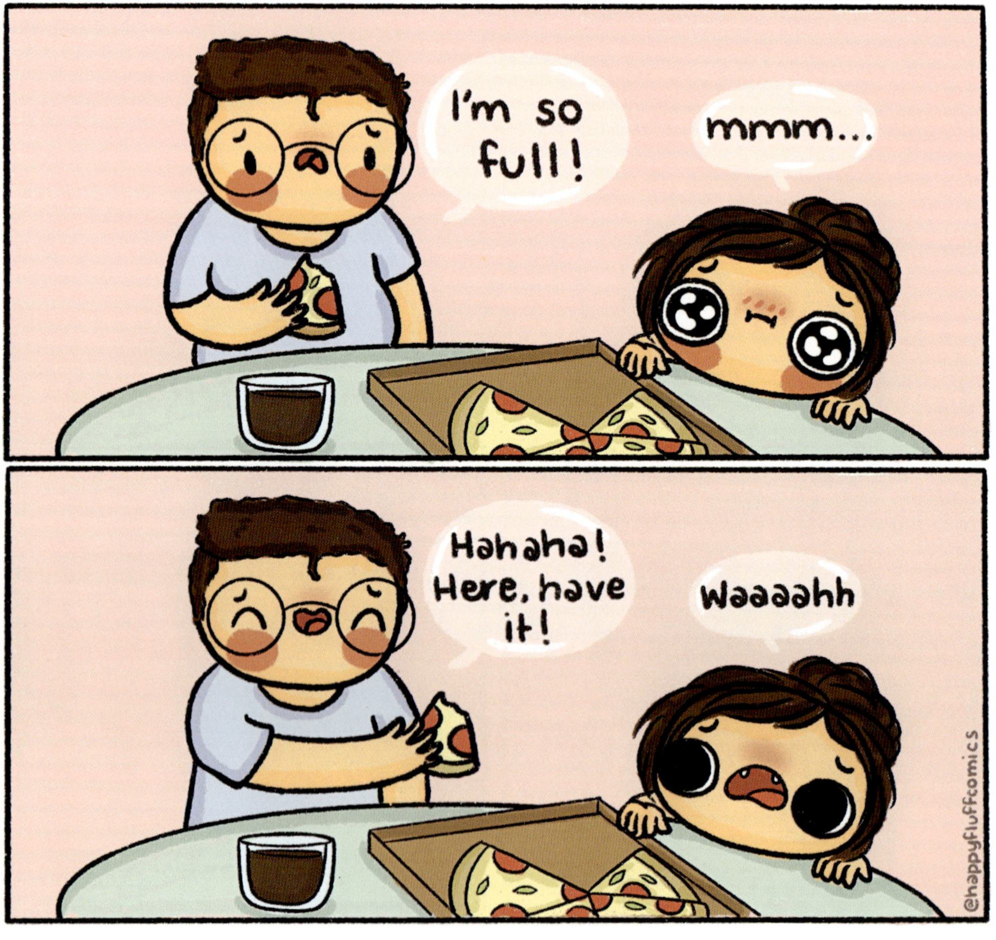
I'm so full!
mmm...
Hahaha! Here, have it!
Waaaahh
@happyfluffcomics

Butt boops

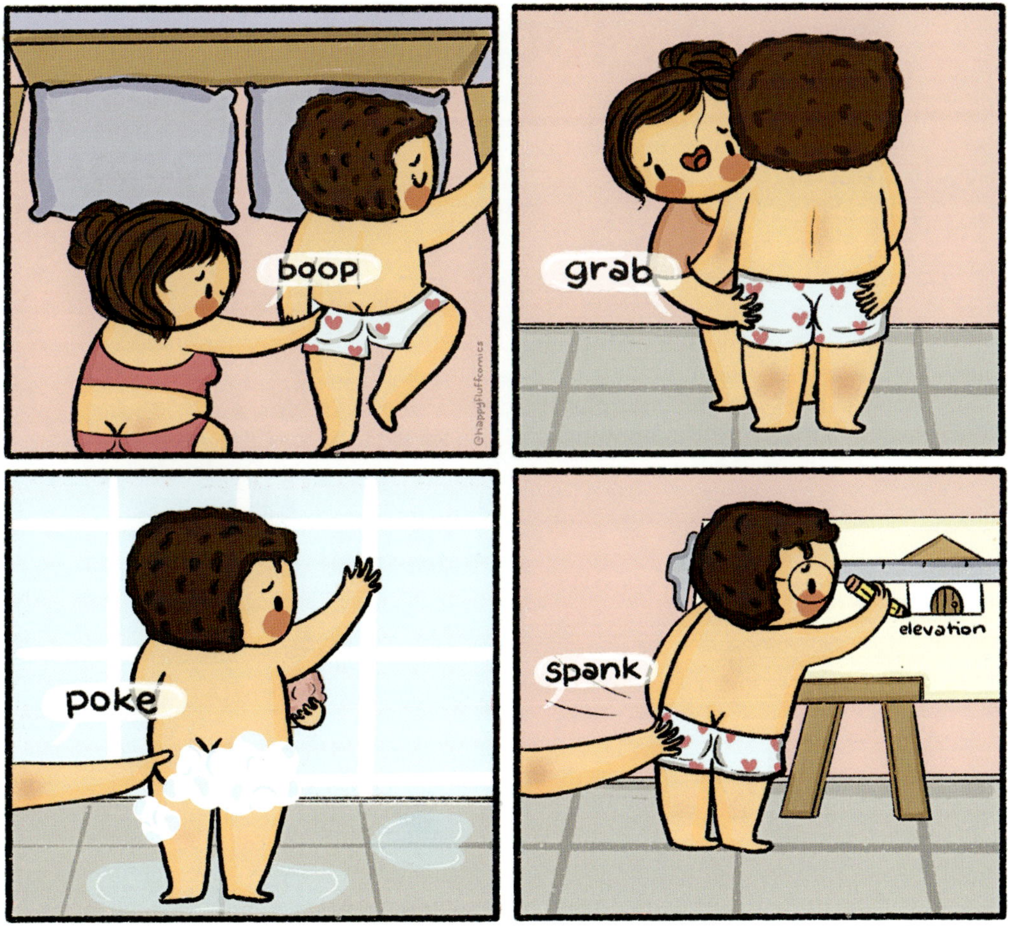
boop
@happyfluffcomics
grab
poke
spank
elevation

4

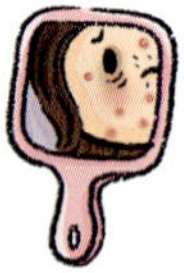

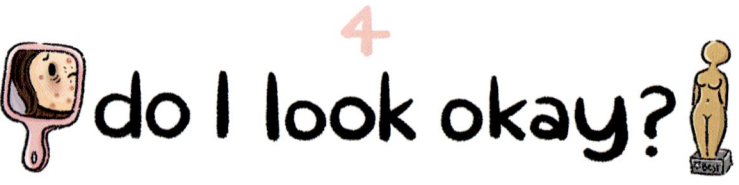

do I look okay?

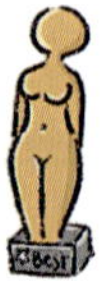

Nothing works out, so you do the next best thing—you pick a tv show and watch it countless times. Until you memorize the lines and build a connection with fictional characters and almost feel like you're a part of their circle. It sounds a lot like a mental illness but it's not that bad . . . you don't have to shave your legs or do your hair. You don't even have to share your food and you get to be ugly in peace, now that's something!

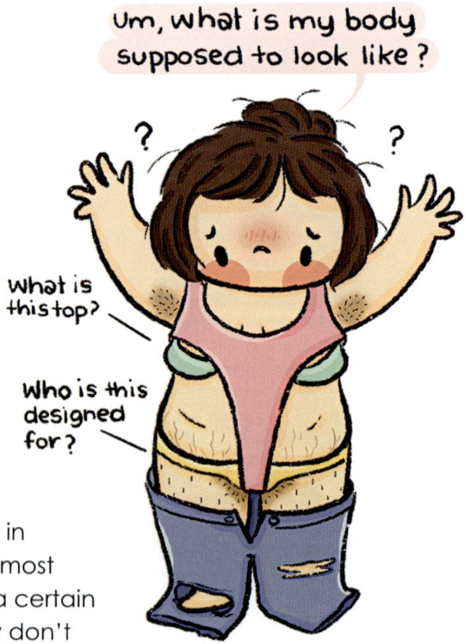

Um, what is my body supposed to look like?
What is this top?
Who is this designed for?

So, you do this for over a year or so and realize that you're 20 kilos heavier, you have blurry vision and none of your clothes fit.

You can't go shopping because you don't want to look at yourself in the mirror and nothing in the store looks good on your body anyways. It almost feels like every piece of clothing is designed for a certain body type. Yeah, there are bigger sizes, but they don't really look flattering on those sizes because they weren't designed to suit them. So you leave the store after having a mental breakdown in the trial room. You're too embarrassed to leave the store empty-handed so you buy some stupid shit you don't even need, like overpriced earrings that turn green in a week.

You don't leave the house any more because your self-esteem is in the toilet. One day you're eighteen and at the best shape of your life, but you're convinced that you're overweight because of your abusive ex-boyfriend from college and almost a decade later, you realize that you'd kill to look like that again. Your body changes faster than you think and suddenly you have all these other health issues—as if depression and anxiety weren't enough. You meet more doctors than friends. Now every conversation you have is centred on your weight and how good you'd look if you lost that excess weight. So, you make excuses and avoid social situations.

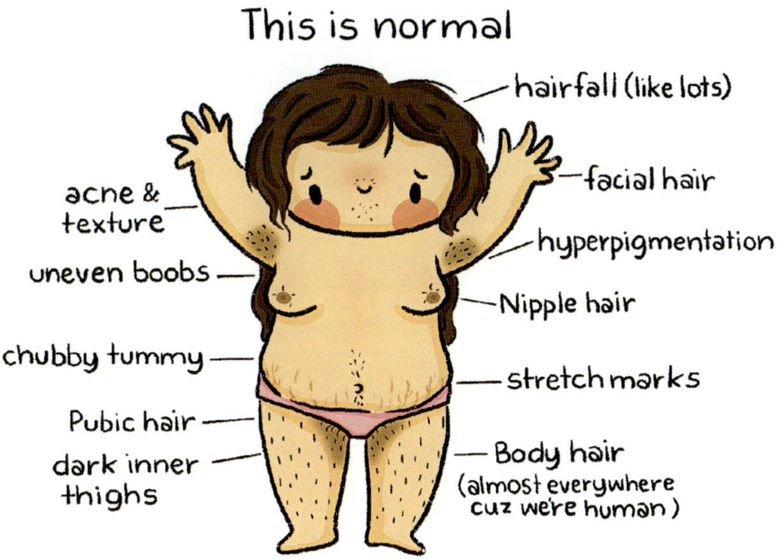
This is normal
hairfall (like lots)
facial hair
acne & texture
hyperpigmentation
uneven boobs
Nipple hair
chubby tummy
stretch marks
Pubic hair
dark inner thighs
Body hair (almost everywhere cuz we're human)

You might have some of these or all of these and more. Either way, you're doing fine. None of these make you unattractive. It just makes you human. A grown woman with body hair . . . WHAT?! Contrary to popular belief, women aren't hairless fairies with airbrushed skin.

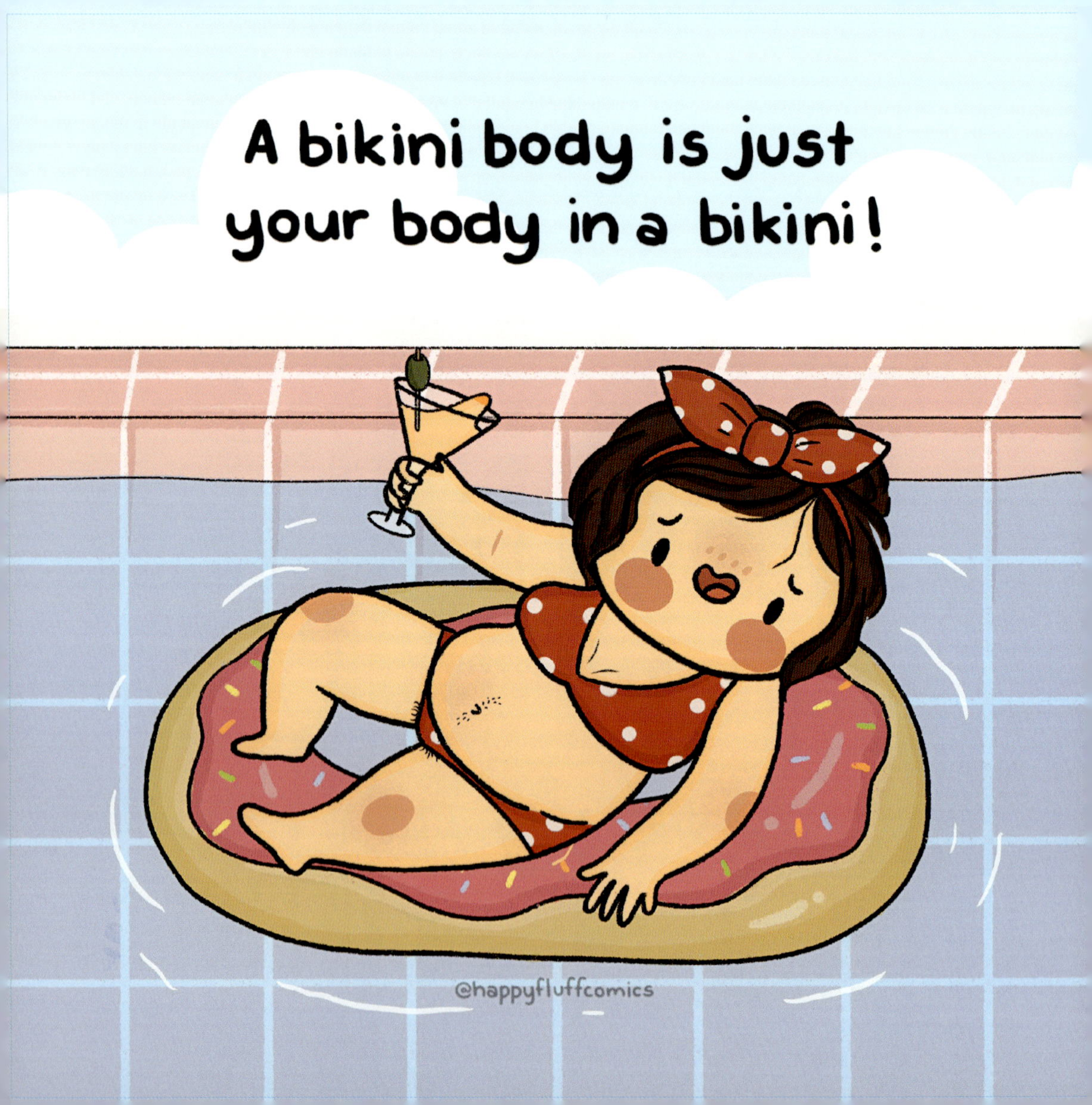
A bikini body is just your body in a bikini!
@happyfluffcomics

You don't have to lose weight to

wear that dress

go dancing

take pictures

get piercings

colour your hair

get tattoos

'why does my neck hurt?'

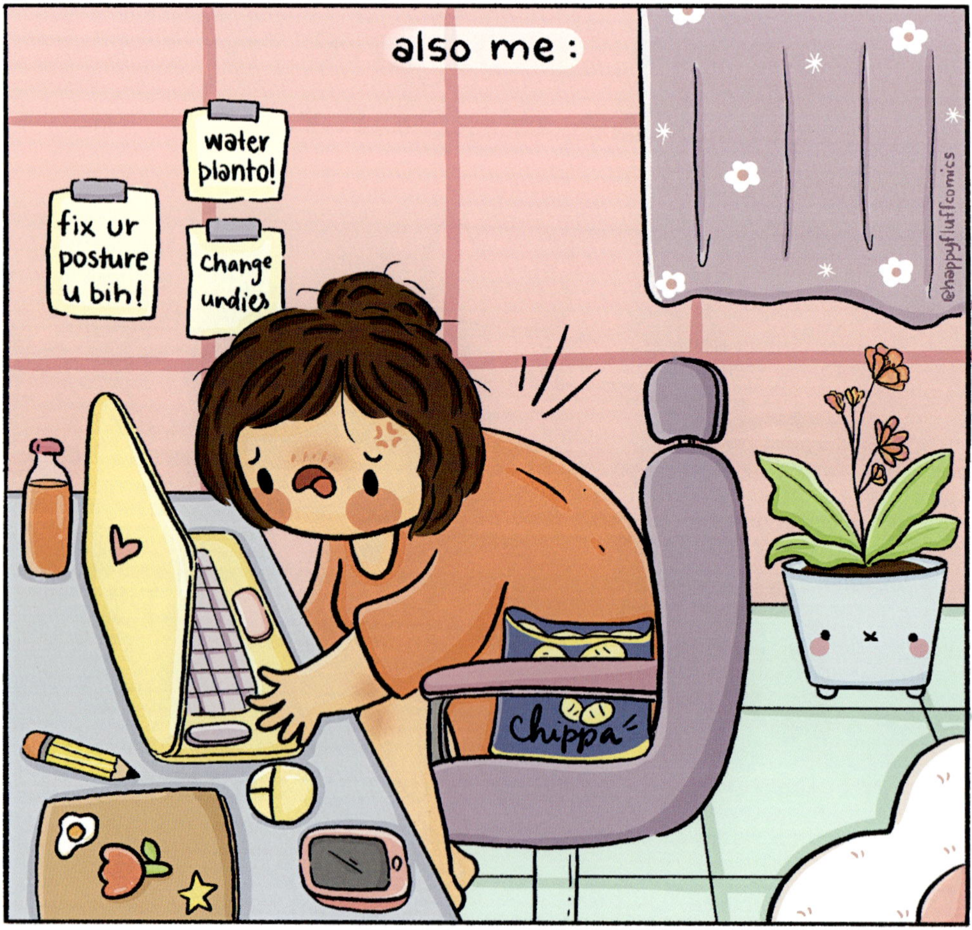
also me:
water planto!
fix ur posture u bih!
change undies
Chippa
@happyfluffcomics

Don't have anything to wear

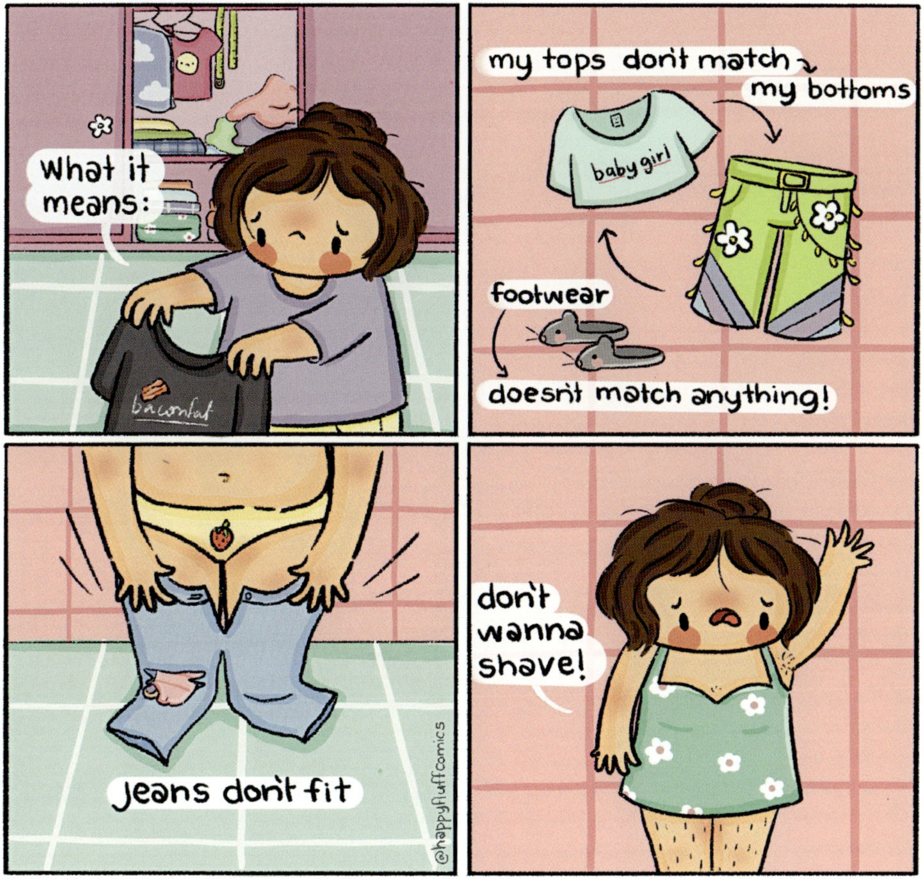
What it means:
baconfat
my tops don't match
my bottoms
baby girl
footwear
doesn't match anything!
jeans don't fit
@happyfluffcomics
don't wanna shave!

new sheets

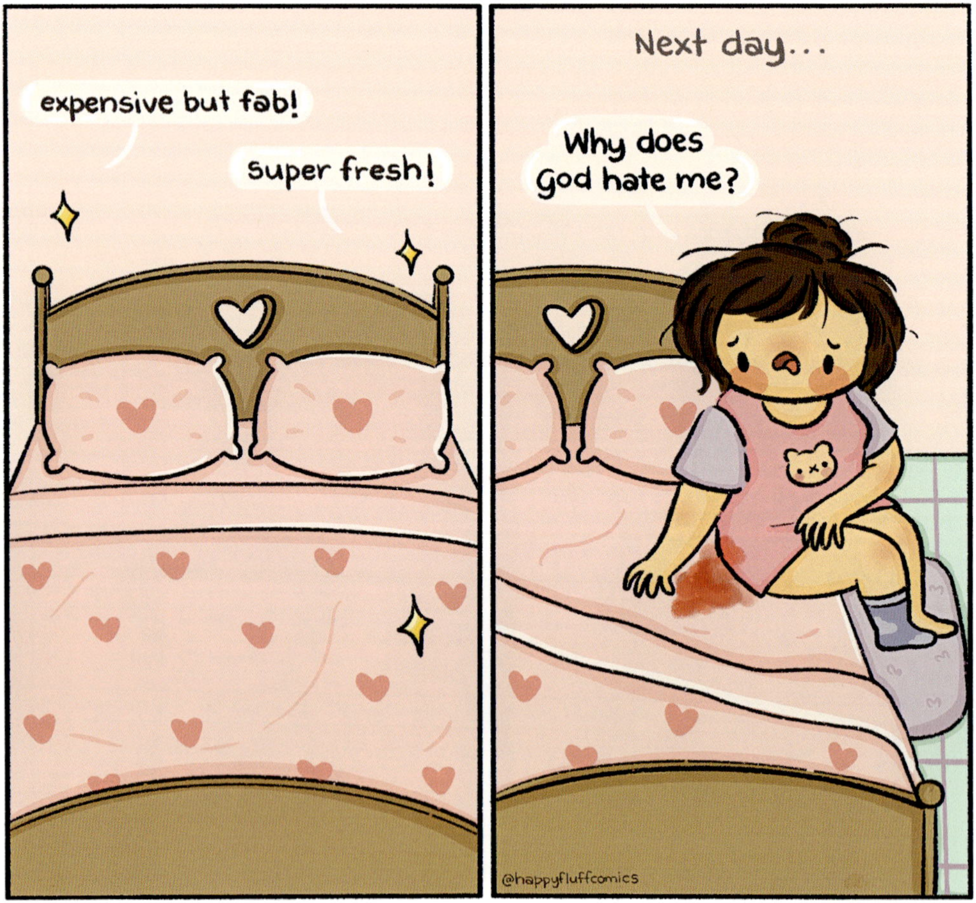
expensive but fab!
super fresh!
Next day...
Why does God hate me?
@happyfluffcomics

Sleeping sideways with earrings

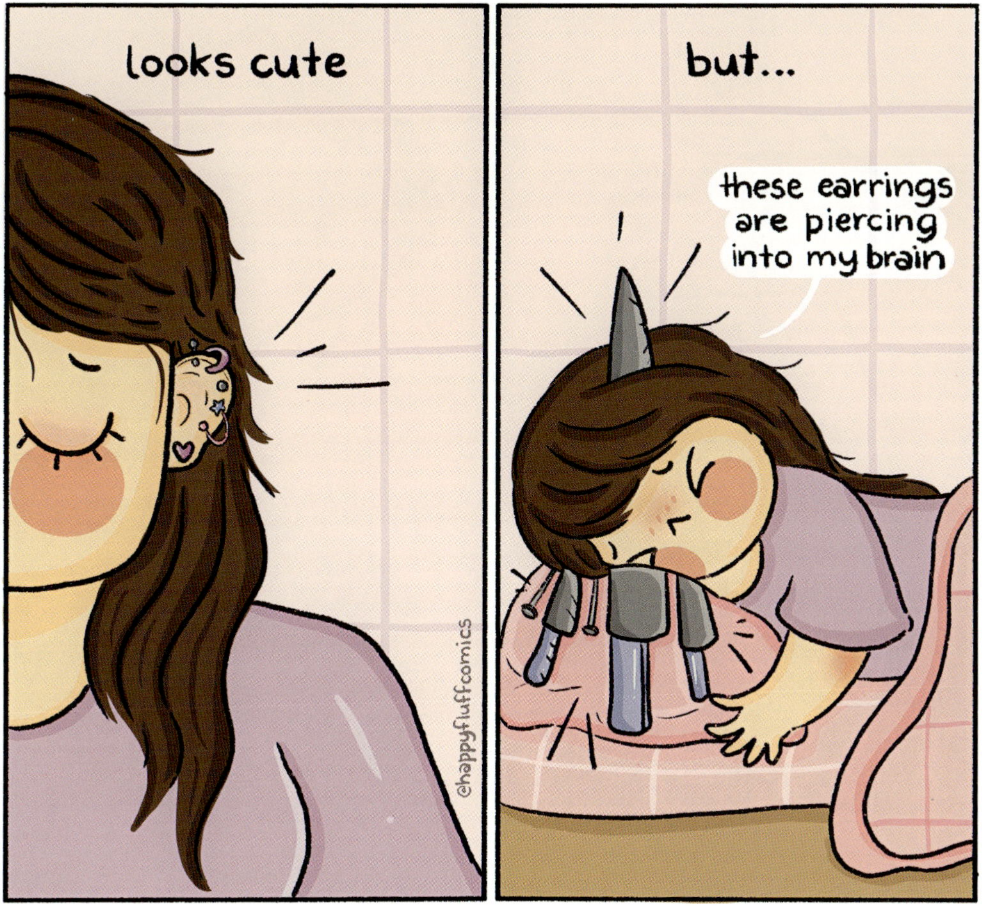
looks cute
@happyfluffcomics
but...
these earrings are piercing into my brain

Skincare

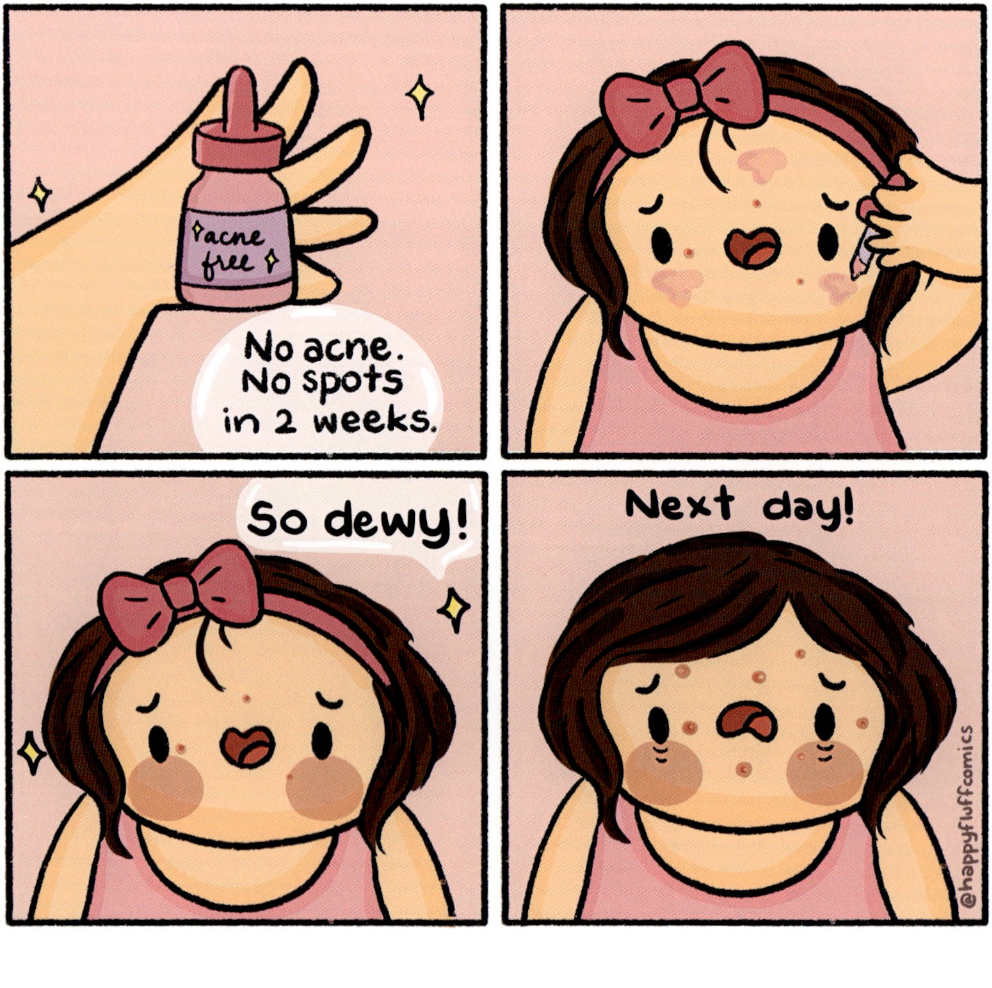
acne free
No acne. No spots in 2 weeks.
So dewy!
Next day!
@happyfluffcomics

Long hair struggles

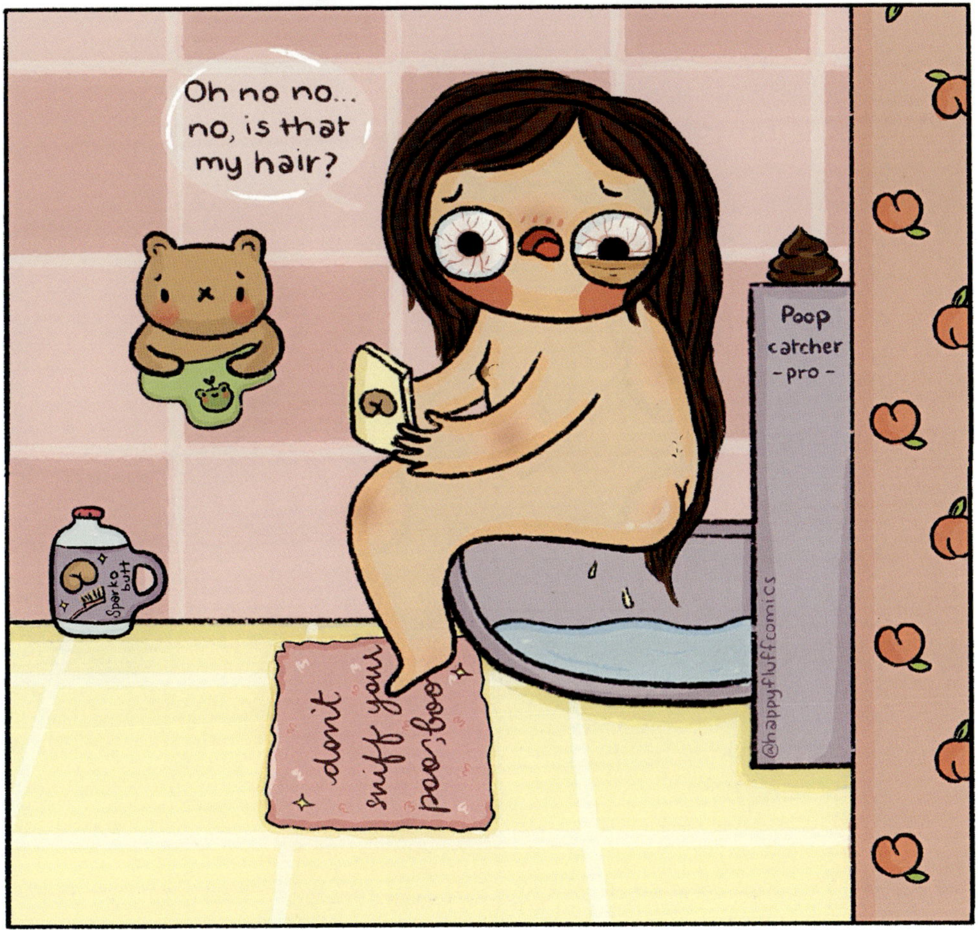
Oh no no... no, is that my hair?
Poop catcher -pro-
Sparko butt
don't sniff your poo, boo
@happyfluffcomics

Me every day

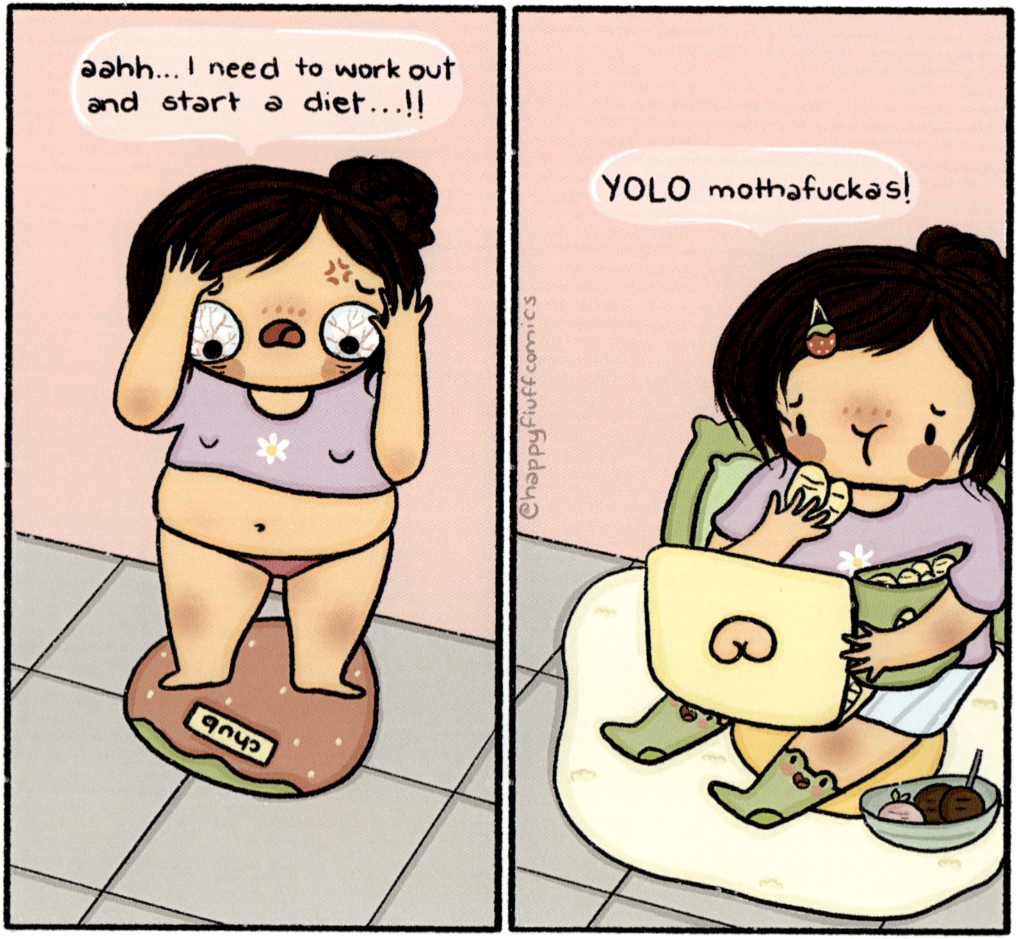
aahh... I need to work out and start a diet...!!
chub
YOLO mothafuckas!
@happyfluffcomics

Hair everywhere!

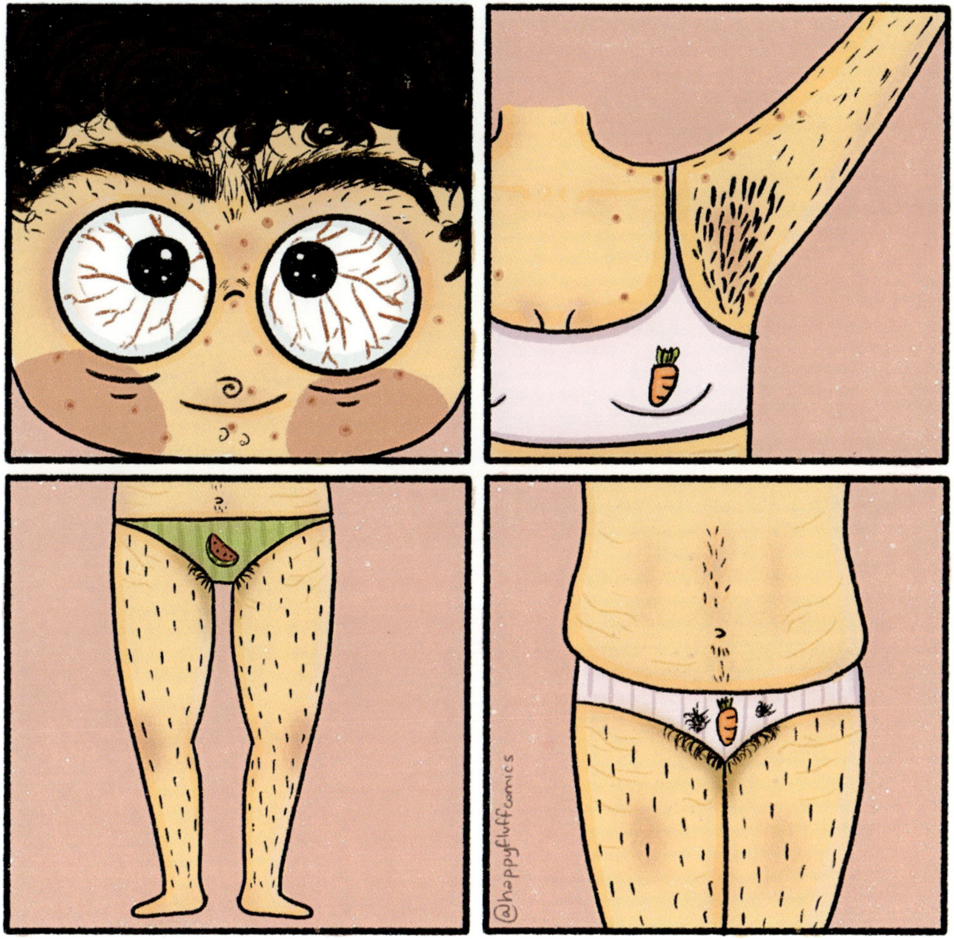
@happyfluffcomics

why shopping is stressful!

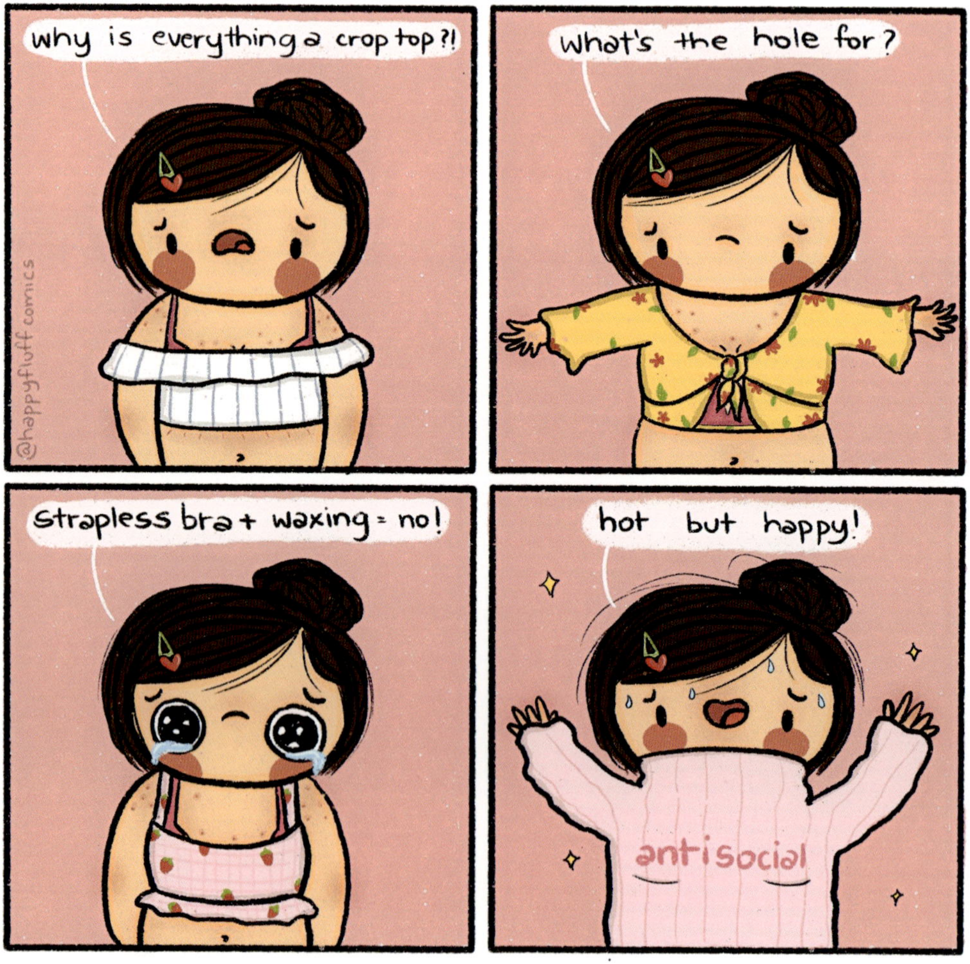
why is everything a crop top?!
What's the hole for?
Strapless bra + waxing = no!
hot but happy!
antisocial
@happyfluff comics

Why I wear black all the time!

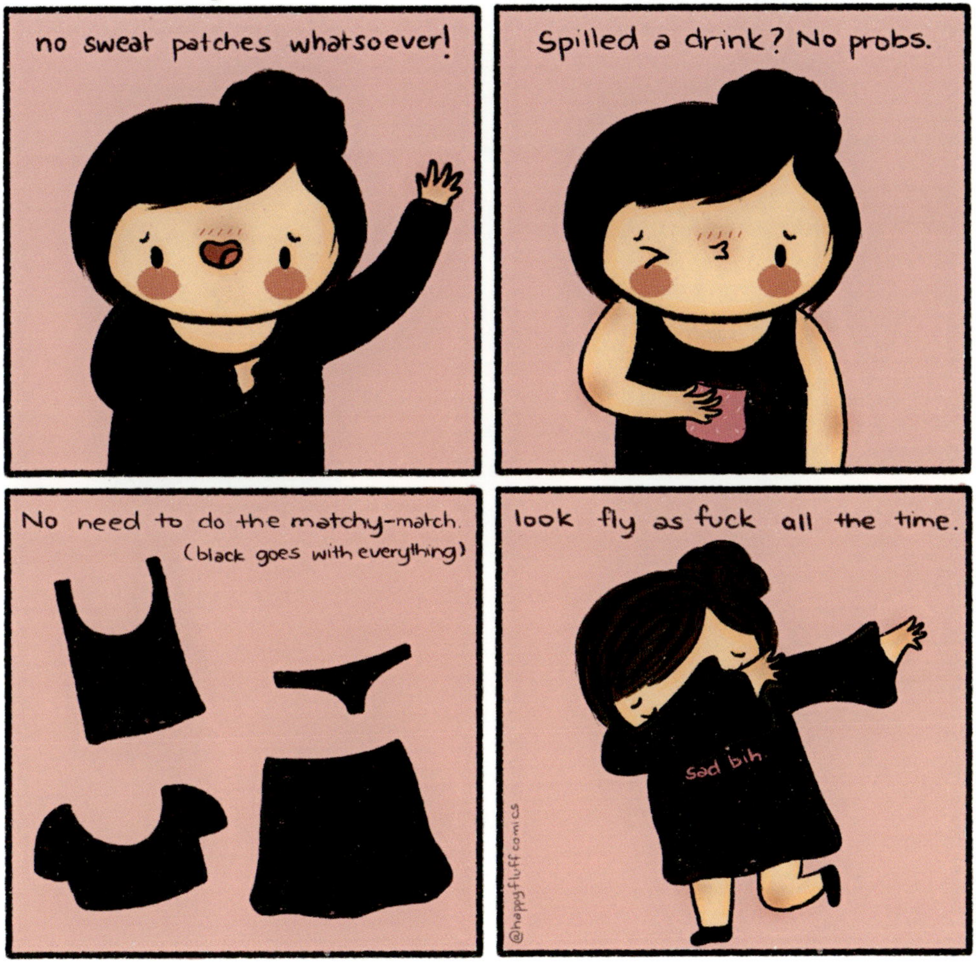
no sweat patches whatsoever!
Spilled a drink? No probs.
No need to do the matchy-match.
(black goes with everything)
look fly as fuck all the time.
sad bih
@happyfluff comics

On the outside

On the inside

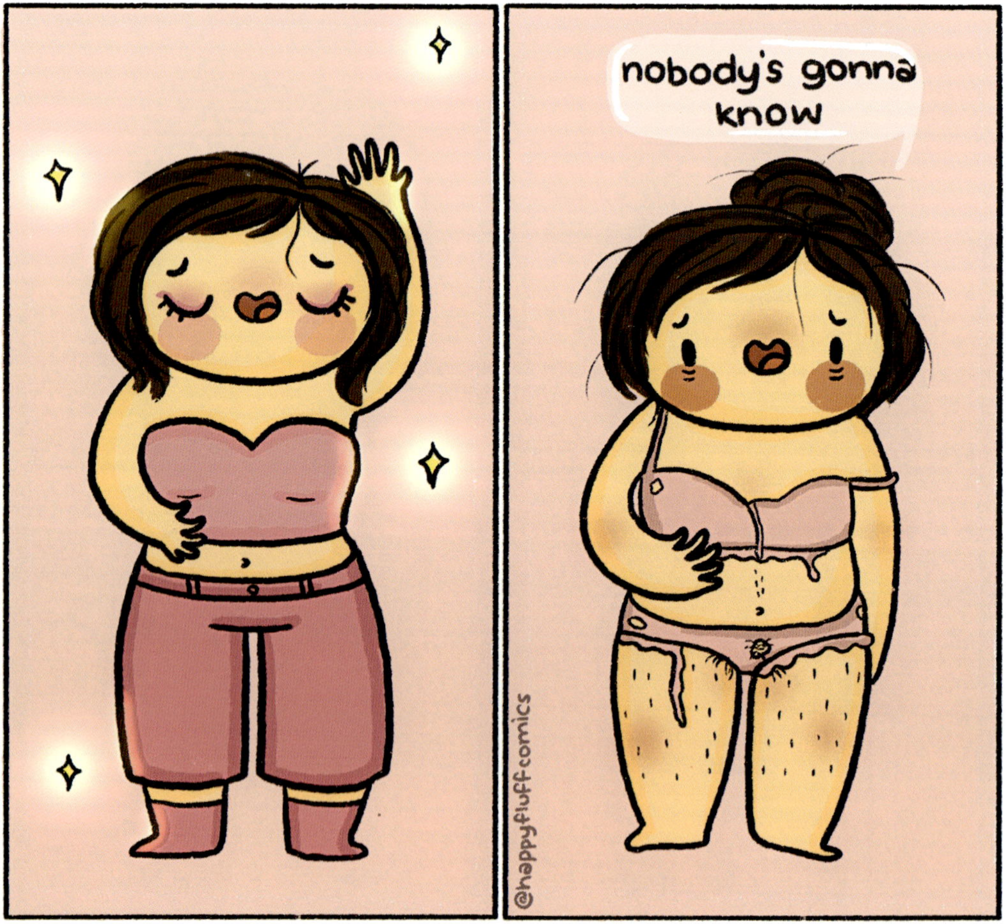
nobody's gonna know
@happyfluffcomics

two types of skinny jeans

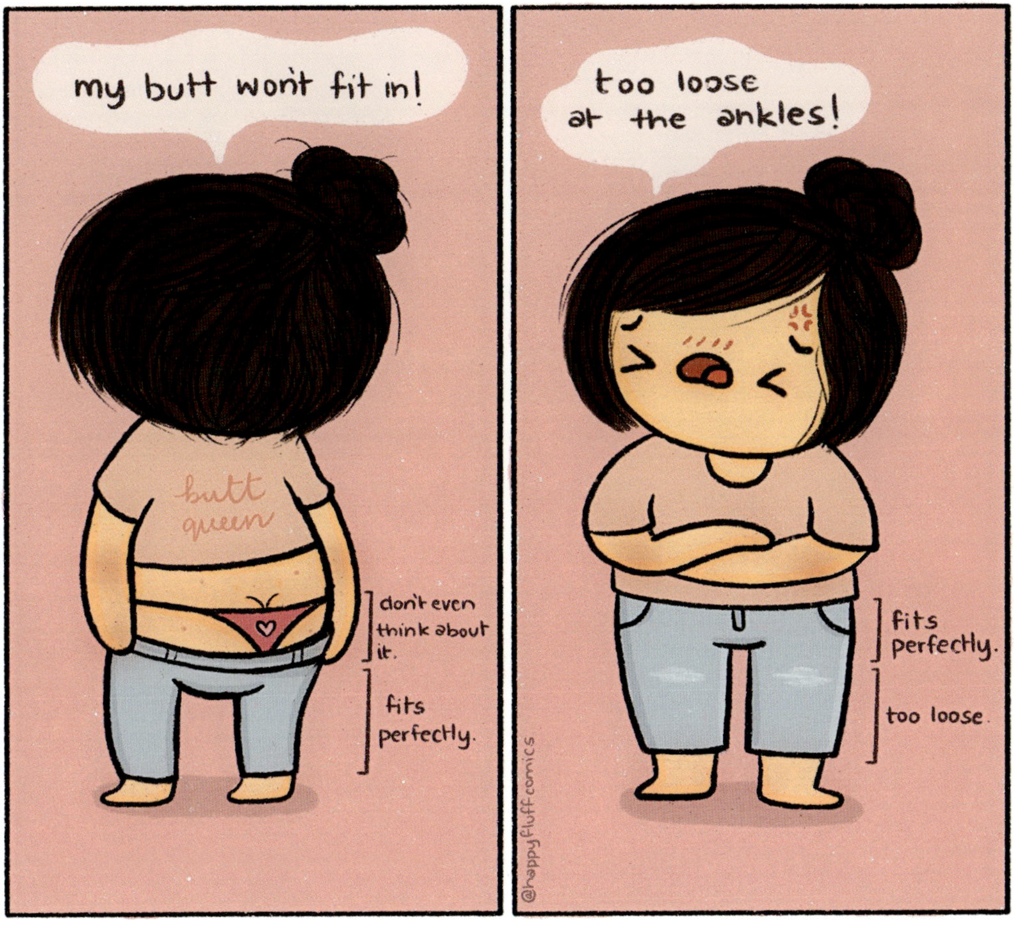

my butt won't fit in!
butt queen
don't even think about it.
fits perfectly.
too loose at the ankles!
fits perfectly.
too loose.
@happyfluffcomics

My mind the whole day

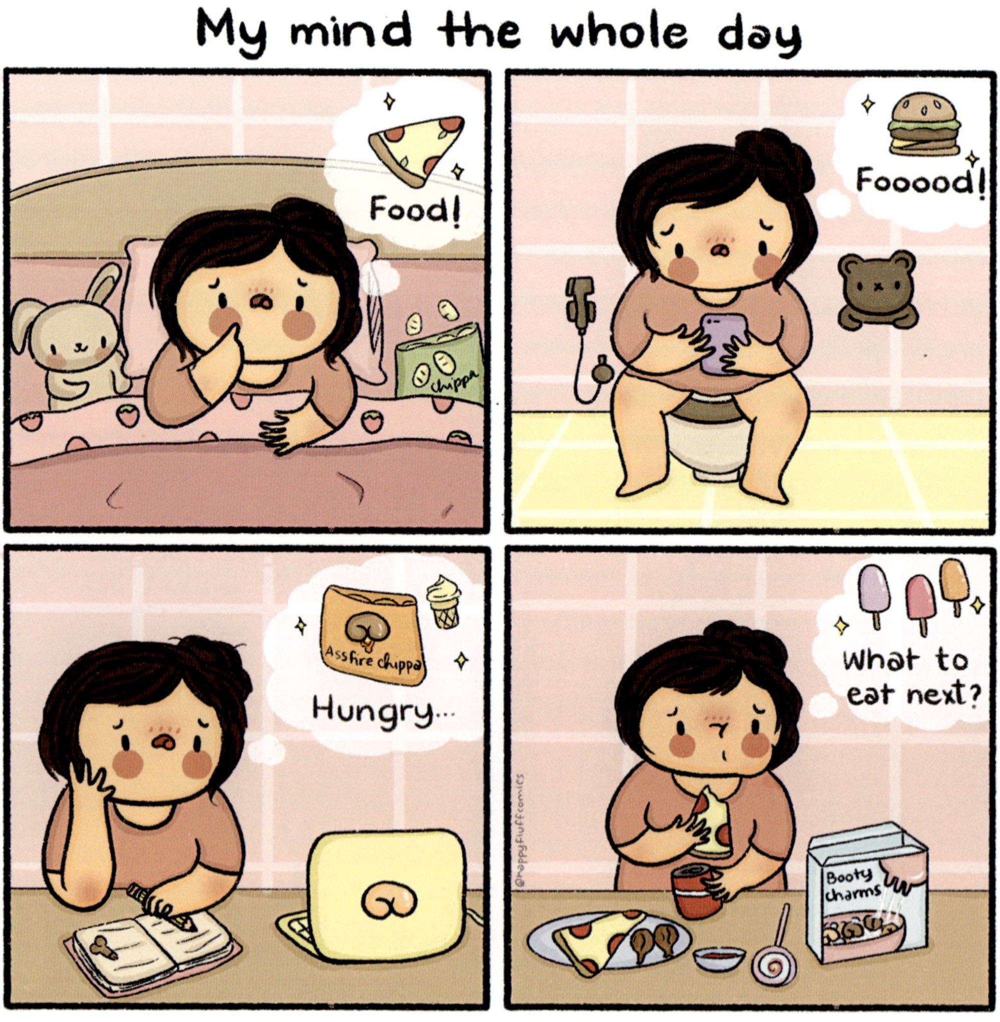
Food!
chippa
Fooood!
Assfire chippa
Hungry...
What to eat next?
Booty charms
@happyfluffcomics

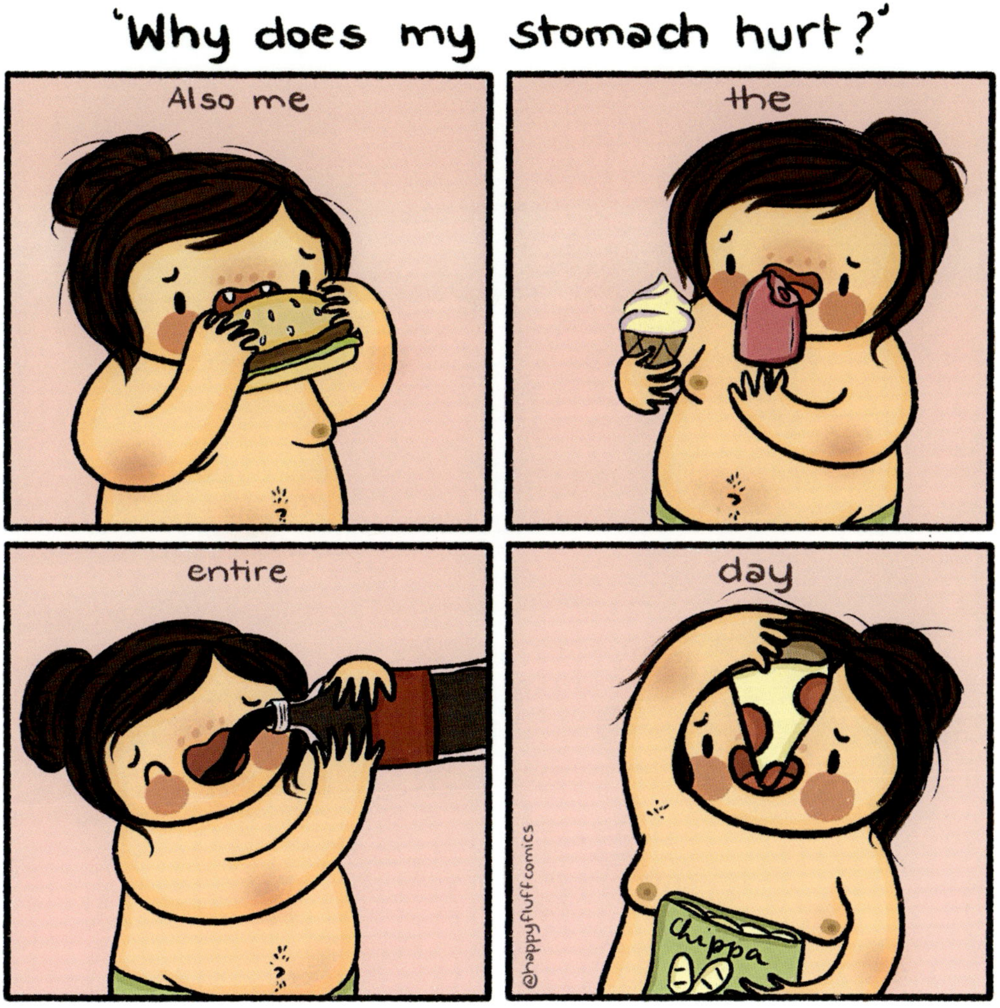
'Why does my stomach hurt?'
Also me
the
entire
day
Chippa
@happyfluffcomics

When you're about to get your period

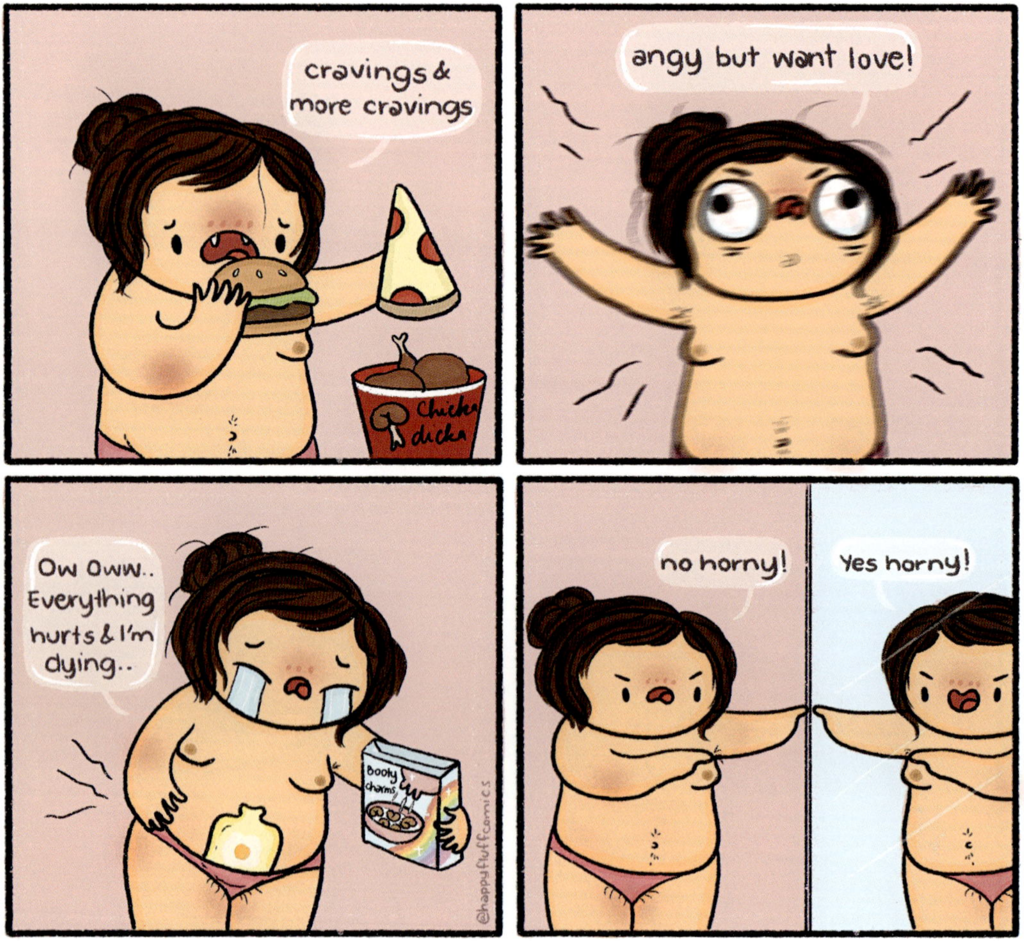
cravings &
more cravings
angy but want love!
Ow oww..
Everything
hurts & I'm
dying..
Booty
charms
@happyfluffcomics
no horny!
Yes horny!

A smol surprise

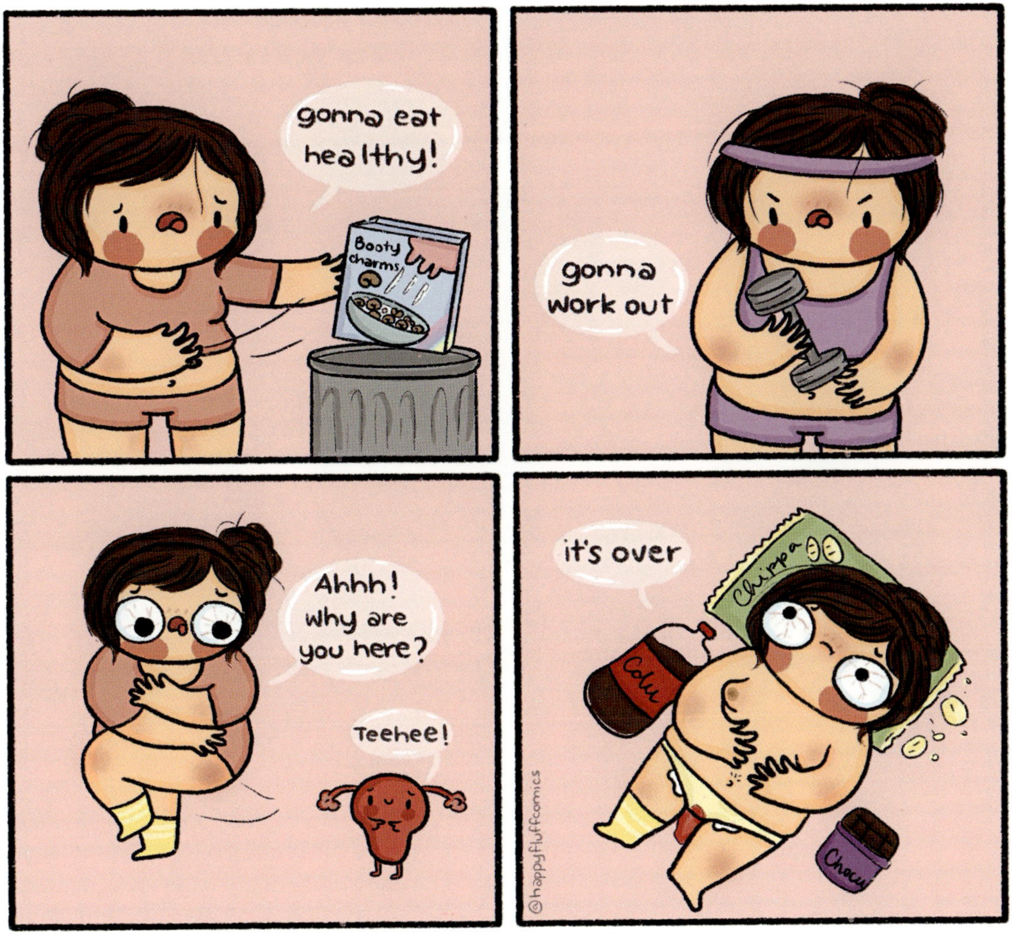
gonna eat healthy!
Booty charms
gonna work out
Ahhh! why are you here?
Teehee!
it's over
Chippa
@happyfluffcomics

Me checking for abs

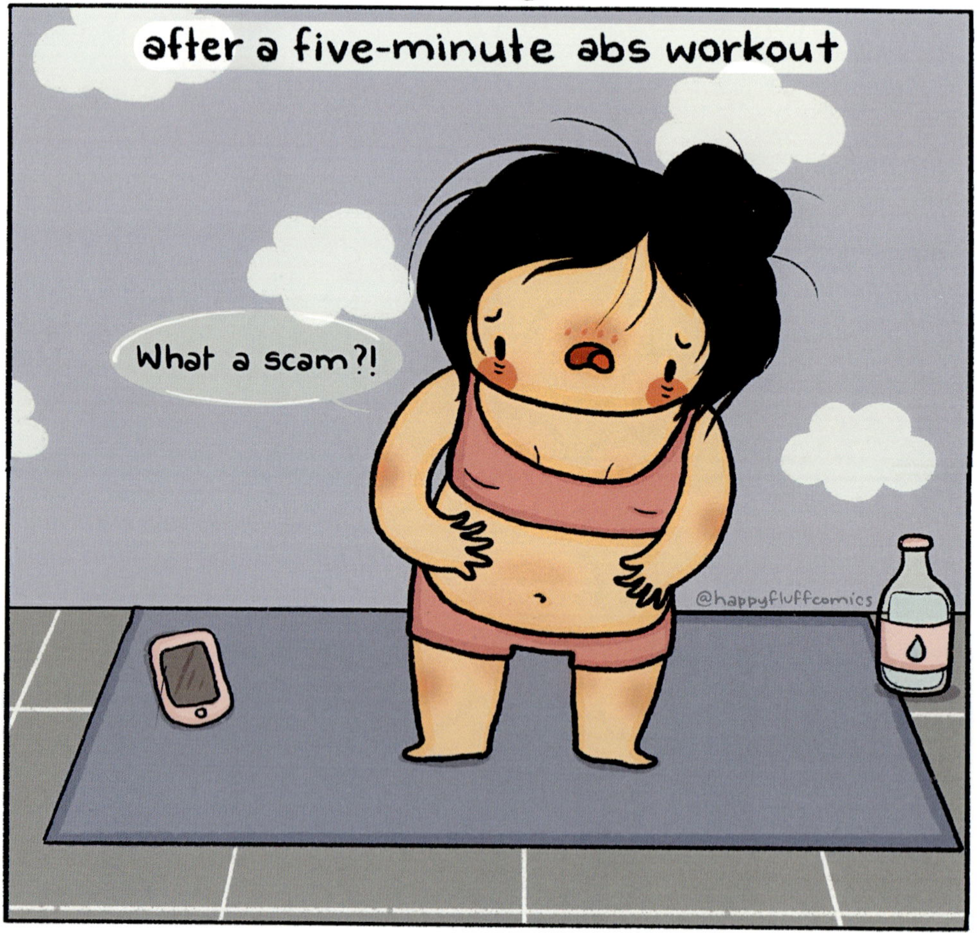
after a five-minute abs workout
What a scam?!
@happyfluffcomics

trying to fit into that pair of old jeans

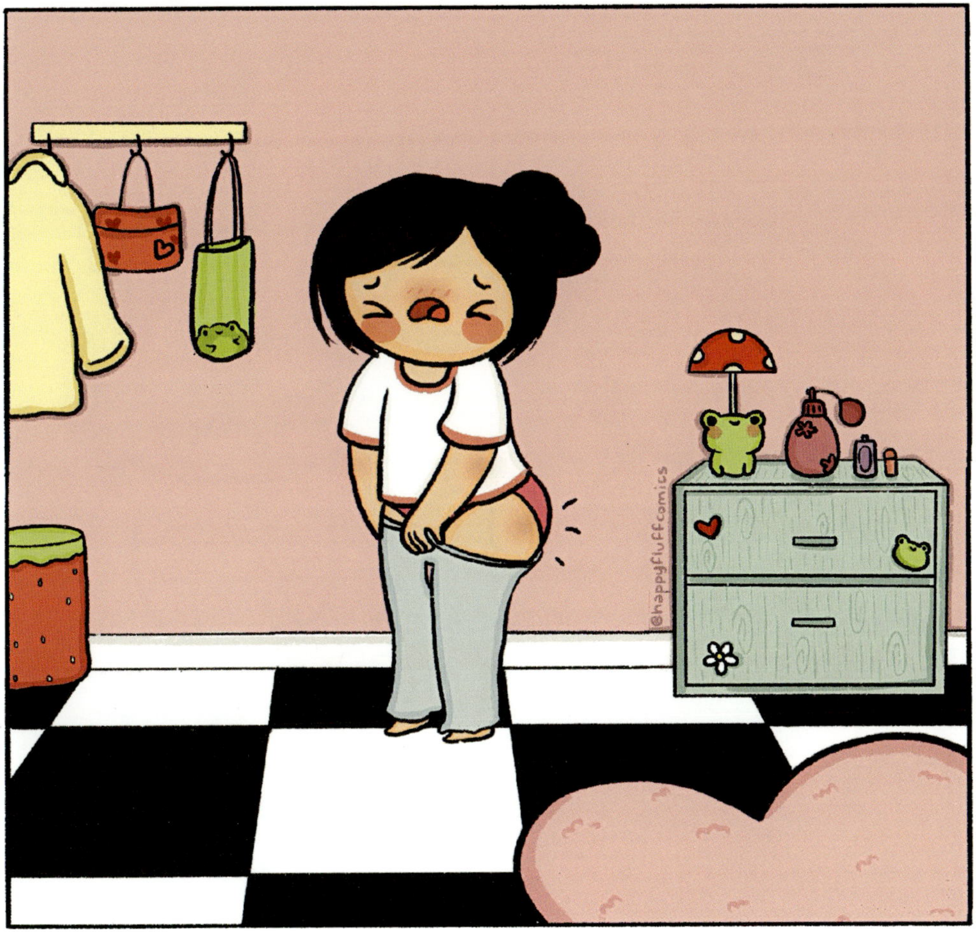
@happyfluffcomics

Shaving down there

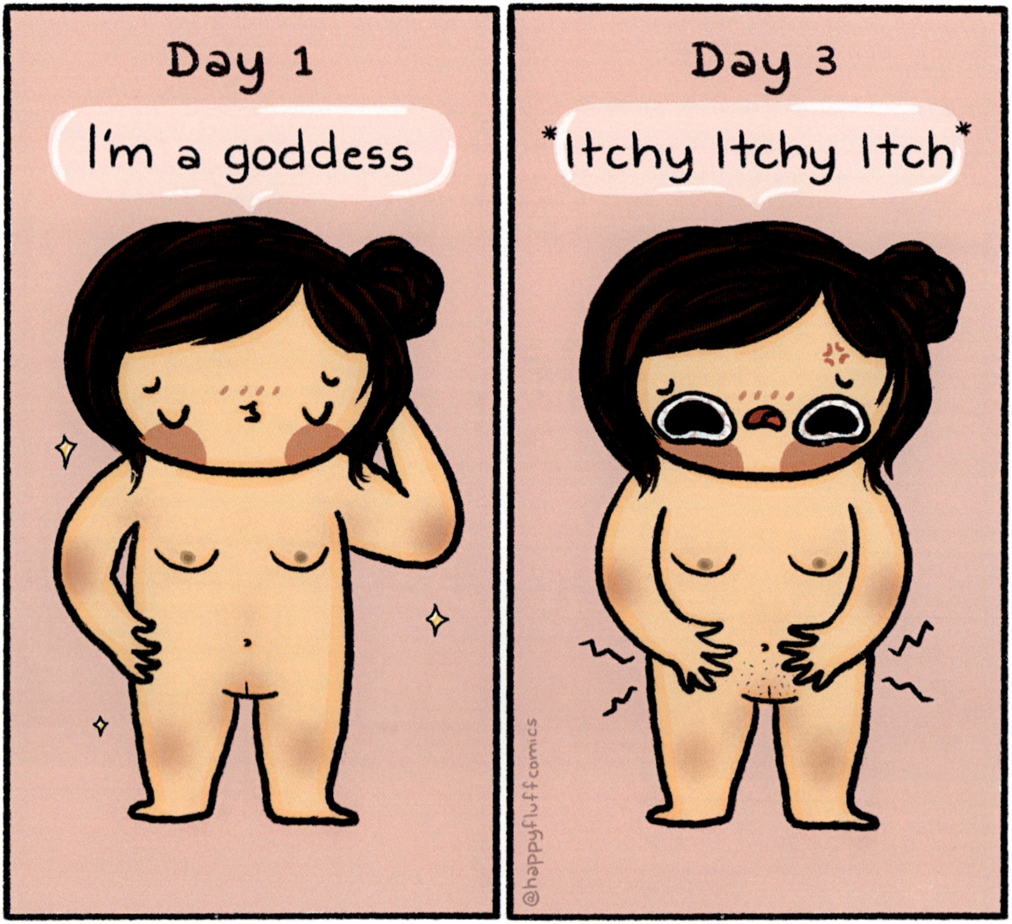
Day 1
I'm a goddess
Day 3
Itchy Itchy Itch
@happyfluffcomics

Nobody's gonna know

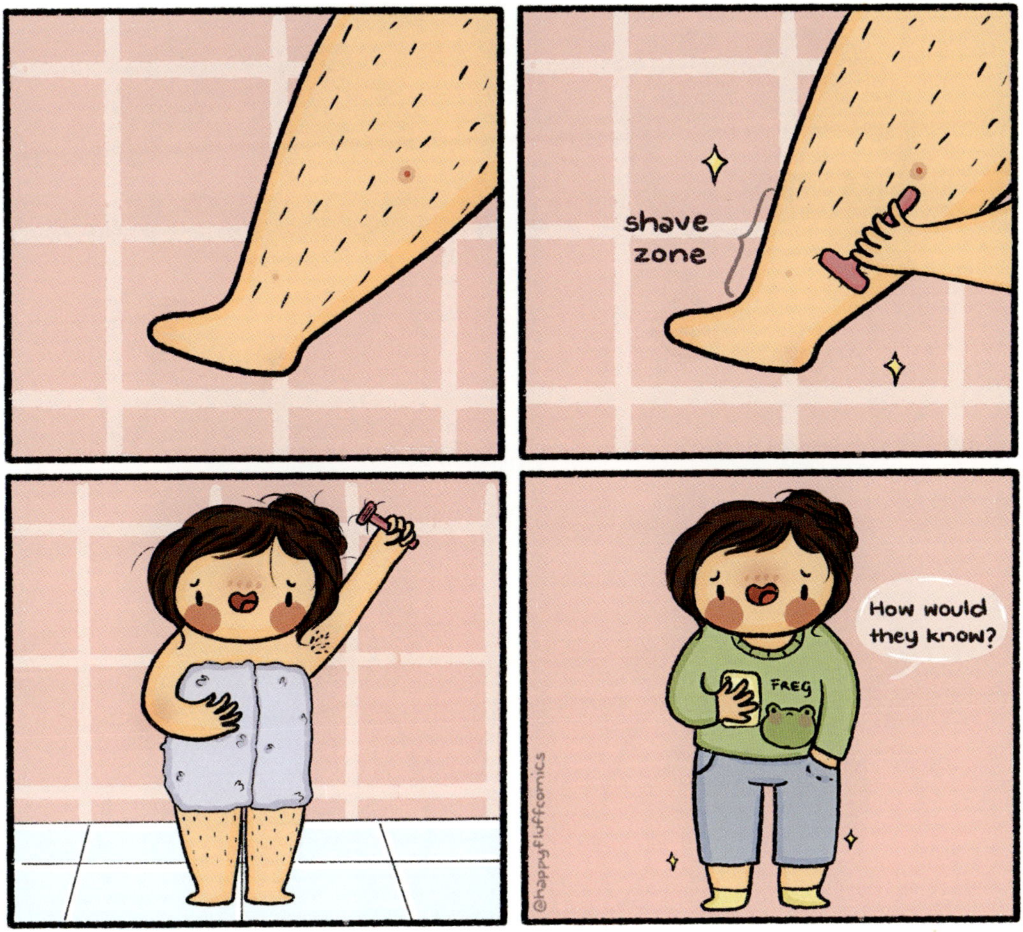
shave zone
FREG
How would they know?
@happyfluffcomics

It never fits

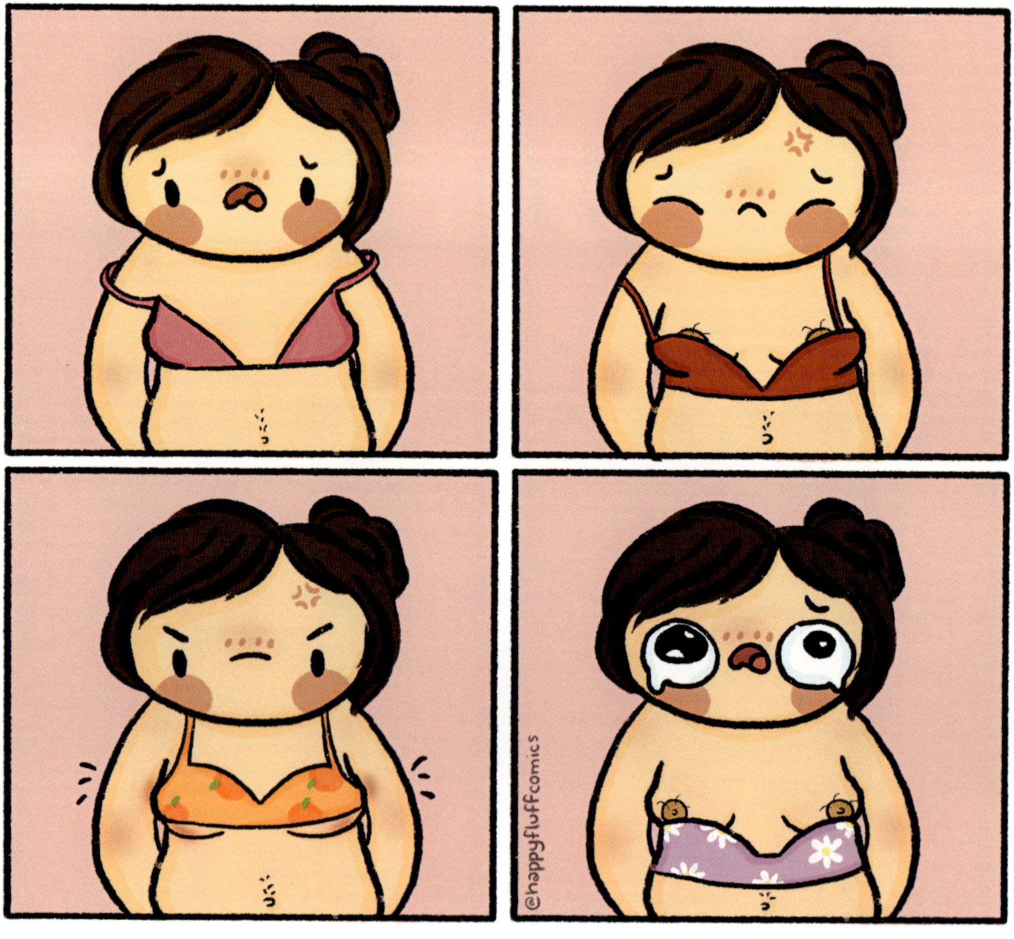
@happyfluffcomics

when you wear matching lingerie

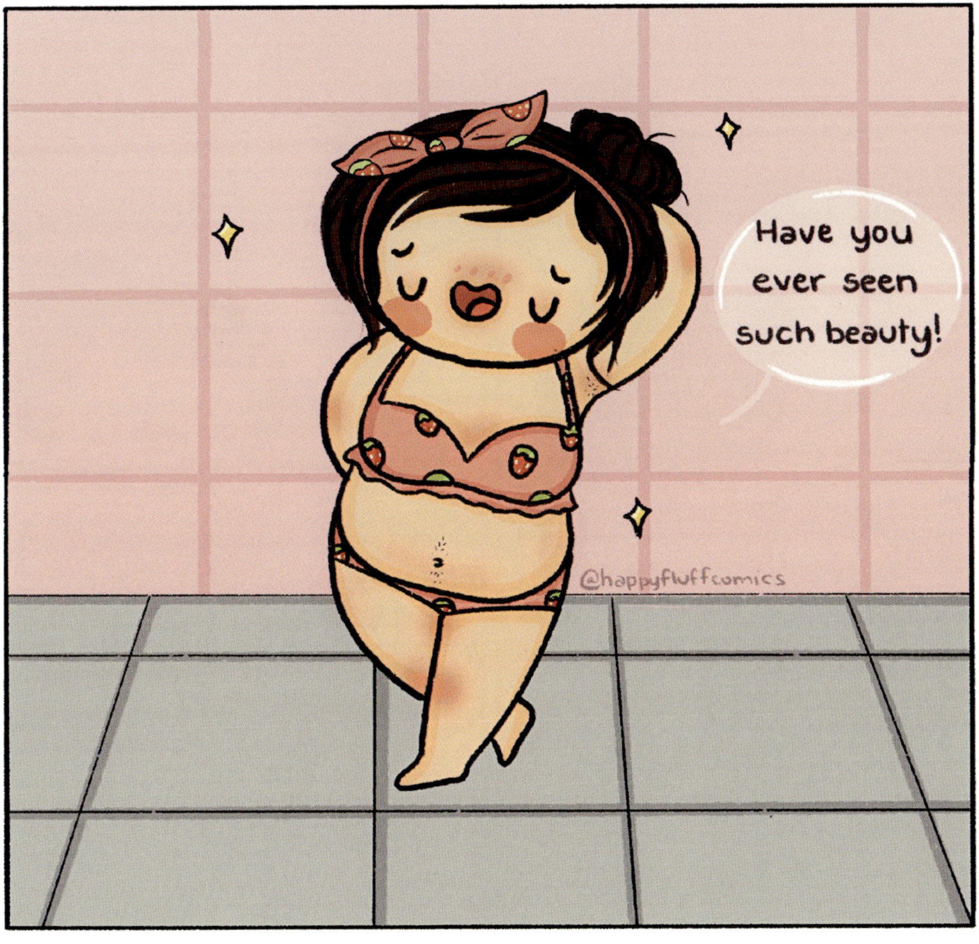
Have you ever seen such beauty!
@happyfluffcomics

Beach body

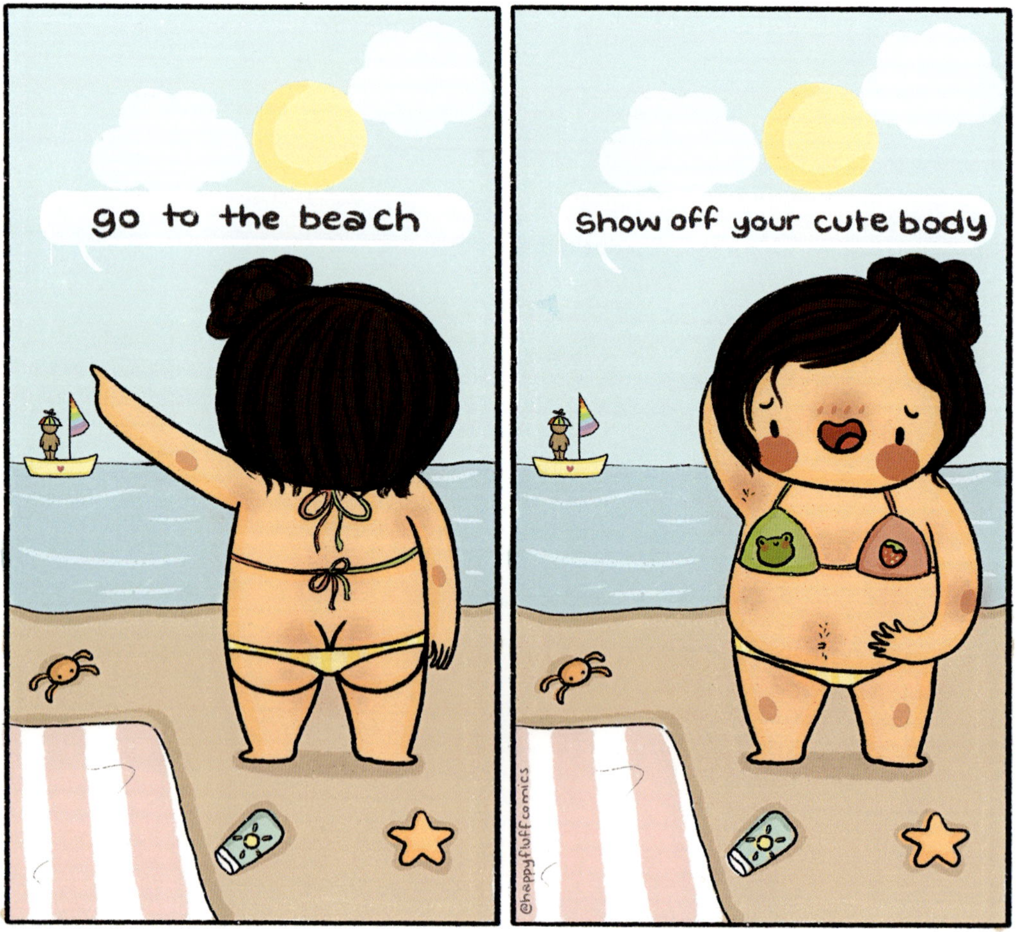
go to the beach
Show off your cute body
@happyfluffcomics

me when I see a mirror

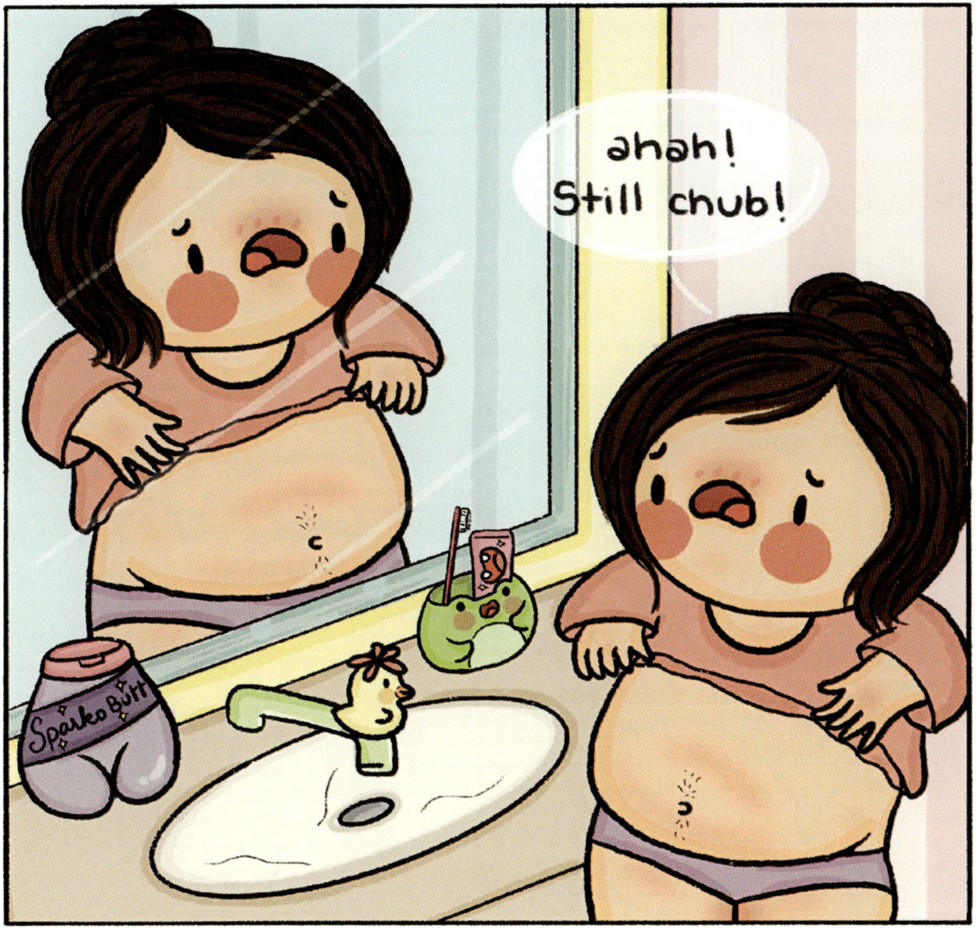
ahah! Still chub!
Sparko Butt

Showering when you're on your period.

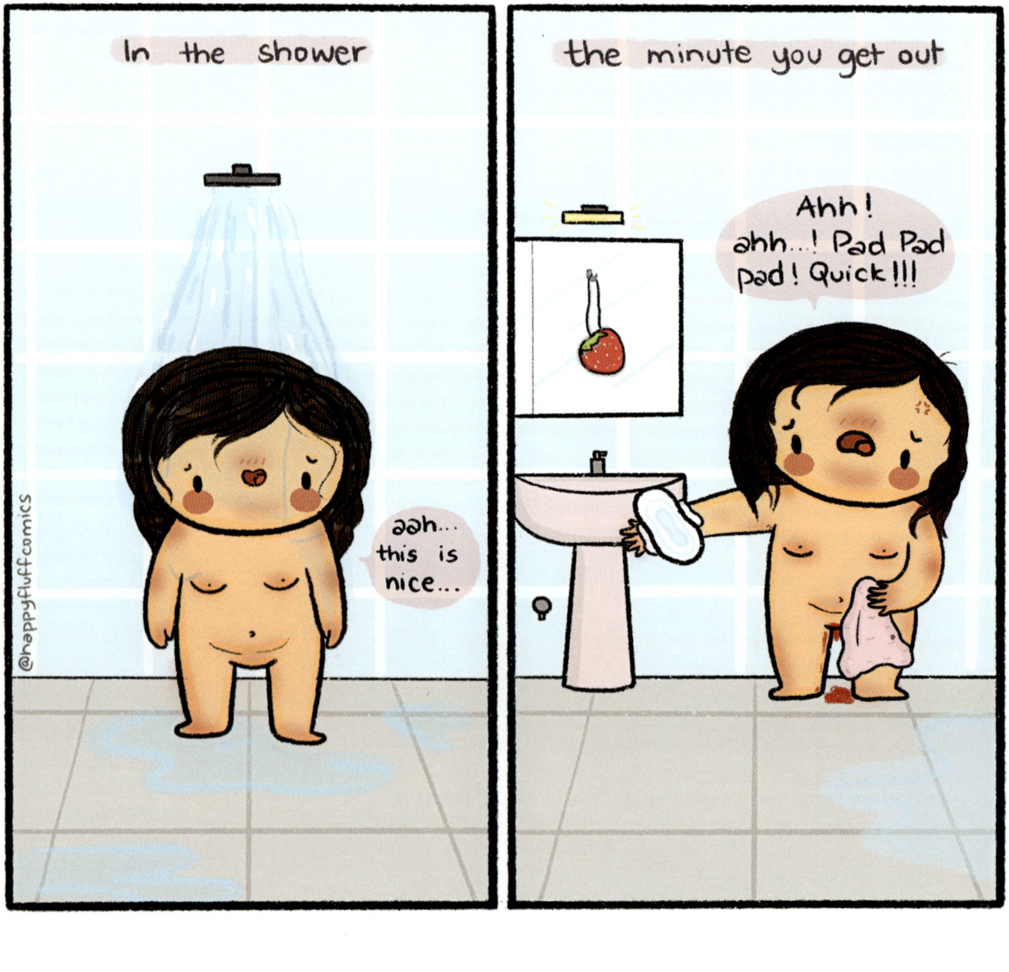
In the shower
aah...
this is
nice...
@happyfluffcomics
the minute you get out
Ahh!
ahh...! Pad Pad
pad! Quick!!!

Me after a minor inconvenience

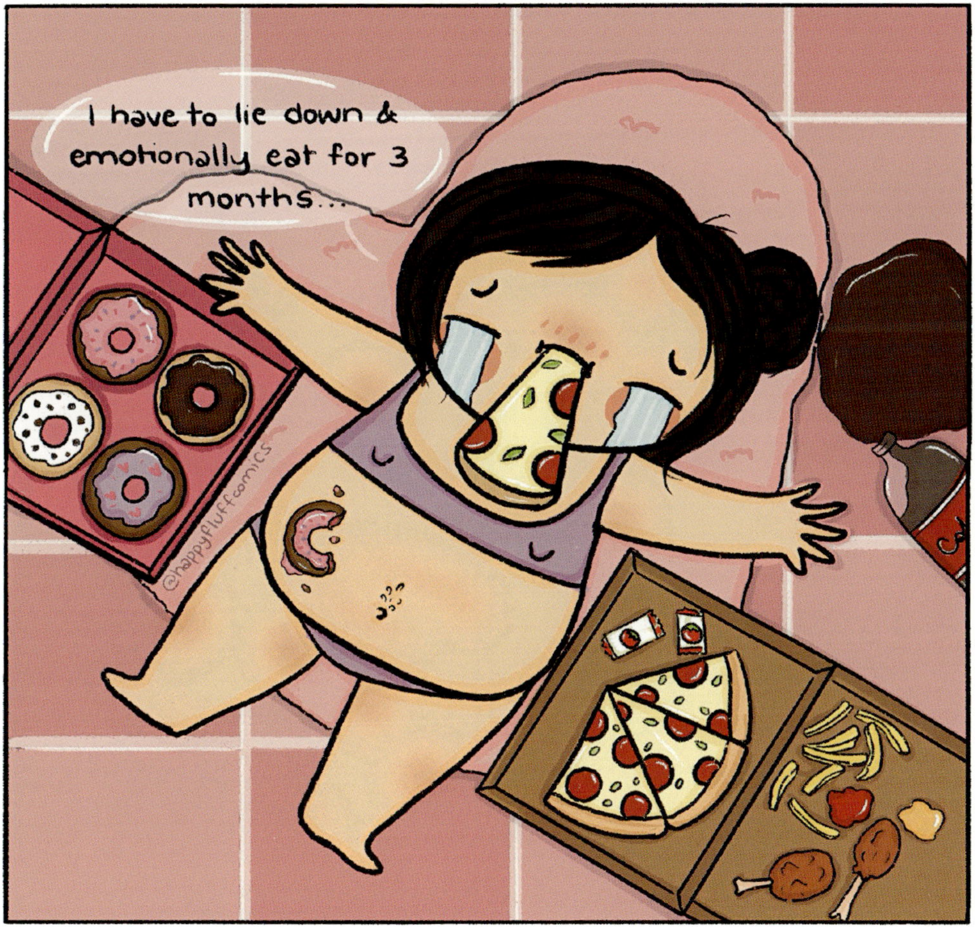
I have to lie down & emotionally eat for 3 months...
@happyfluffcomics

Getting your period

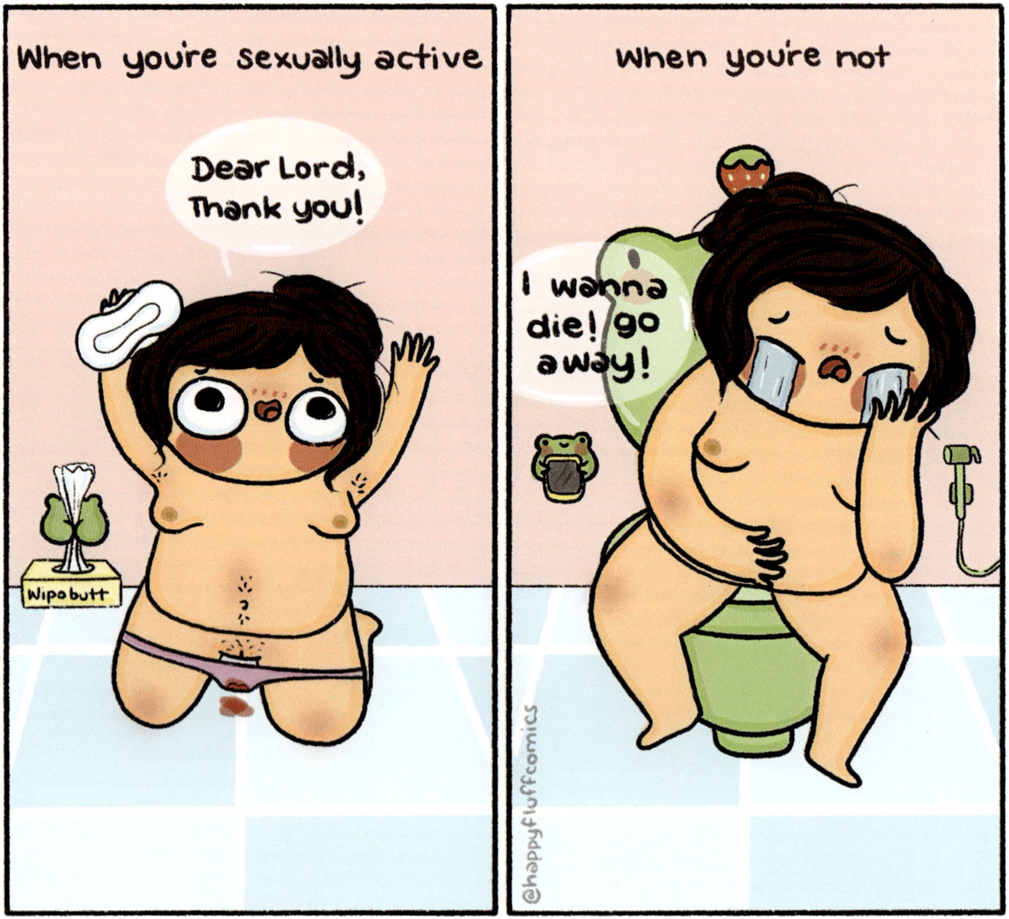
When you're sexually active
Dear Lord, Thank you!
Wipobutt
When you're not
I wanna die! go away!
@happyfluffcomics

first day of your period

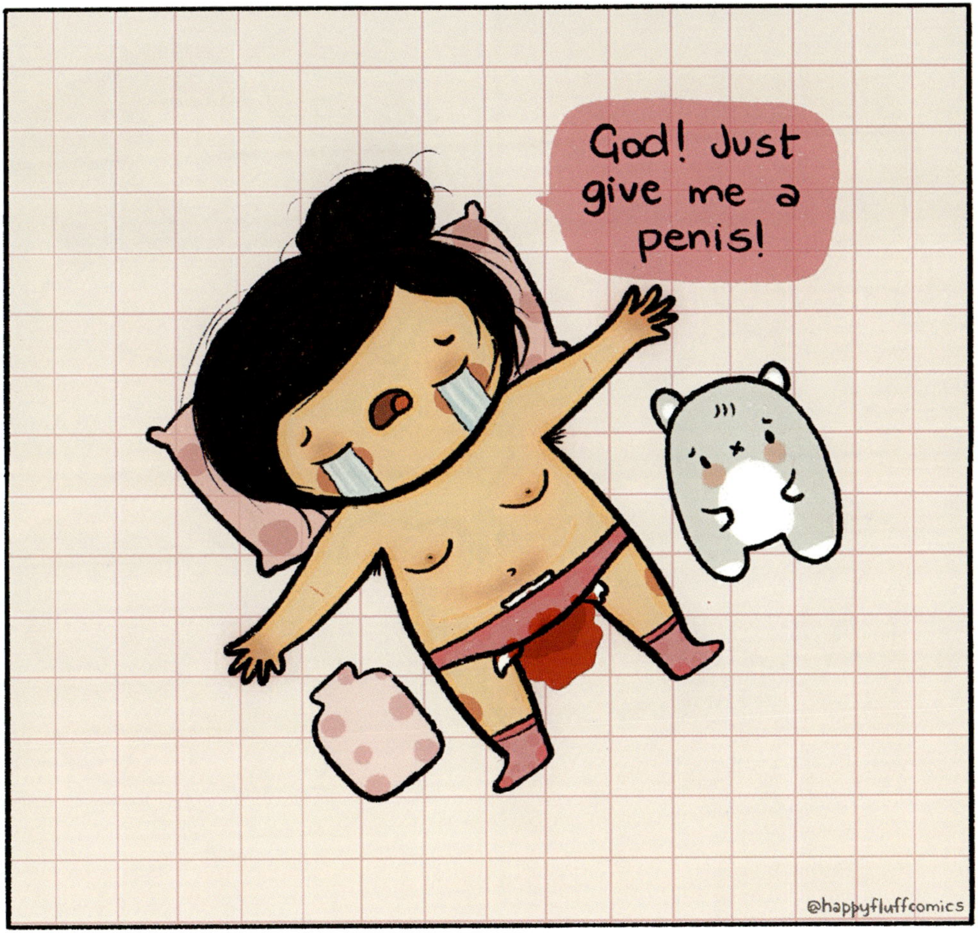
God! Just give me a penis!
@happyfluffcomics

‘Why does my back hurt?’

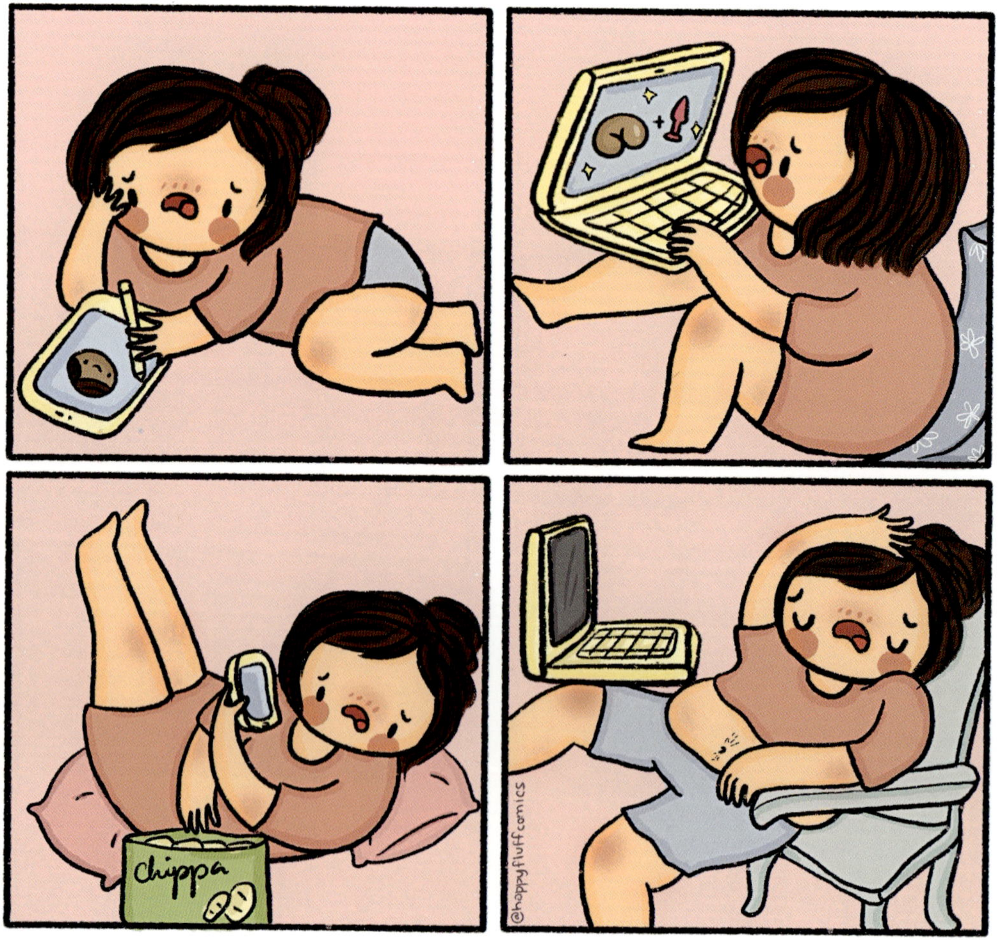
Chippa
@happyfluffcomics

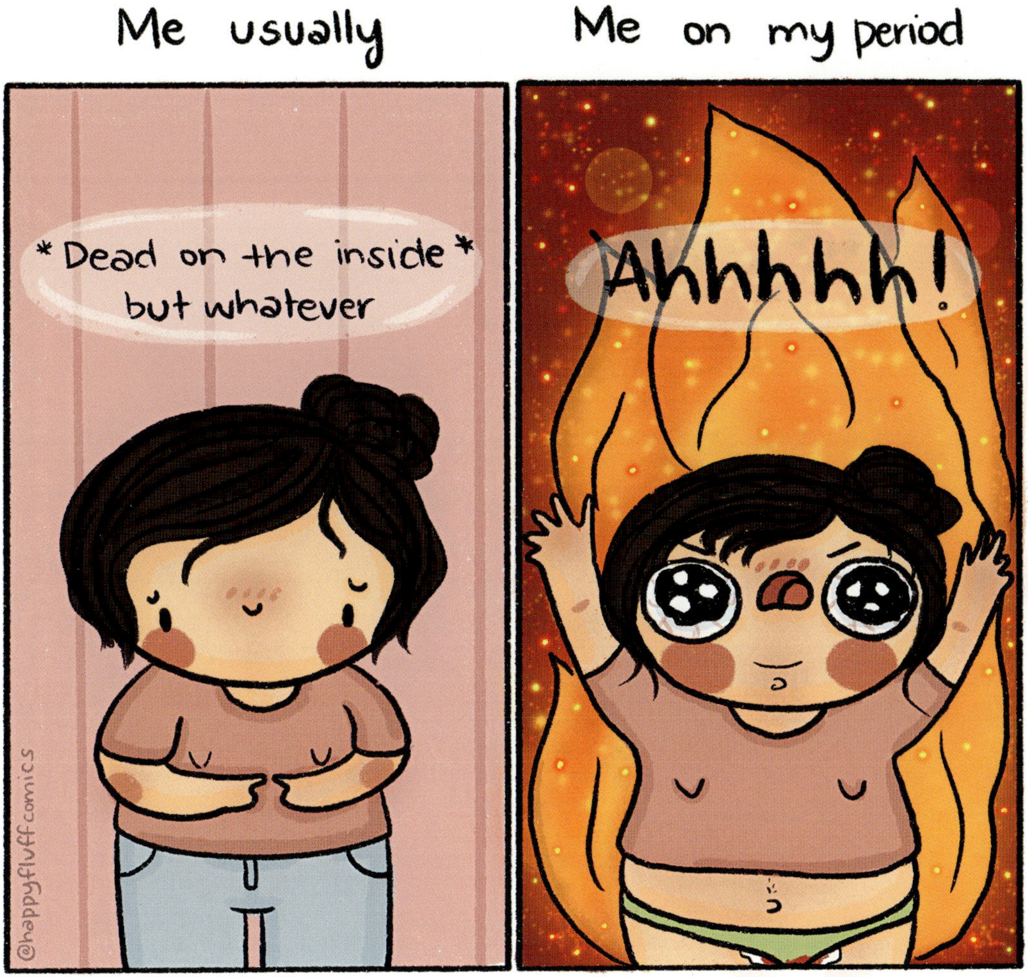
Me usually
* Dead on the inside *
but whatever
@happyfluffcomics
Me on my period
Ahhhhh!

'Food gives you energy'

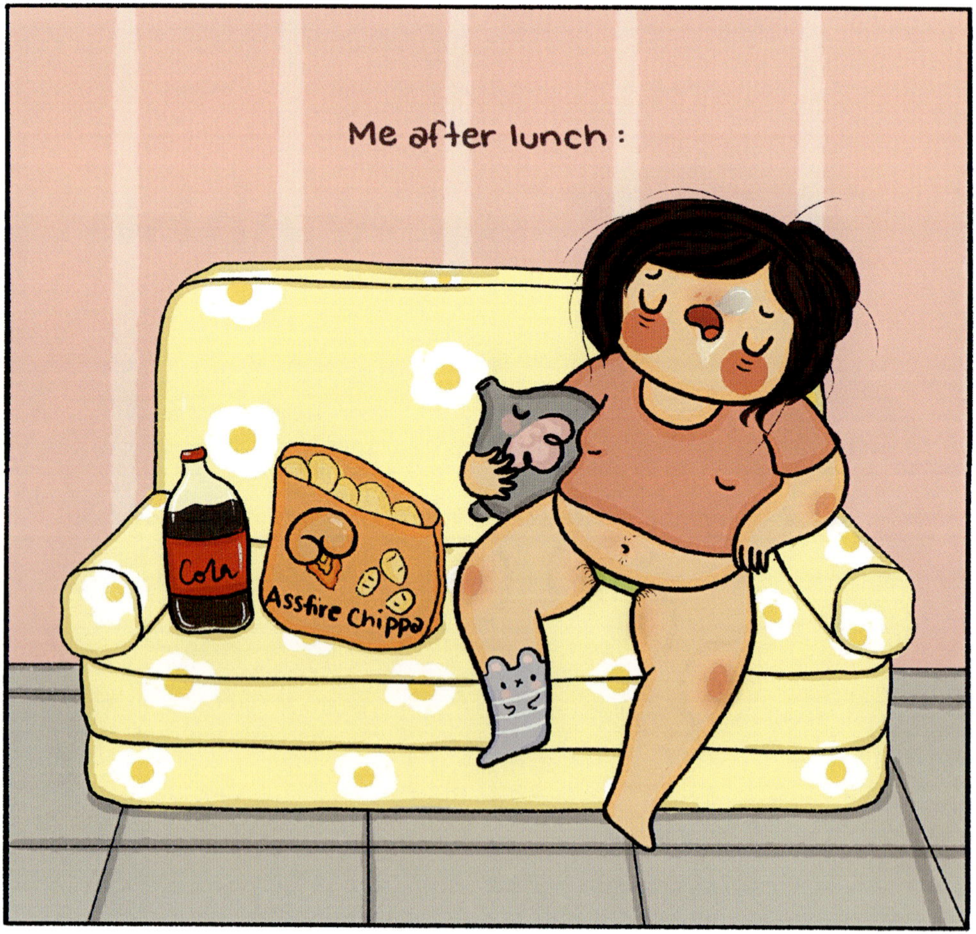
Me after lunch:
Cola
Assfire Chippa

How I work out

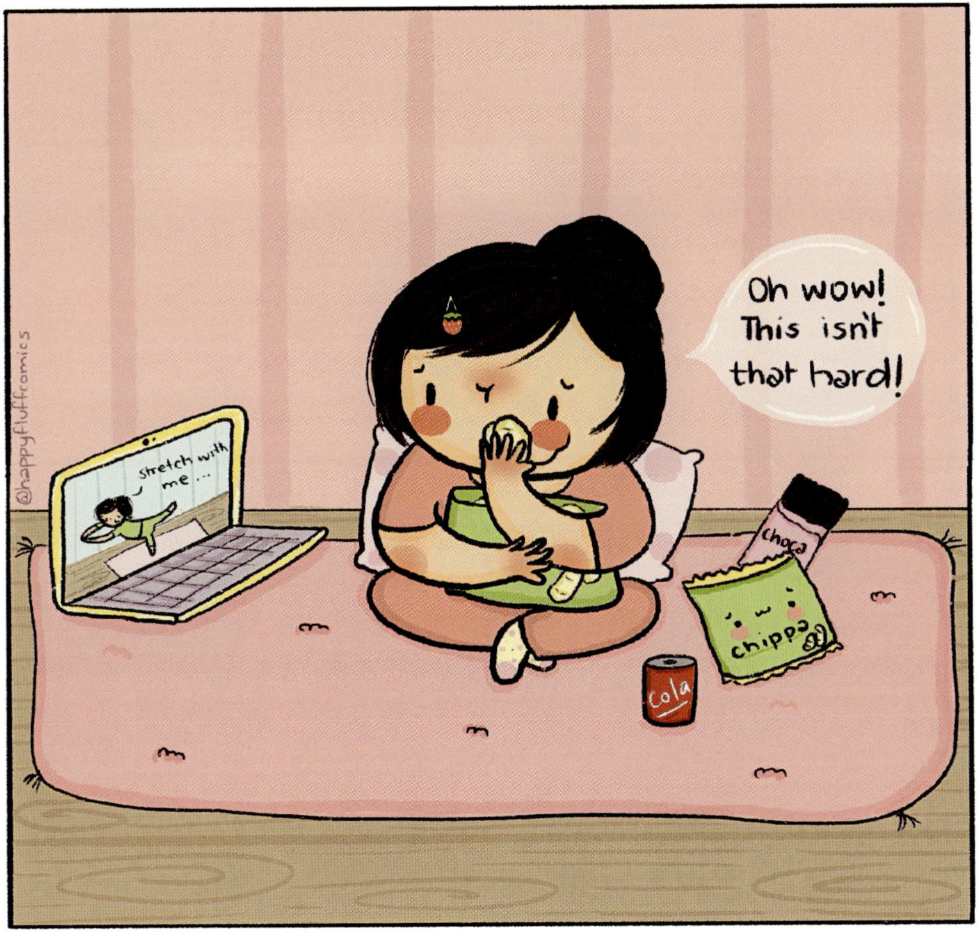

@happyfluffcomics
Stretch with me...
Oh wow! This isn't that hard!
Choca
chippa
cola

shaving down there

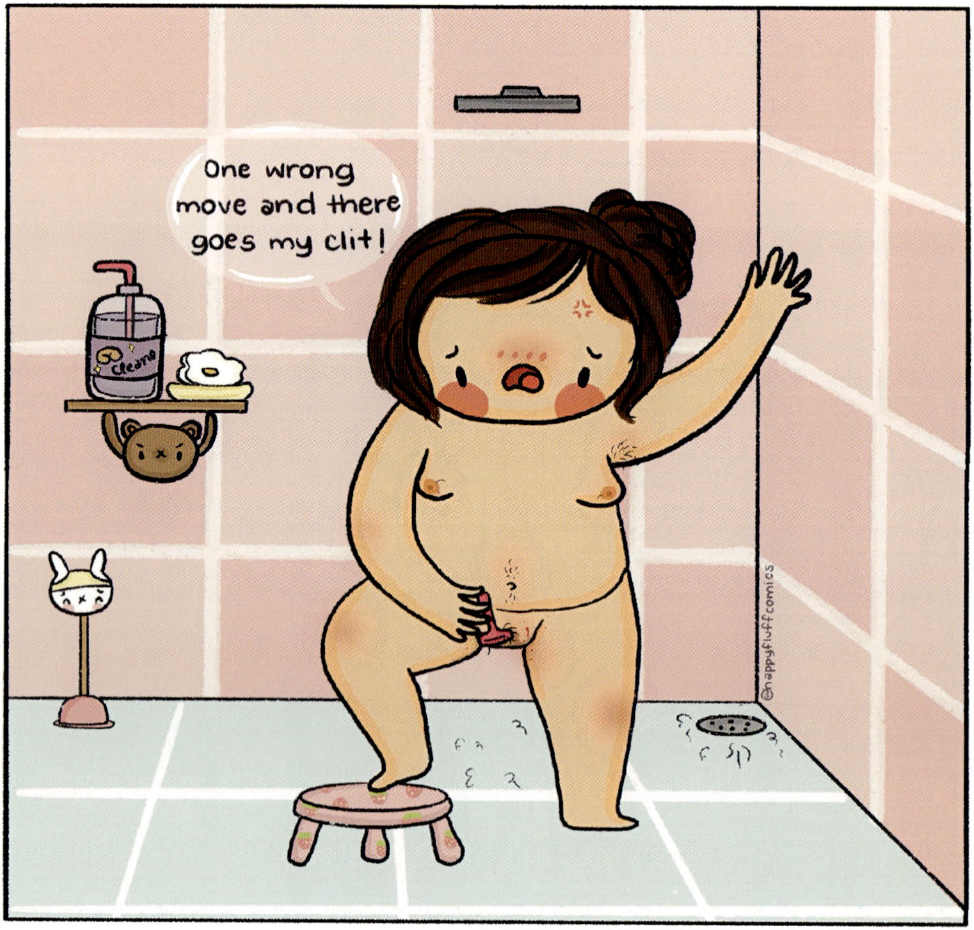
One wrong move and there goes my clit!
Cleano
@happyfluffcomics

Things that are normal

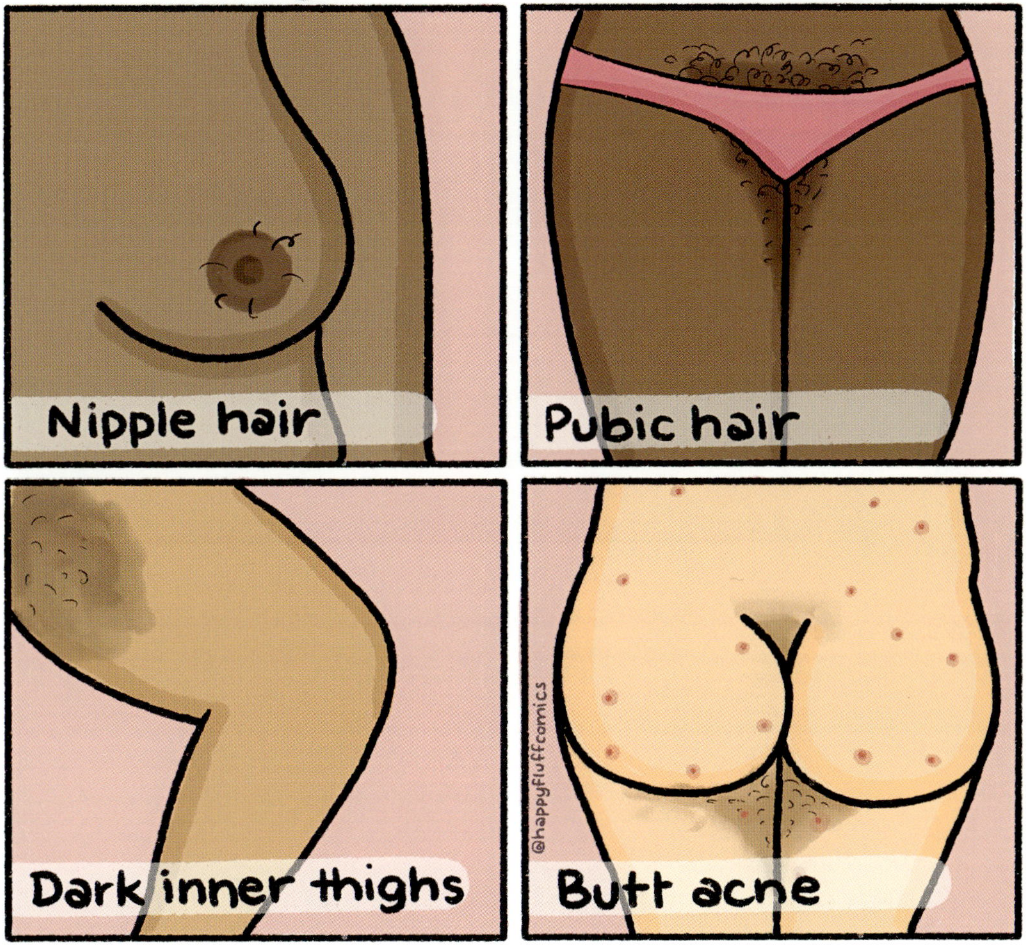
Nipple hair
Pubic hair
Dark inner thighs
Butt acne
@happyfluffcomics

5

what's wrong with my mind?

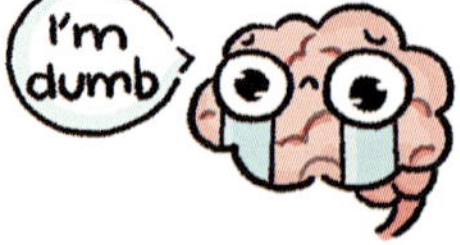
I'm dumb

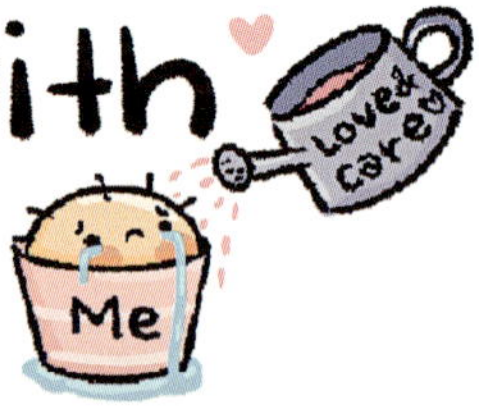
Love & care
Me

Your depression gets worse and you can't get out of bed or work, so your mom drags you to a new doctor. For some reason, this doctor has lesser empathy than all my high-school bullies combined. She looks at me with a straight face as I'm sobbing and says that she doesn't believe in a diagnosis because that's just a label. What does that even mean? So, I sob some more because I have to pay for this now.

My last therapist was nice . . . until she wasn't. Finding a new therapist is so exhausting. Every time you meet a new therapist, you have to go through all the traumatic events of your life again. Sometimes more than once because your therapist forgets to take notes. Eight or so sessions later you realize that they're not helping at all. All you do is vent and I could do that with a friend . . . for FREE.

So, you ask them for a treatment plan because you're running out of money. There's a slight change of tone because you asked them to do their job. So I assumed they're mad at me and disappeared off of the face of earth even though I had a paid session left because I can't stand people being disappointed in me.

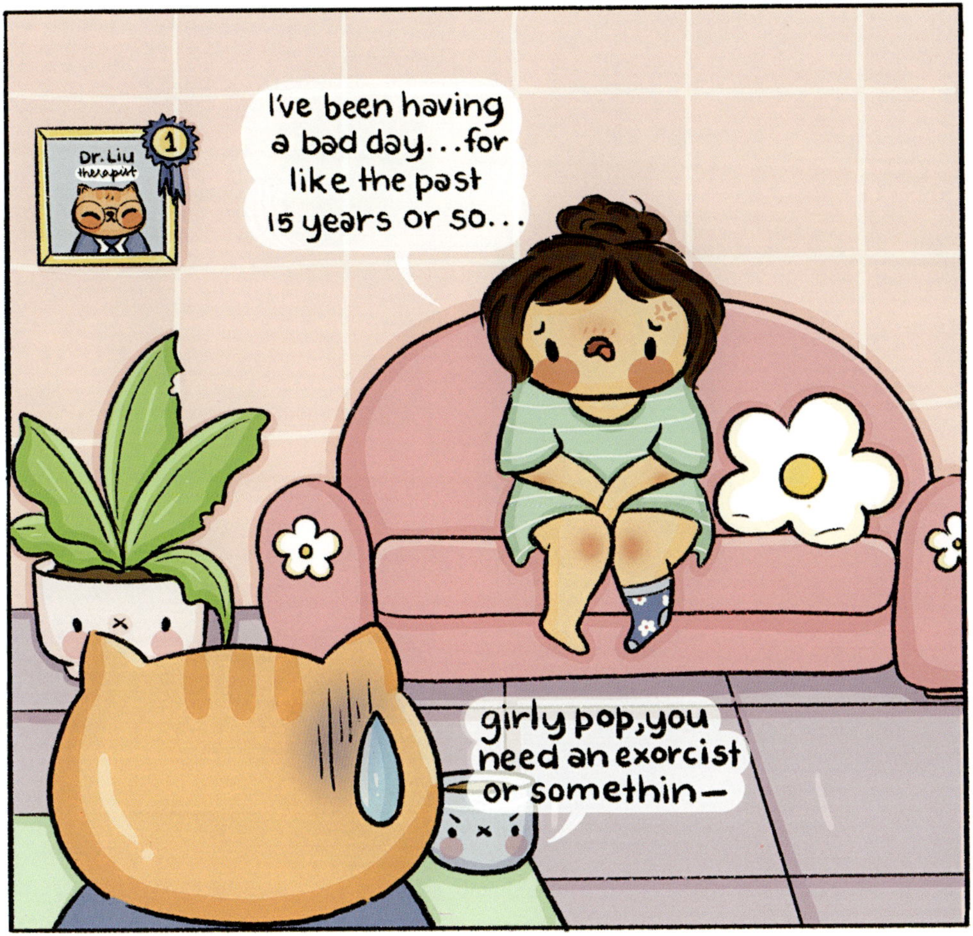
Dr. Liu
therapist
1
I've been having a bad day...for like the past 15 years or so...
girly pop, you need an exorcist or somethin—

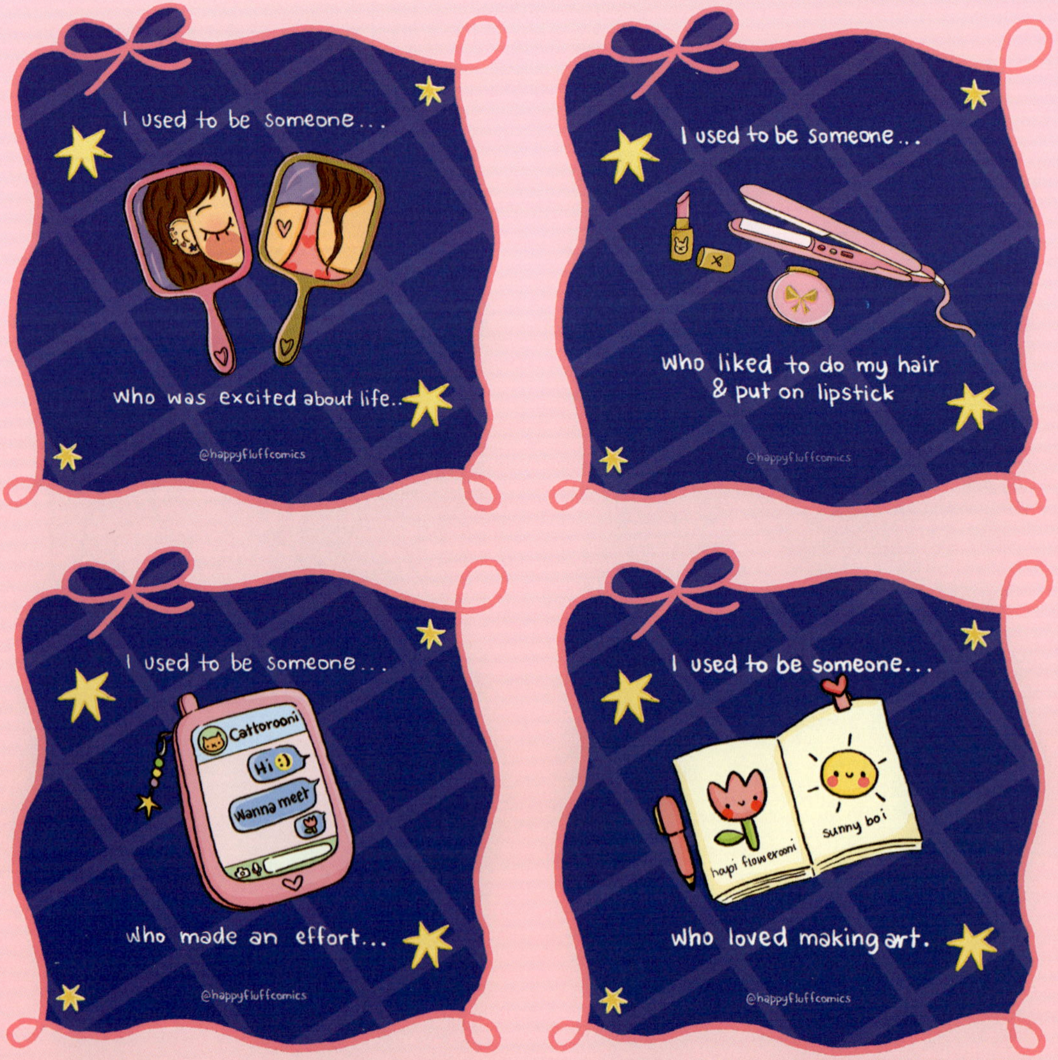
I used to be someone...
who was excited about life...
@happyfluffcomics
I used to be someone...
who liked to do my hair
& put on lipstick
@happyfluffcomics
I used to be someone...
Cattorooni
Hi :)
Wanna meet
who made an effort...
@happyfluffcomics
I used to be someone...
hapi flowerooni
sunny boi
who loved making art.
@happyfluffcomics

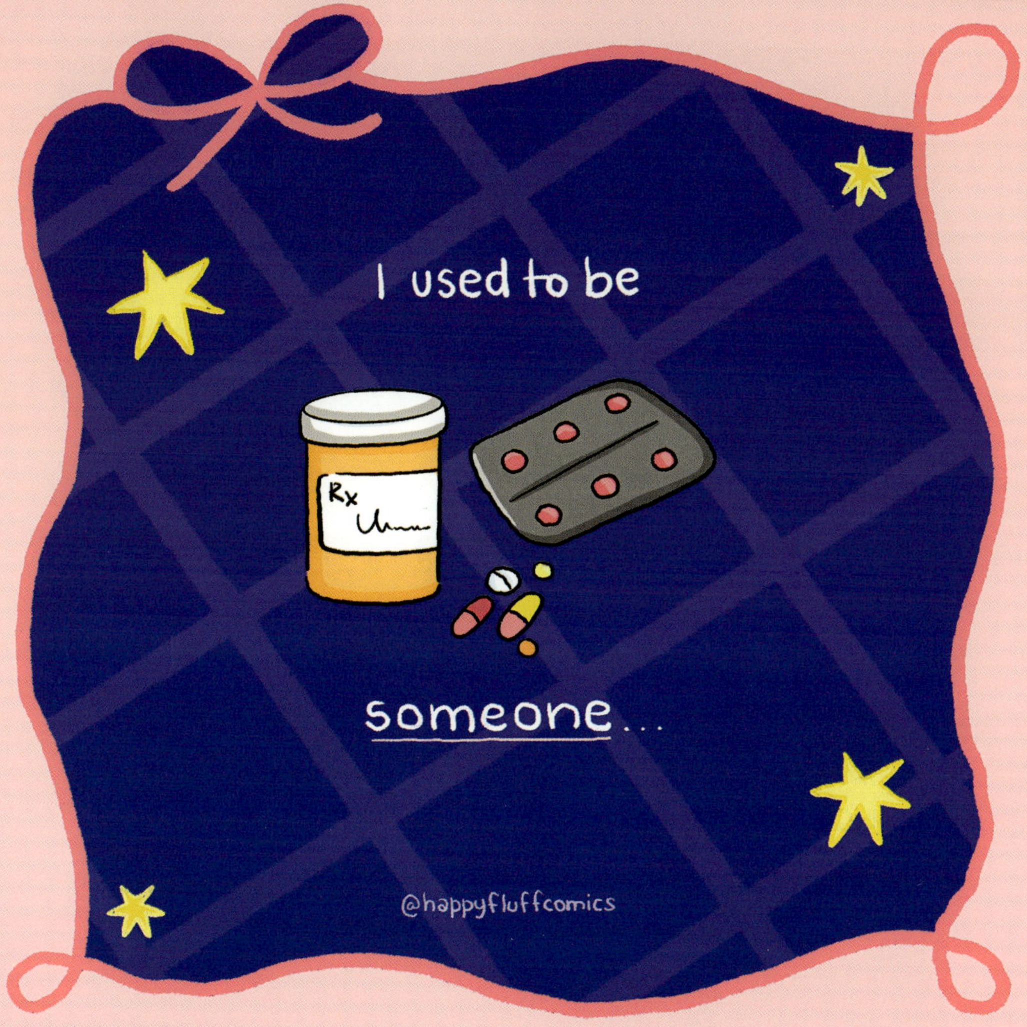
I used to be
Rx
someone...
@happyfluffcomics

I felt grossly judged when my doctor asked, 'Why do you need a diagnosis? It's just a label.' Would she ask the same thing to a patient who has a physical illness? I don't think so. This isn't a quirky trait I want to flaunt. It's something I struggle with every day. Something that stops me from living my life the way I want.

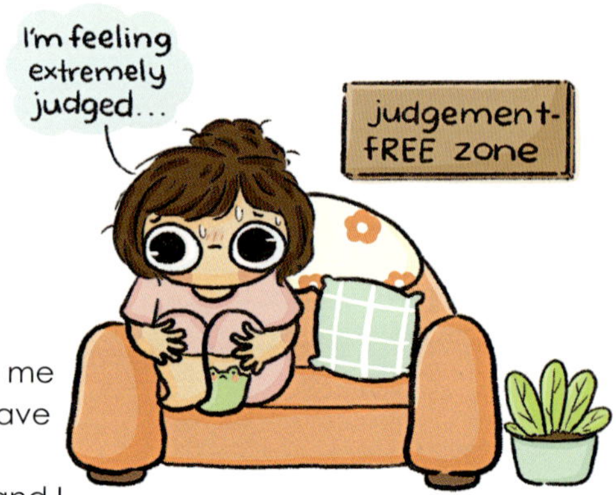
I'm feeling extremely judged...
judgement-FREE zone

Also, how is a doctor or a therapist going to help me if they don't even know what the problem is? I have been going around in circles for the past seven years because I didn't have a proper diagnosis and I couldn't find the right help.

Different doctors and psychologists specialize in different areas of mental health. So, a diagnosis will help me find a specialist who can actually help me instead of paying for five sessions and finding out this isn't their area of expertise.

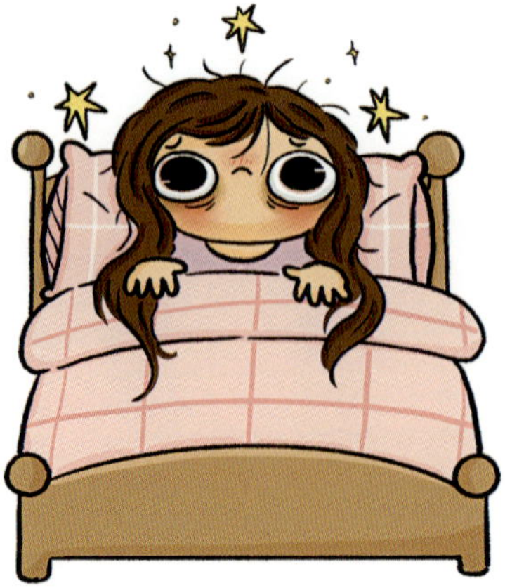

The main reason is to get to know myself better so I can stop being so hard on myself. Maybe I can never fit in or be social or make eye contact or eat things with weird textures. But I'll know this is why I am the way I am and it's not because I'm a freak or a weirdo. That will help me have some empathy for myself. Right now, life feels like a blurry dream where everything feels real and I can't control anything that's happening. I can't wake up either and I'd really like to wake up.

Mental health issues are largely misunderstood due to the lack of awareness and stigma. People often say that mental health issues aren't real and that it's just attention-seeking behaviour. In reality, you almost never get any positive attention from talking about your struggles. Most of us don't prefer to talk about it because we're harshly judged or even laughed at by our own family and friends. Many people don't want to date or be friends with someone who's struggling. So I don't think it's attention-seeking behaviour; it could be a cry for help.

I get that it's hard to relate to things one hasn't experienced. But I really wish people had more compassion and empathy towards others.

It's important to know that recovery isn't linear. There'll be some bumps along the way. But you'll get there some day. It's hard to be hopeful on most days because you keep failing. On days like that, you have to read a good quote or watch an inspiring movie and pretend to be optimistic even if you're the biggest pessimist on this planet waiting for the worst to happen (like me).

Mental disorders are not adjectives

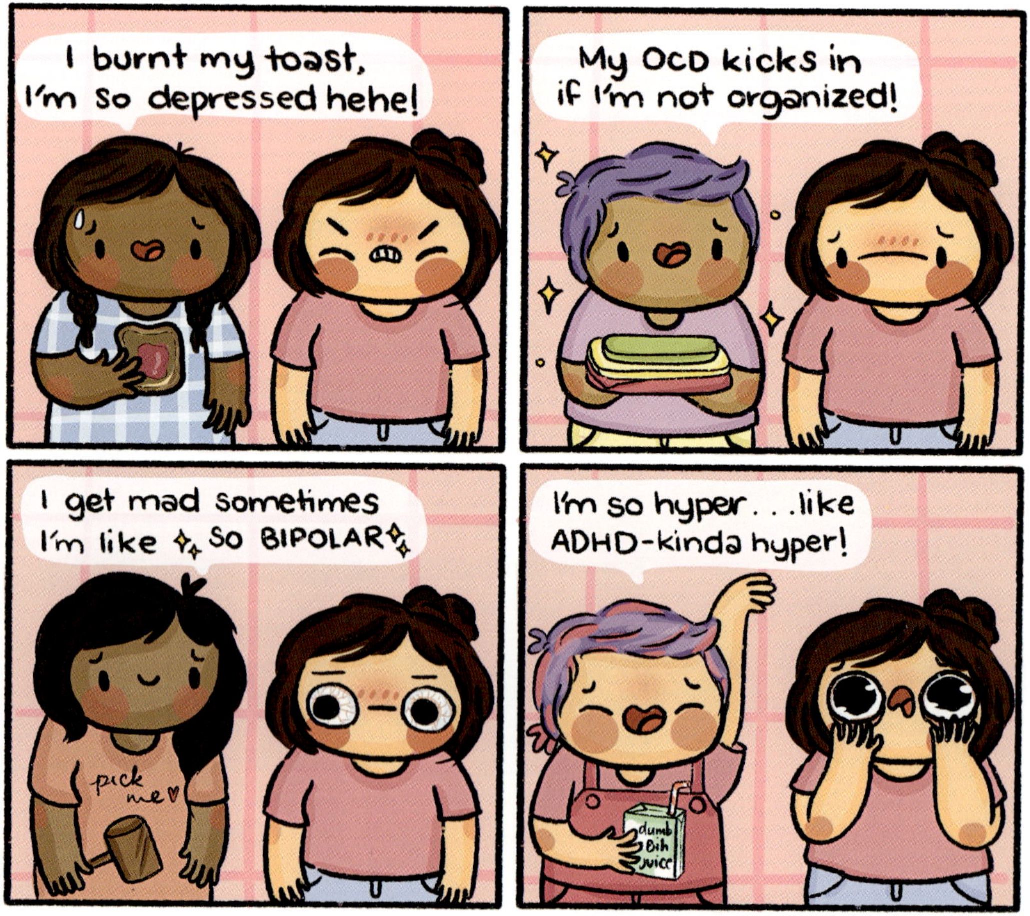
I burnt my toast, I'm so depressed hehe!
My OCD kicks in if I'm not organized!
I get mad sometimes I'm like SO BIPOLAR
pick me
I'm so hyper. . .like ADHD-kinda hyper!
dumb Bih juice

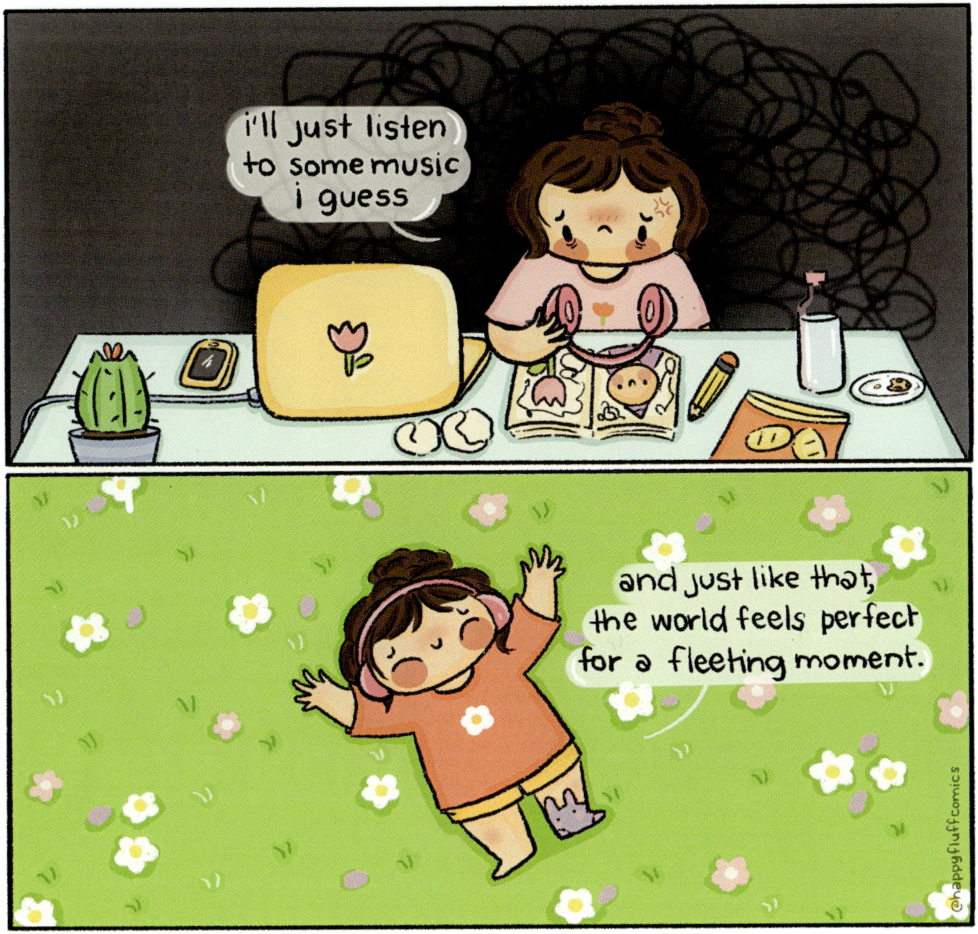
i'll just listen to some music i guess
and just like that, the world feels perfect for a fleeting moment.
@happyfluffcomics

6

taking care of yourself

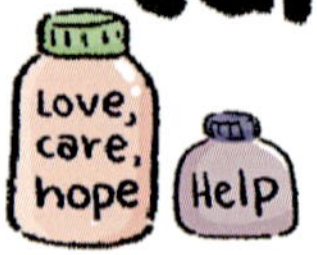
love, care, hope
Help

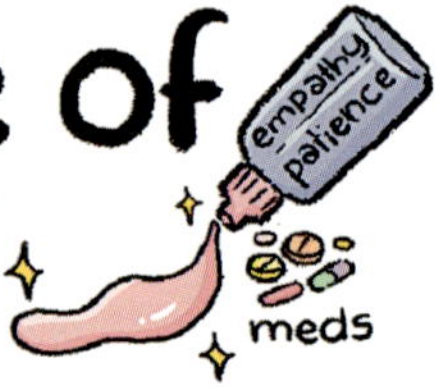
empathy
patience
meds

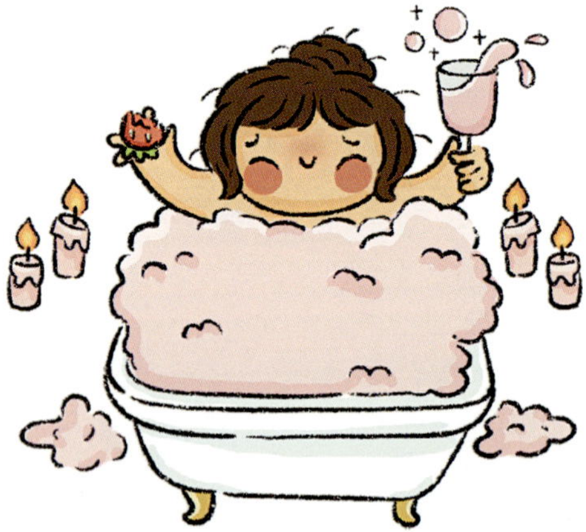

Self-care isn't just about sitting in a fancy bathtub drinking pink champagne. Well, it could also be that if you own a bathtub and have pink champagne lying around. But for most of us, it's harder than that.

Some of us are too depressed to brush our hair so forget running a bubble bath. It's okay if all you did today was sit up straight in bed. May not seem like much to most people, but that's still progress.

It's hard not to compare yourself with people from school or college. Especially when they're shoving their success stories down your throat via Instagram. But their success doesn't have any impact on your life. Just because your fifth-grade bully is winning at life doesn't mean that you're losing. It definitely feels bad, but it doesn't hurt your success one bit.

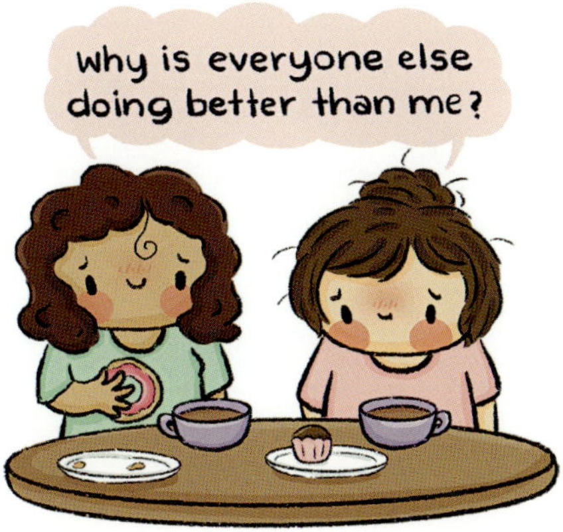
why is everyone else doing better than me?

I'm very insecure about everything in life and I can still say that my twelve-year-old self would be a little proud to see how far we have come. If you write down things you have achieved so far, I'm sure you'll find a thing or two to be proud of.

I may not be super successful, but I have definitely made progress. It's a bit slow, but I'm getting there. We're not in a race, so take your time to achieve your goals. I know that society expects us to reach certain milestones with age, but we can never measure up to society's standards because there'll always be someone who's better than us.

It's important to give yourself the same love you give others. Because the only person who can save you is yourself. You can't do that if your brain keeps telling you mean things. I know it's hard to control your thoughts or to train your brain to be more positive. Trust me, I know because as I'm writing this book, my brain is telling me that it's garbage and I should set it on fire.

All we can do is try our best. If you fail, go to sleep and try again tomorrow. ♥

🚨 Reminder 🚨

Bad days—
survived

You have survived
every bad day
you've had.

Hard tasks—
completed

You have overcome
every task that
felt impossible.

You'll figure this out,
because you always figure it out. 🩷

❀ acknowledgements ✉

A big thank you to everyone who has been a part of this journey.

My sweet boys: Thank you to my pug, Yoshi and my cats, Teefie and Dalgo, for making me feel alive (and for checking to see if I'm alive every morning).

My lovely family: Mummy, Pappa, Aloo, Uncle and Amma, thank you for always being patient with me and for all the endless cups of tea that kept me going.

My best friends: Zebha, Raveena, Ashwathi and Vaishalee, thank you for always being there for me no matter how repetitive and annoying I am.

My favourite human: Yash, you deserve a cat-shaped medal made of gold and diamonds for listening to every thought I've ever had. Thank you for the endless supply of plushies, *snackies* and our *talko* time that keeps me going.

My tiny community on Instagram and Patreon: Thank you for believing in me and making all of this possible.

Team at Penguin: Thank you, Gurveen, for offering me this book deal. Thanks to my lovely editor, Manali, for answering all of my annoying questions. A special cookie for everyone who has worked on this book. Thanks for making this happen.

Scan QR code to access the
Penguin Random House India website

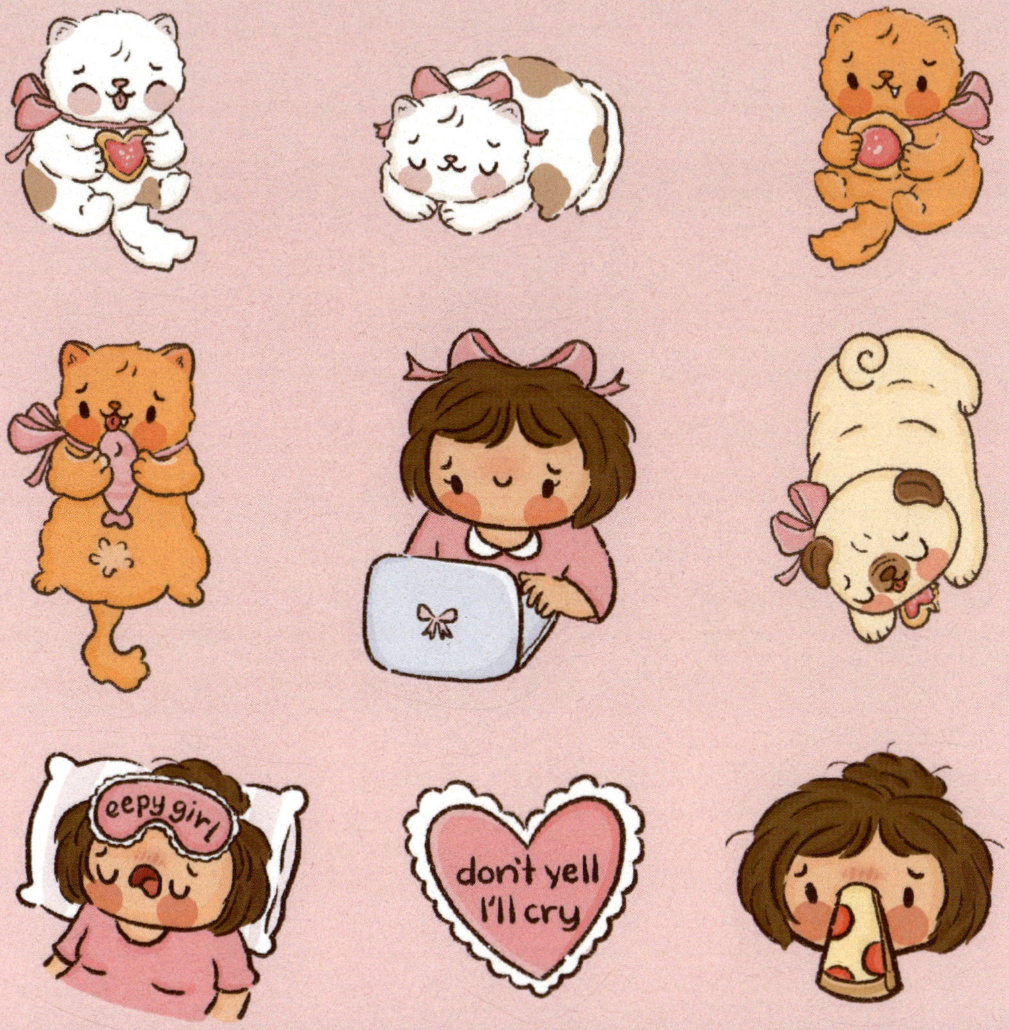
eepy girl
don't yell
I'll cry

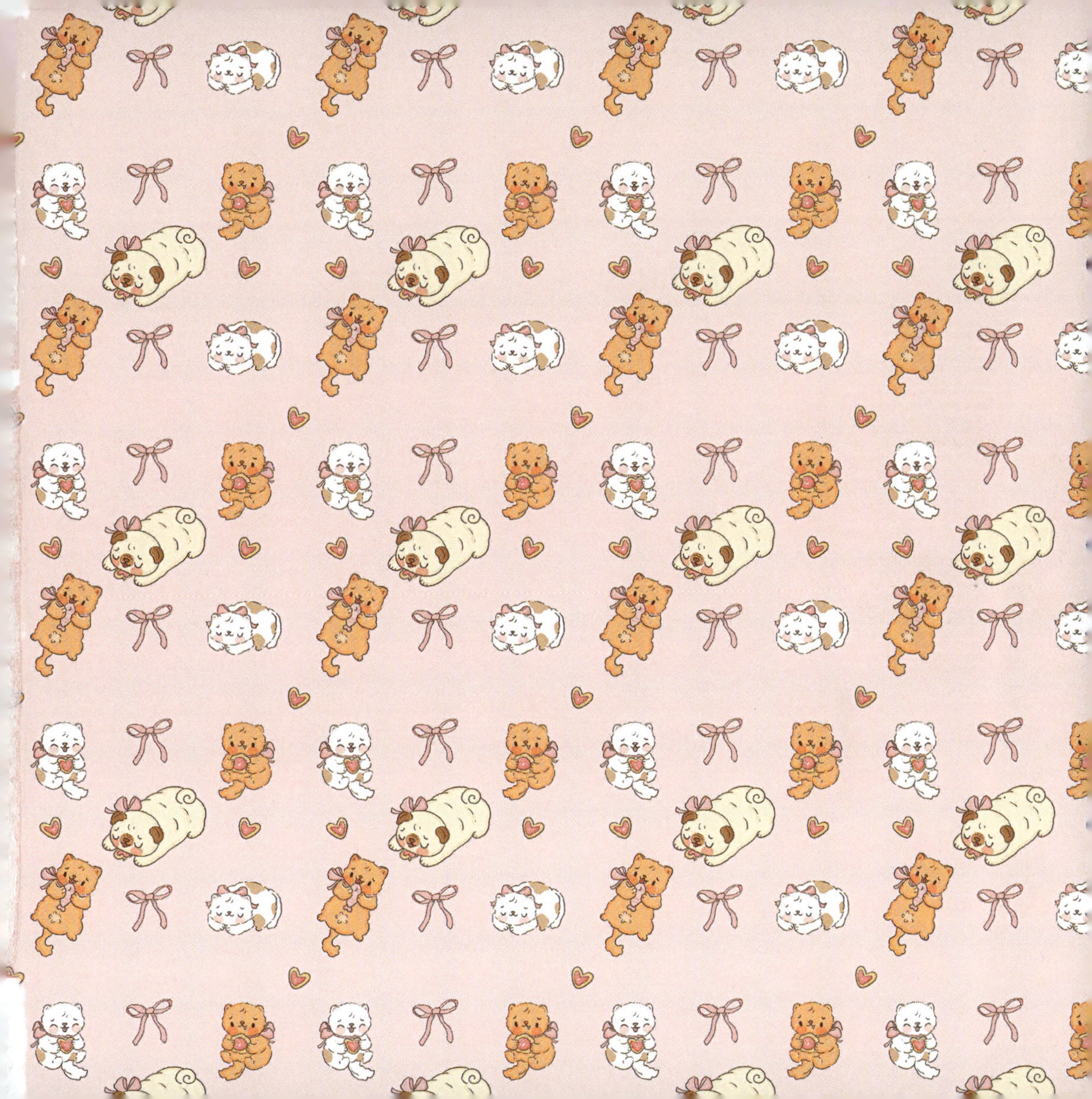

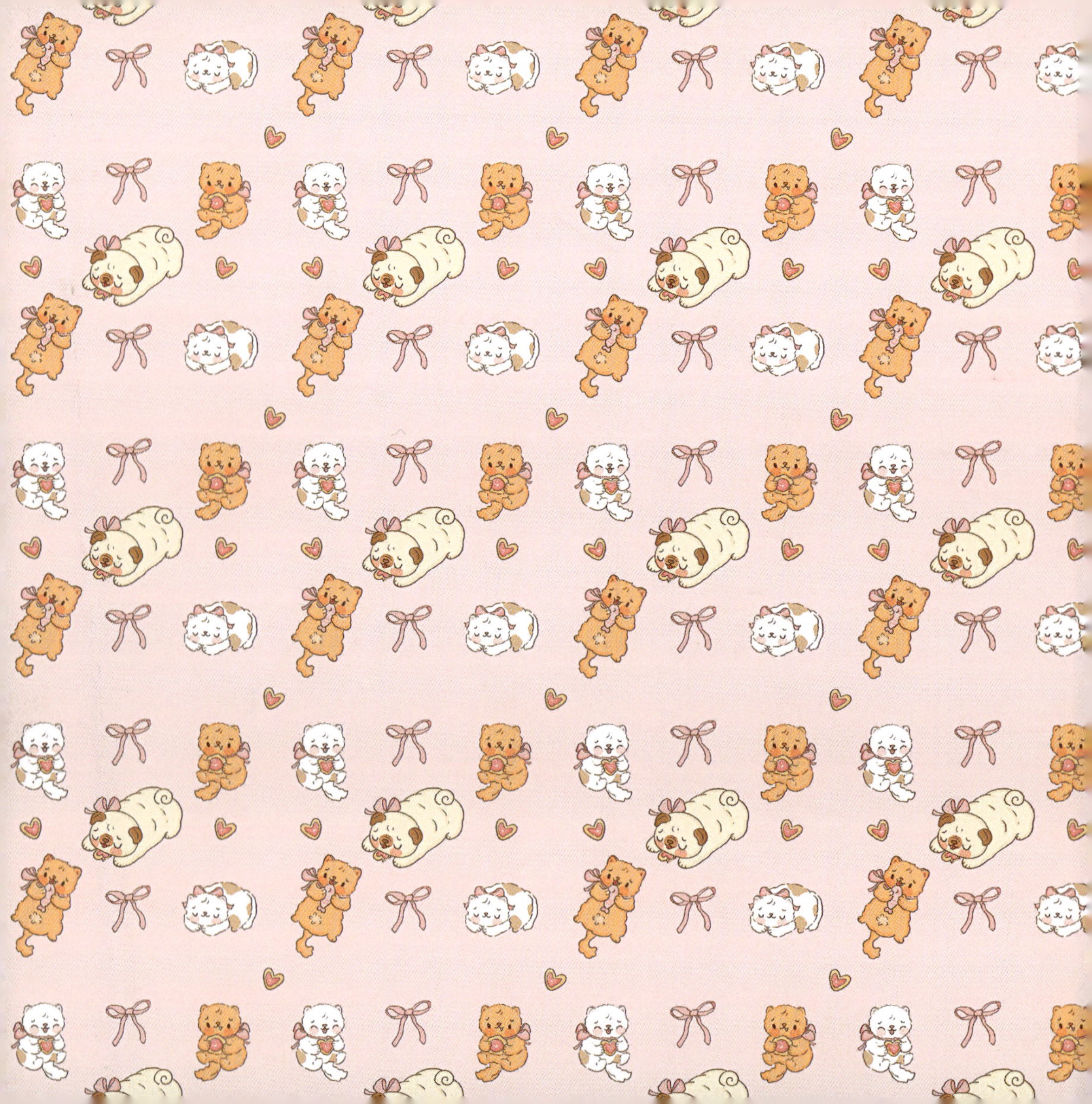